Anarchy & Order

Anarchy & Order

The Interplay of Politics and Law in International Relations

James C. Hsiung

LYNNE RIENNER PUBLISHERS

BOULDER
LONDON

To the memory of
Oliver J. Lissitzyn (1912–1994)

Published in the United States of America in 1997 by
Lynne Rienner Publishers, Inc.
1800 30th Street, Boulder, Colorado 80301

and in the United Kingdom by
Lynne Rienner Publishers, Inc.
3 Henrietta Street, Covent Garden, London WC2E 8LU

Library of Congress Cataloging-in-Publication Data
Hsiung, James Chieh, 1935–
Anarchy and order : the interplay of politics and law in international relations / by James C. Hsiung.
p. cm.
Includes bibliographical references and index.
ISBN 1-55587-571-8 (hardcover : alk. paper)
1. International relations. 2. Law and politics. 3. Anarchy.
I. Title.
JX1391.H78 1997
341—dc21 97-13584
CIP

British Cataloguing in Publication Data
A Cataloguing in Publication record for this book
is available from the British Library.

Printed and bound in the United States of America

The paper used in this publication meets the requirements of the American National Standard for Permanence of Paper for Printed Library Materials Z39.48-1984.

5 4 3 2 1

Contents

Preface

Politics and law intersect in the international system as in the domestic. But books written on international politics since the 1970s rarely, if ever, touch on international law. Conversely, as if in return courtesy, recent writings on international law by and for scholars out of the Anglo-American tradition show even less enthusiasm for the political underpinnings of the law. Moreover, as academic fads and fashions come and go, the subject of international organization seems to be avoided at all costs by most writers in the International Relations (IR) literature.[1]

I have chosen for the focus of this book precisely the interstices and linkages between international politics and international law. As used in the title, *anarchy* is a shorthand label, which, in agreement with the neorealist first premise, denotes the state of our Westphalian system and the context in which world events unfold in the absence of a central authority. *Order* suggests the common urge of states for a modicum of stability and predictability in their mutual relations, which leads to the genesis of international law. Without the proper functioning of the latter, there can scarcely be normal transfer of people, goods, capital, and technology across national boundaries, the stuff of which much of international relations is made. Where the context requires, discussions will extend to international institutions as they provide a forum in which international political battles are fought within the confines set by their respective organic laws and general international law. Although not extensively treated, these excursions are sufficient, I think, to illustrate the inevitable linkage of law, politics, and institutions (international organization) in the "extended family" of the IR field. Knowledge of this complex interrelationship is indispensable to an untruncated understanding of the reality of world events surrounding us.

While the book does not purport to be an exhaustive explication of any of the themes introduced, it will have accomplished its purpose if it has illustrated the inadequacy of any monofactor (e.g., power alone) analysis. Beyond that, the book will have made a contribution if it helps demonstrate the inherent need in the IR field for a broader approach that can transcend the running debates between neorealism and neoliberalism and that is potentially capable of bridging them. As such, this is an antifaddish book: it addresses a fundamental question concerning the integrity and coherence of IR as a field. To the layperson, it tries to show the perils of turning a blind eye to the law/politics interplay in studying international relations.

The wide-ranging coverage of the book is a function of its purpose: I hope to show that the kind of linkage I discuss is much more extensive than one might think intuitively. By addressing a wide spectrum of these areas of convergence, I hope to make a convincing case for the importance of international law (and organization) to the study of international politics.

A few words are in order about the organization of the book. Part 1 sets international law in systemic perspective, showing the logic of the paradoxical relationship between anarchy and order in our Westphalian system. The introductory chapter provides the theoretical background and justification of the book. It discusses two themes in particular: (1) the two responses from the institutionalist perspective to the Realist and Neorealist paradigm,[2] built on the central premise of anarchy—the Policy Science approach to international law propounded by Harold Lasswell, Myres McDougal, and associates (see Chimni 1993, 73ff.) and, more recently, the resort to settled practices (some codified in treaty form) known as "international regimes" (Krasner 1985); and (2) the political parameters of international law in historical contexts, taking off from the legacy left by the Kaplan and Katzenbach classic (1961) but bringing things up to date.

Staying within the systemic perspective, Chapter 2 addresses the security dilemma—a perpetual problem facing all nations in an anarchic system—and how international law, through eliciting iteration and changing the strategic choice for the players, can have a mitigative effect on the otherwise intractable problem.

Part 2 deals with self-help and systemic order. *Self-help* is a derivative of systemic anarchy and is responsible, along with the security dilemma, for much of the violence and lawlessness in the world. Chapter 3 shows how states' collective preference to outlaw war has created a restriction under international law on their self-help discretion, limiting the use of force to instances of self-defense only. Chapter 4 shows that international law not only conduces to the maintenance of systemic equilibrium, but also mitigates international conflict by providing for alternative modes of pacific settlement of disputes and by laying down certain minimal standards in the waging and conduct of war.

Part 3 looks at the general theme of sovereignty and its restraint. Chapter 5 deals with the restraint of sovereignty in a number of ways, including the voluntary and reciprocal curtailment of sovereignty by states, as in the extension of immunities to other sovereigns and their diplomatic and consular agents, for the sake of facilitating their mutual relations. Likewise, international law lays down guidelines for demarcating jurisdictions and resolving jurisdictional conflict; it sets common standards for state responsibility, such as in the treatment of aliens and their interests. In these areas, international law offers a constraining effect on systemic anarchy. In Chapter 6, it is shown that the rise of human rights as an issue in international politics is both a result of the politics/law interplay and evidence of the ascendancy of the individual's status internationally, the latter being evidence itself of state sovereignty (self-help) in check.

In Part 4, under the rubric "Rise of Community Interests," I use two areas to illustrate that, despite systemic anarchy and their consequential self-help discretion, states do occasionally show a willingness to accept certain community interests over and above their own, such as in decolonization (Chapter 7) and environmental control (Chapter 8).

Part 5, "Summary and Conclusions," also has two chapters. Chapter 9 looks at three traditions in the evolution of international relations and their modern influence: Hobbesian, Kantian, and Grotian. After examining their links to the subfields that make up the traditional staple of the IR field[3]—international politics, organization, and law—the chapter ends by questioning whether available evidence does not show that modern Neorealism, under the Waltzian influence, is actually more Hobbesian than Hobbes; and that the three traditions, and the IR subfields they anticipated, should really belong to an integral whole. The final chapter offers both an overall review of the lessons to be drawn from the preceding chapters and a close-up look at the likely trends of the international system into the twenty-first century, accentuating the unfolding interrelations between politics and law.

Many legal cases are cited in the text, reflecting my belief that international law is not just what official documents or pundits say it is; it has to be tested in concrete cases decided by judicial tribunals or crystallized through state practice. Rather than explaining each case, which would make the book much too long, I provide a list of the cases mentioned, citing sources where they can be located. As I hope that the book can appeal to different levels of academic instruction, I am mindful of beginners as well as more advanced readers. And, as I am addressing two distinct audiences—the international politics experts and the international lawyers—I have on occasion to explain some basic concepts in one discipline to the other—hence, the recurrent references "to the uninitiated."

* * *

I owe a heavy intellectual debt to a number of people, including colleagues and former mentors. Special mention has to be made of Oliver J. Lissitzyn, who as my mentor at Columbia University some three decades ago first showed me the way to wisdom on the question of the law/politics linkage. He continued to be an inspiration even after I had started my own career, teaching in the various IR subfields. Some of the major ideas in this book reflect his influence. My only regret is that the book was not completed before his death, at the age of 82, in 1994. The book is dedicated to his memory.

In writing a book that draws on several traditions, I have had the privilege of receiving help from unexpected quarters. For example, Steven J. Brams, my colleague at New York University (NYU), provided expert game-theory input; and John C. Matthews III, at the Center for Science and International Affairs, Harvard University, offered useful comments early on, especially with reference to the rational-choice and international-cooperation literature. Similar debts are owed to others, but I cannot possibly acknowledge them all here.

As this book in part reflects the kinds of questions that came up in my IR classes, I wish to acknowledge the contributions of my students spanning several generations, to an extent that, I am sure, they would not realize. I am also thankful to NYU for granting me a sabbatical in which to complete the writing part of the project. Of course, the ultimate responsibility for any remissness lies solely with me.

My final debt is to my wife, Betty, for showing graceful understanding, forbearance, and unrelenting support during the throes of my book writing, when the computer and daily loads of notes and materials seemed to receive my exclusive attention.

Notes

1. As a field of study, I capitalize "International Relations." On the downplay of international organization in the IR field in recent decades, see Rochester 1995, 203; and Kratochwil and Ruggie 1986, 753.

2. Throughout this book, "Realism" capitalized is used to refer to realism associated with the Morgenthau (1985) tradition, whereas capitalized "Neorealism" denotes the particular school under the influence of Kenneth N. Waltz (1979).

3. I say "traditional," because the addition of international political economy (IPE) is only a relatively recent development, considering the history of the IR field.

Part 1

International Law in Systemic Perspective

1

Introduction: Neorealism and International Law

This book deals with an anomaly in the field of International Relations (IR). Contemporary IR literature, dominated as it is by the Realist school and its more recent Neorealist offspring (Keohane 1986), often treats international law as a fiction or at best a separate entity that may not be relevant to international politics (Boyle 1985, 3–16; Ringmar 1995). Yet the fact is that in the actual realm of international relations there is scarcely an event or issue in which law and politics are not intertwined (Henkin 1968, 13–23; Perkins 1981). The anomaly is only bound to deepen given the fact that, as Boyle (1985, 15) bluntly reminds us, in the mainstream IR profession today, very few professors of international politics possess even a rudimentary training in international law.

The discourses in this book proceed on the central premise that international relations would not be possible if the world community did not a priori have a set of common standards of behavior. Call it a code of conduct, if you will; this set of norms defines what is acceptable behavior for actors on the international scene. (*Actors* here is a generic term for nation-states, international organizations, and other nonstate actors, such as multinational corporations, whose actions and interactions constitute the international relations we study.)

This minimal set of common norms, otherwise known as international law, is necessary in that it helps establish an indispensable, albeit largely invisible, structure of "quasi-authoritative communications" (Coplin 1968, 17) where the expectations of vital decisionmakers in the international community converge. Without it there would be no assurance of a modicum of order and predictability for the movement of people, goods, capital, and technology across national boundaries, the stuff of which international relations are primarily made.

As Lissitzyn (1965, 3) points out, "On a continent divided into many small states and increasingly dependent on distant lands for supplies and markets, domestic law alone could not provide the necessary modicum of security. There was a need for standards of official conduct that would be recognized and normally followed by all governments." In the same functional vein, Lissitzyn suggests that international law serves to prevent the unnecessary friction between governments and irrational destruction of values and resources (p. 4).

If we can thus agree on the necessity, nay, indispensability, of a minimal set of common norms for determining what is acceptable normal behavior in international relations, we are not far from agreeing that international law is a necessary ingredient of those relations or at least something never far behind in the background of those relations. As will become obvious in the following chapters, the *interplay* between law and politics (and institutions) in the international domain is the focus here. It is also the conceptual thread that ties the book together.

Law and Politics in International Relations

The debate regarding the place of international law in international politics is by no means new. The ineluctable relationship of law and politics in international relations history was, for example, explored in depth in *The Political Foundations of International Law* by Kaplan and Katzenbach (1961), which remains a classic in the post–World War II era. And there is no dearth of treatises on the relevance of international law (Deutsch and Hoffmann 1971; Joyner 1984; Ringmar 1995), or on the politics of international law in foreign policy (Forsythe 1990; Perkins 1981; Beres 1987). At the other extreme, there are those who advocate international law as a measure of all things in the international system. Just as Kelsen (1945) argued for the autonomy of general international law before, Kocks (1994) more recently made an eloquent plea for international law as a "system structure." A theory of international politics, he argued, should equate international structure with the legal principles regarded by states as imposing binding constraints on their strategic actions. Though couched in more modern social-scientific terminology, Kocks's thesis recalls Kelsen's exaltation of general international law as a depersonalized sovereign watching over the conduct of nations in their mutual relations. More important, Kocks explicitly criticizes the Neorealist equation of the international structure with the distribution of capabilities (power) across the system of states.

Reconceptualizing law and politics is nothing new, either. It began with Lasswell and McDougal's (1943) effort to put law back on track by creating a "policy science" combining law and politics. This endeavor was carried on with renewed zeal later by McDougal, as he found that the onset of the Cold War had sidelined international law by the political realists' emphasis on "the importance of naked power" (McDougal 1953, 137). If this policy science of the "New Haven School," as the Lasswell and McDougal approach came to be known, skewed international law too much to the side of political process (Burley 1993), Falk (1970) came up with another answer. While continuing the effort at redefining law in relation to politics, Falk sought to redress the balance between Kelsen's (1945) autonomy of international law and McDougal's paradigm of law as a political decisionmaking process.

A new generation of legal scholars have since tried to integrate international law with political theory, to make it more palatable to political scientists (Brilmayer 1989; Burley 1993). These are lofty endeavors to bridge the gap between the disciplines of international law and political science. They in general responded to what Burley calls a "resurgence of rules and procedures in the service of an organized international order" (p. 205) following the end of the Cold War. Their appearance testifies to a post–Cold War euphoria best described by Franck (1992) as a "post-ontological era."

This book, however, does not purport to duplicate what these other works have done. In contrast to the works by legal scholars, some of them just cited, this work is a political scientist's—nay, a realist IR student's—response to and commentary on the Neorealist nonchalance toward international law. Its claim to distinction, if any, lies in its very acceptance of Neorealism's idiom and metaphor of "anarchy" (i.e., lack of a world government over and above the states), working within its paradigm rather than outside or against it. My aim is to focus on the indispensable role and practical significance of international law—but in the language Neorealists use. Accepting the Neorealist paradigm, however, is not the same as accepting its inherent Hobbesian opposition of anarchy and authority. Onuf and Klink (1989) have cogently critiqued the Hobbesian dichotomy and proposed instead a single "paradigm of rule." Although Onuf and Klink focus primarily on what they call the overlapping web of hierarchical, heteronomous, and hegemonial layers of international relations, their paradigm of rule seems only a step away from Kocks's thesis. Both theses share a similar dissatisfaction with the Neorealist paradigm of anarchy and, to varying degrees of conviction, suggest an alternative perspective, making "rule" or international law a point of departure for any analysis of relations in our Westphalian system.

But, in this book, I take the Neorealist anarchic metaphor as a given and attempt to address international law as an integral part of international politics. I do so by pointing out that some of the crucial Neorealist inferences or conceptual associations are unsubstantiated. By the end of the book, I hope to have shown that the Neorealist theory, contrary to an extreme view held by some of its critics, need not be condemned to oblivion. Instead, it can renew itself by merely adding to its first premise (the power equation) a normative desideratum (rules and values) that equally motivates and guides the behavior of nations. In this spirit, my criticisms of Neorealism, which may seem harsh at times, are ultimately constructive in intent.

I first offer a brief but composite sketch of the Neorealist paradigm of systemic anarchy and its views on international relations flowing from the anarchic premise. Only after we have seen the case Neorealism makes for *anarchy* in the international system can we come to grips with the system's crying need for *order.* Accepting the Neorealist premise, I would argue that, paradoxically, the anarchic nature of the system of states necessitates states' quest for order. Here lies the genesis of that body of norms defining what is acceptable behavior—i.e., international law—in the anarchic system, Neorealist disclaimer notwithstanding.

The Neorealist Paradigm

Neorealism's challenge to international law arises from its postulated polarity of law and power in its paradigm,[1] inherited from the Realist school. The latter rejects law in international politics in the name of power (Morgenthau 1960, 144) or of diplomacy (Kennen 1954). With its added concern for structure, Neorealism sees in the international system the overriding attribute (called "ordering principle") of anarchy, or lack of a supranational authority such as a world government would embody (Waltz 1979). From this central premise comes a derived attribute of the anarchic system, namely *self-help,* which is the most reliable means available to each of the component units (nation-states) for its own survival. The dictate of self-help makes the quest for *power* a sine qua non for statecraft. How a particular international system stands out from another variant also depends on how power is variably distributed across the system. Thus, international relations in this paradigm become power relations. On the surface of it, the reflex of self-help by states would leave little or no room for international law.[2]

From its structural perspective, Neorealism views the system's component units (states) as positional, or positioned relative to one another according to the power distribution across the system, which in turn anticipates (in fact, almost determines) how states act and interact. Within this structural logic, Neorealists following Waltz's (1979) lead have built a parsimonious and even airtight theory of international relations, seeing all behavior of states as being system induced—that is, determined by the system's power distribution pattern. Because I return to the Neorealist theory in various contexts in later chapters, I shall note only one more thing here: that my discussions of Neorealism, in terms of both its merits and deficiencies, are invariably geared to the ultimate question of its self-renewability.

Some resourceful political scientists, it is true, did try to modify structural realism by deriving a theory of international institutions from Realist premises and in the process reinvented international law in rational-choice language. They adeptly substituted for *international law* the term *international regimes* (Krasner 1982). Regimes are defined as the principles, norms, rules, and decisionmaking procedures around which actor expectations converge in a given issue area (p. 186f). Others, such as Kratochwil and Ruggie (1986), introduced the concept of "international governance" to ameliorate the postulated anarchic situation. *International governance* is defined as the "coordination of group activities so as to conduct the public business . . . consistent with national sovereignty" (p. 753). Hence, it provides the raison d'être and a functional basis for "international regimes."

But in the conceptual development of international regimes, though redirecting attention to the usefulness of international institutions, regimes-oriented IR scholars have been able to avoid mentioning the term *international law* for a decade or so. While the theory of regimes is an answer to the Neorealist premise of systemic anarchy, which calls for collective action (in lieu of a world government), it skirted the issue of the polarity of law and politics instead of tackling it head-on.

For one thing, the regimes theory avoids altogether the Neorealist inference about self-help and power pursuit from the anarchic premise. In the following pages I show how the Neorealist inference is false and unsupportable by either facts of reality or even the inherent logic in Neorealist structuralism itself.

International Law Despite or Because of Systemic Anarchy?

There is in Neorealism, I would argue, a neglected but crucial link between the condition of anarchy and the place of international law. To appreciate this point, let us consider two extreme hypothetical cases. First, let us assume the existence of an international system that has a world government functioning very much like the federal government in the United States. Although in this system the condition of anarchy is absent, it (paradoxically) would not have an international law as we know it. Instead, it would have a "world law,"[3] something resembling the federal law in the United States writ large on a world scale. The other extreme case would be if the system should resemble, say, the ancient land of Africa, being a loose geographic collectivity of various clusters of population (tribal units) with little or no substantive interchange. International law would not obtain in this situation for two reasons. One, there would be no need for any body of common norms to serve as a guide because of the lack of interaction. Two, even if something approximating a body of common norms should exist among these tribal units, it would not be inter-national law per se, because the various clusters of population were not nation-states. At best, it would be inter-tribal law.

Hence, inter-national law, by definition, can exist only in an international system of nation-states such as ours, in which each state is sovereign and knows no higher authority ("anarchy" in the Neorealist parlance), yet in which there is enough contact among the states to warrant a body of norms to guide their mutual relations (hence, order). Reasoning within this logic of structuralism, one finds that anarchy and order go hand in hand. Contrary to the Neorealist deduction, the condition of anarchy in our Westphalian multistate system is, paradoxically, a prerequisite for our modern international law. In the first place, anarchy creates the coequality of states, by dint of their being coequal sovereigns with no higher authority. As sovereignty is absolute and exclusive within each territorial state, sovereign coequality defines the relationship across national boundaries among the system's component units. Sovereign coequality is indicative of another systemic quality, namely that there is no "vertical" accountability, only horizontal accountability, between its various coequal units. This is so because the decentralized system has no superordinate-subordinate relationship (due to systemic anarchy), but only coordinative relationship among its component units (states). Thus, inter-national law is both a product, and a guide for conduct, of these coequal units in their mutual, coordinative relations under conditions of anarchy. Thus viewed, it would be inconsistent with even the inherent logic of Neorealist structuralism to claim that systemic anarchy so catapults power to the fore that it denies a relevant place for international law. The irony is, however, that despite this logical demonstration, many IR scholars inducted into the Neorealist tradition seem to be blind to this natural link between anarchy and order, i.e., between international politics and international law in our anarchic system.

Let us now reformulate the phenomenon more precisely, using the Neorealist idiom and language: In this *anarchic* system, each of the component units (nation-states) enjoys *sovereign* authority within its territorial confines. But, for practical needs, these units voluntarily enter into mutual relations of exchange, the conduct of which gives rise to a universal consensus on the pressing need for order in the system. The dictate of order—so that there will be the least friction among states and the least destruction of values (Lissitzyn 1965, 4)—requires that states surrender part of their sovereignty as a price they pay for the sake of orderly relations in the larger community. This partial sacrifice of sovereignty, for the sake of order, is reciprocal and dictated by self-interest. Hence, community order and self-interest of states are not ipso facto opposed. Yes, in the anarchic system, states may have to resort to *self-help* to ensure their own survival. And to ensure that they will have the wherewithal with which to resort to self-help, states have to be concerned with the pursuit of power. Just as community order and a state's self-interest are not ipso facto opposed, it would be hardly convincing to dichotomize a state's self-help and community order, as Realists tend to do.[4] Self-help and public order can equally conduce to the survival and well-being of the nation-states. If order is maintained because states, out of enlightened self-interest, should voluntarily observe the common norms of acceptable behavior, it obviates the need by individual states to resort to self-help for the protection of their interests.

Realists, however, show a general nonchalance to this point because of their preoccupation with the dictates of self-help and power alone. As Nardin (1992) puts it in slightly different language, a "shared purpose" among states, such as trade or mutual defense, gives rise to certain "common rules" such as those of diplomatic practice or international law, which in turn lead to a clear definition of roles and relations in "practical association." The participants in a practical association may have shared purposes, he adds, but it is common rules, not shared purposes, that define their relationship (p. 20). Hence, their origins (shared purposes) may fade and vanish, but, the common rules, once formulated, continue to define international relations until they are revised or replaced by a new set of norms.

Furthermore, in the anarchic Westphalian system, it behooves nation-states to keep the various dictums—such as state sovereignty, international order, and self-help—in balance, for the sake of normalcy in their mutual relations. Nowhere is this point better expounded than by the International Court of Justice (ICJ) in the *Corfu Channel* case (Merits) in 1949.[5]

In this first post–World War II case brought before the ICJ, the question the court was called upon to address was not just whether Albania had the sovereign right to lay mines in its own territorial waters, where the strait joined two parts of the high seas (hence, forming an international channel). Nor was the question just whether Britain had the right to resort to self-help when it sent in a minesweeping force to the strait three weeks after an explosion (caused by the Albania-laid mines) damaged a British warship in innocent passage. In fact, Britain alleged that its minesweeping operation was an exercise of its right of intervention and, more important for our discussion here, its right of "self-help" in the interest of justice. In a split decision, the court first found Albania responsible under international law for the explosions and the damage and loss of life resulting from them. Its claim of sovereignty over its own territorial waters notwithstanding, Albania was under an obligation not to create conditions hazardous to foreign ships making innocent passage through an international channel. The court, nonetheless, also found the alleged British act of self-help in violation of Albanian sovereignty.

The lessons for international law that can be deduced from the court's decision are threefold:

1. Order versus justice: While Albania's unannounced minelaying, though within what it considered its own territorial sea, violated international public order, the British self-help violated the procedures accepted under international law for determining justice in international disputes (that is, the determination should not be unilateral).

2. International order versus state sovereignty: Albania may have violated, and did violate, international public order by an act that posed danger to foreign ships sailing through its territorial sea exercising the right of innocent passage. But the British act of self-help (minesweeping) nevertheless violated Albanian sovereignty. One wrong (violence to international order by a state) did not justify another wrong (violation of the culprit state's sovereignty). And, self-help would not be justifiable, provided there were procedures available for redress under international law. Hence, the code of conduct we call international law prescribes not only the standards of acceptable behavior, but also the procedures for determining whether and how self-help is upheld (see the section "Unilateral Action Versus Community Approval" later in this chapter). The stricture that no state should impose on another state its interpretation of what is permissible behavior is well-established (cf. Jesse Lewis claim). In an anarchic system, this only makes sense, because systemic anarchy creates juridical equality between states, according to which no sovereign state should be subject to another sovereign state's interpretation of what is right behavior. In a system characterized by horizontal accountability and coordinative relations, no one state is juridically inferior or superior to any other. Therefore, only a third party can legitimately make such a definitive determination in the event of a dispute, provided the said third party's jurisdiction is accepted by the disputant parties. This presumptively impartial third party may be either a tribunal (standing or ad hoc), an arbitrator, or simply another state playing a mediating role under prior agreement by the disputant states. I emphasize jurisdiction by "agreement" of the disputant states precisely because of the issue of juridical equality as defined above. Membership in an international organization like the United Nations confers ipso facto prior consent on it. Hence, no ad hoc agreement is necessary to establish its jurisdiction in case of a dispute between member states.

This discussion, I hope, will serve to illustrate that international law is consistent with the anarchic reality of our Westphalian system as well as with the logic inherent in Neorealist structuralism. It is unfortunate that Neorealists, as Realists before them, who presume an unwarranted dichotomy of power and law, should consider international law either useless or irrelevant.

3. One state's sovereign rights versus another state's: Although the British self-help violated Albania's sovereignty because the locale of the British minesweeping was in the latter's territorial sea, the Albanian state also should be held responsible under international law because its minelaying was in a section of its territorial sea that links two parts of the high seas. The act should no longer be viewed as simply a sovereign act within domestic jurisdiction, but one that jeopardized the safety of the international maritime community. International law, it is safe to infer from the ICJ judgment, seeks to balance not only the rights of individual states, but also the interests of any one state against those of the larger community. Moreover, international law has to have these balanced concerns in order to answer the common urge of states for order and stability in the conduct of their mutual relations in an anarchic system as a whole.

National Interest and International Law

A related question is: If international law is so concerned with community order and the balance between community interests and state sovereignty, as shown above, does it mean that the Realist assumption regarding the law's incongruity with "national interest" (Morgenthau 1981, 144) is valid?

To answer this question, we first have to examine the reasoning behind the assumption. At first blush, the Realist inference that states in an anarchic system have to resort to self-help puts power in opposition to international law. Since to the Realists the pursuit of power is the essence of national interest (Morgenthau 1985, 5), anything perceived as having the potential of restraining power would therefore be detrimental to national interest. Hence, Morgenthau (p. 291ff.) sees international law in the context of "limitations of power." International law, in this view, is a potential hindrance to both foreign policy discretion and the pursuit of power by states. However, on closer examination, the Realists' assumed opposition of international law to national interest need not be true, for three reasons.

The Partisan Dimension

First, the Realist misperception is the result of ignoring what Chimni (1993, 46) calls the "partisan dimension" of international law. Without getting prematurely into the complex subject of the sources or the making of international law, let me say that Chimni is suggesting that in reality the more powerful states "are able to write their interests into the law." In his anxious attempt to show why the Realist dichotomy of law observance and national interest is untenable, Chimni's allusion to the "unneutral contents" of international law may have been slightly overstated. His reference is skewed to what the more powerful states can do in furthering their interests by making sure that only those contents favorable to them would be incorporated into international law. I wish to point out, however, that despite the onslaught of the alleged "tyranny of the majority" in the United Nations and other similar multilateral treaty-making forums, the more powerful states always have a recourse open to them for the protection of their interests should international law be perceived as being inimical to them. The recourse is to withdraw their consent to the new norms being hatched.

The United States, for instance, chose not to become a party to the Convention on the Law of the Sea (CLOS III) of 1982. The Reagan administration denounced the treaty in December 1982, saying that it would sabotage private enterprise by requiring U.S. private companies that mine seabeds to pay hefty royalties to help Third World countries that could not afford to do such mining. But holding out only increased Washington's bargaining power, so that other nations, principally those in the Third World, were willing to renegotiate the terms of the treaty (e.g., lowering the royalty rates) to ease the way for America's belated joining (*New York Times,* March 10, 1994, 10). By a 1994 agreement, CLOS III was in effect amended to accommodate U.S. interests (Oxman 1994).

Again, withdrawal of consent to protect a state's interests from an allegedly offensive lawmaking treaty is made both necessary and possible by our anarchic multistate system. Anarchy and horizontal accountability combine to decentralize the lawmaking process, in that the states whose behavior is to be regulated by international law are also the collective creators of its norms. For this reason, McDougal (1960) aptly describes international law as characterized by "functional duality" (i.e., states are bound by the law they have a part in creating) and by "competing claims and mutual tolerances" (for lack of a world government as final arbitrator). For the layperson, a few words are in order for this decentralized lawmaking process and the obligatory bases of international law.

Sources and binding force of international law. International law consists of norms created by both treaty and custom, which are known as two of the three principal *sources* of the law; the third is "general principles of law recognized by civilized nations" (Parry 1965, 28–108).[6] With treaty law, the scope and extent of its binding force is easier to determine, because a treaty is binding only on states parties to it (*pacta sunt servanda*). With customary international law, however, the answer is not so cut-and-dry. Whether a customary norm, or a set of customary norms, has acquired the status of being part of *general* international law binding on all states depends on whether it passes the test of collective *opinio juris* (cf. *Western*

Sahara case). This is a reference to a required general consensus of states showing their willingness to be bound by a particular norm, which may owe its origin to an international custom established through repeated state practice or to a declaration hailing from a universal forum such as the United Nations (Higgins 1994, 22f.). Demonstration of a commitment to be so bound (*opinio juris*) is necessary to establish that a repeated practice is evidence of custom with the force of law, lest the practice be an act of political expediency (*Asylum* case). In the case of multilateral declarations, such as resolutions of the UN General Assembly, there must be demonstration that the supporting votes cast for the resolutions indicated a collective *opinio juris* and that, equally important, those casting the majority vote represented the major groupings of nations in the world (*Western Sahara*), including the most powerful ones.

The Western industrial countries chose, for example, not to associate themselves with certain resolutions adopted in the United Nations General Assembly with heavy support of Third World nations. One such example was Resolution 3281 (XXIX): "Charter of the Economic Rights and Duties of States." It was one of a series of UN General Assembly resolutions on states' permanent sovereignty over natural resources and their right to nationalize. That charter, in particular, sought to change traditional (Western-influenced) international law, which required an expropriating state to pay "adequate, prompt, and effective" compensation to the foreign principals whose property was the target of expropriation. The new charter, however, would require only "appropriate compensation" to be paid according to the domestic law (not international law) of each state initiating an expropriation decree. A test case came when Libya, in the wake of these UN resolutions, promulgated in 1973 and 1974 certain decrees purporting to nationalize all the rights, interests, and property of two international oil companies in Libya. The companies, invoking the arbitration clause of the concessions, requested the president of the International Court of Justice to appoint a sole arbitrator to hear and determine the dispute over whether the Libyan act of nationalization violated international law. The sole arbitrator delivered an award in favor of the companies.

In this test case (*Texaco Overseas Petroleum et al. v. Libyan Arab Republic*), the arbitrator noted that the adoption in the UN General Assembly of Resolution 3281 (XXIX), proclaiming the Charter of Economic Rights and Duties of States, showed "unambiguously that there was no general consensus of the States with respect to the most important provisions and in particular those concerning nationalization." The charter was adopted by 118 votes to 6, with 10 abstentions. The particular clause mentioned above (i.e., "appropriate compensation" to be determined by domestic law), the arbitrator pointed out, was voted by 104 to 16, with 6 abstentions, "all of the industrialized countries with market economies having abstained or having voted against it."

The Charter of Economic Rights and Duties, therefore, did not become *corpus juris gentium* because it was opposed by the most important Western countries (Belgium, Federal Republic of Germany, France, Israel, Italy, Japan, the Netherlands, Portugal, Spain, the United Kingdom, and the United States). In addition, a large number of the developing countries (Barbados, Côte d'Ivoire, Ghana, Haiti, India, Indonesia, Malawi, Malaysia, Nepal, Nicaragua, Philippines, Rwanda, Singapore, Sri Lanka, Thailand, and Turkey) also abstained. Hence, the charter lacked the necessary consensus (collective *opinio juris*) to become part of general international law, the arbitrator concluded.

Thus, the withdrawal of consent by the Western industrial nations to the Charter of Economic Rights and Duties effectively rendered inapplicable the purported new norms the said charter sought to create. Withdrawal of consent can therefore be an effective way of protecting the national interests of the industrial countries, as was affirmed in the *Texaco Overseas Petroleum* case. The Realist postulation of an antithetical relationship between international law and national interest is therefore not supported empirically in this light.

In the second half of the twentieth century, even the less powerful states have an increasing voice in the making of new norms of international law so that their interests too are accommodated under the law. One example is the extent of concession made by the more powerful states to the landlocked and powerless countries in the negotiations for the new law of the sea. For the first time in history, landlocked countries now enjoy a right of access to and from the sea, which entails the "freedom of transit through the territory of transit States by all means of transport" (CLOS III Art. 125). This development is remarkable in view of what had prevailed during the centuries before the advent of CLOS III in 1982. By definition, a landlocked state is a country with no seacoast. Under the social Darwinism prevailing in traditional international relations, a landlocked state would have no right to the sea whatsoever. It was literally at the mercy of its neighboring countries (i.e., transit states) whose territories its nationals and goods would have to traverse to get to the sea and back. Whatever convenience the transit states chose to grant to a landlocked state was not a right for the latter, but an act of grace or good will. But the CLOS III grants all landlocked states an unequivocal "right of access to and from the sea," which is backed up by rights of transit through neighboring countries.

Hence, either from the more powerful states' point of view, or from that of the powerless states, it makes no sense today for any country to consider its national interest to be unequivocally at odds with international law.

Interpretation

The second reason the Realist dichotomy of international law and national interest is unwarranted is that international law requires interpretation by states. Oftentimes, by seizing the interpreting initiative or otherwise asserting claims within permissible bounds, nations, especially the more powerful ones, can press international law into serving their own interests. Even Morgenthau (1985, 298), in a different context, agreed that international law allows room for different interpretations. The example he gave was the length of a coastal state's territorial sea. Until it was definitively settled in CLOS III of 1982, general international law simply allowed a coastal state to claim a stretch of waters to be its territorial sea, without specifying how far it should extend. The rise of the Soviet bloc and later of a multitude of Third World countries brought with it a challenge to the traditional "canon shot" (3-mile) rule. For a time, there were competing claims of 12 miles and in some cases even 200 miles asserted by these two blocs, respectively, as against the 3 miles claimed by the Western states. While the principle of territorial sea remained universally accepted, the inexactitude of international law as to its length lent itself to conflicting interpretations by states.

Other examples include the different doctrines adhered to by the United States versus European and other countries on (1) the question of "expatriation" (i.e., explicit renunciation of one's former nationality) in cases of naturalization, and (2) the legal ground for determining nationality: *jus soli* (by the soil on which one was born) versus *jus sanguinis* (by one's father's blood).

Another example concerning interpretation was the extent of sovereign immunity enjoyed by foreign states. Until the onset of the Cold War by 1950, the United States had always accepted the doctrine of absolute immunity (*Berrizi Brothers Company v. S.S. Pesaro*). But, increasingly, the Soviet bloc countries' practice of state trading presented a problem. Their state trading firms, hiding behind the shield of sovereign immunity, were beyond the reach of U.S. courts in the event of commercial disputes with U.S. companies.

The U.S. shift to the alternative restrictive doctrine on foreign immunity came in 1952. In what came to be known as the "Tate Letter," named after acting legal adviser Jack B. Tate, the State Department, on May 19, 1952, informed the world that henceforth the United States would follow the restrictive theory in considering requests from foreign governments for the grant of sovereign immunity (Department of State *Bulletin* 26 [1952]:984). The new position, in contrast to the classical absolute theory, makes a fine distinction between *acta imperii* and *acta gestionis*, or between public acts and private acts of foreign governments. Only public acts would henceforth be immune from the jurisdiction of U.S. courts.

Hence, the cloak of sovereign immunity surrounding all foreign trading firms was lifted. Since there were no international standards on what exactly constituted *acta gestionis* (commercial or private acts), however, it was left up to the law of forum. Congress filled the vacuum in 1976 by enacting the U.S. Foreign Sovereign Immunity Act (90 Stat. 2891; *ILM* 15 [1976]:1388). The act defines a "commercial act" by reference to its "nature," not "purpose" (Sec. 1603 [d]). Hence, the mere engagement in something tantamount to a prima facie commercial act by a foreign sovereign or its agent will, ipso facto, disqualify it from immunity, although the "purpose" of the act may be to further the foreign sovereign's political interests (hence, arguably public).

Thus, we see that the United States in the present case was able to protect its national interest through giving a specific meaning to an unspecified norm of international law. Not only that, where a lacuna in international law left much leeway to the law of forum, the U.S. Congress rose to the occasion with domestic legislation. This concrete example substantively invalidates the Realist claim that international law is inimical to the protection of one's national interest.

The World Context

The third reason the Realist dichotomy of international law versus national interest is both empirically and analytically unfounded is that it is oftentimes in a state's interest to see international law being upheld by the world community. This gets to the heart of the Realist power politics hang-up, which, as we shall see, turns out to be a power politics dilemma.

Unilateral Action Versus Community Appraisal

The lack of a "common power" (Lieber 1988) over and above the states in our anarchic system means there is no central enforcement agency. Unilateral action (i.e., a form of self-help) by individual states, such as the more powerful ones are often inclined toward, provides a remedy of sorts. However, in the anarchic system, a specific violation of international law by one country—if it should stem from a unilateral action of self-help—is apt to invite reciprocal or competitive counterviolations by opponent states. At least it supplies a justification for other states reciprocally to engage in like violations. This eventuality may not be to the interest of the first state succumbing to the power politics impulse at the expense of international law, which leads to a dilemma.

As Boyle (1985) argues, violations by the United States, even in disputes with minor powers like Sandinista Nicaragua and Castroite Cuba, not only give these latter countries a perfect excuse for similarly disregarding international law, but, even worse, they also jeopardize the ultimate sanctity of international law per se, because violations invite counterviolations (pp. 171–295). Boyle sees that the United States has the most to lose by its participation in a reciprocal cycle of violation and counterviolation because it undermines the very international legal order that Washington helped to build after the end of World War II (p. 267).

To bring things up to date, the United States and the world reacted violently to Iraq's armed invasion of Kuwait in the summer of 1990. But, for its part, the United States had invaded Panama less than nine months before, in December 1989. In that earlier armed invasion carried out by 24,000 U.S. troops, 1,000 to 4,000 Panamanians were killed. Thousands more Panamanians were arrested, including union leaders, university professors, government officials, journalists, and military personnel. Each was known to be a defender of Panamanian independence and sovereignty and opposed to the U.S. invasion. The crowning event was the abduction of Panama's chief of state, General Manuel Noriega, to the United States for trial by a U.S. court (Independent Commission of Inquiry 1991). There may not have been a causal relationship between the 1989 U.S. invasion of Panama and the Iraqi invasion of Kuwait a year later. But to the extent that the first event may have encouraged the latter, the coincidence and the close succession in which the second invasion followed the first would seem to support Boyle's argument that one unilateral violation of international law offers an imprimatur to counterviolations or copycat violations. The U.S. "loss" in this case is not just in the abstract, but can be measured by the billions of dollars the United States had to spend to finance Operation Desert Storm, not to mention the additional billions of dollars contributed by allies from Saudi Arabia to Japan and others.

Fortunately for Washington, Saddam Hussein did not have the political wisdom, nor apparently the advice of capable international law experts, to offer a neat, legalistic, defense of his Kuwaiti invasion by pounding on the precedent set by the U.S. move in Panama. What if Saddam Hussein had made a case in self-defense by arguing that, by its own similar violation of international law, the United States had forfeited its right to condemn Iraq's action? The United States, in that case, would have had a lot explaining to do to the UN Security Council, whose sanctions it presently sought against Iraq. Saddam Hussein did not exploit this U.S. "feet of clay" angle but instead used an "internal affairs" defense, based on Iraq's questionable claim to Kuwait as "lost" Iraqi territory (Schachter 1991b, 453; *U.N. Chronicle,* December 1990, 10). He chose to do so probably for a practical reason, namely, the U.S. invasion of Panama had been conducted in total secrecy and against the regime of an alleged drug trafficker (Noriega). Such details as the Panamanian casualties and the circumstances of the U.S.

invasion had been withheld or denied for months by the U.S. government, which finally conceded under pressure in September 1990 (Independent Commission 1991, n. 1). Washington was lucky because the Iraqi invasion of Kuwait took place on August 2, or before the world heard a final disclosure of the local casualties and other details in the Panama invasion. So, without full knowledge, Saddam Hussein could not make too much of the U.S. precedent in justifying his own misdeed before a world forum. But that does not rule out the possibility that the earlier invasion may have inspired and emboldened him to follow suit.

Washington was also lucky, because the Iraqi invasion took place in 1990, following the fall of the Berlin Wall and the collapse of East European communist regimes the previous year. The end of the Cold War was thus irrevocably confirmed. The next day of the invasion, August 3, it was possible for the United States to secure a joint communiqué with the Soviet Union condemning the Iraqi invasion (*New York Times,* August 6, 1990). Iraq lost a veto-wielding champion in the Security Council, in which the Soviet Union had habitually spoken against the West and in behalf of Third World clients during the Cold War. Nevertheless, the moral from the rapid succession of these two invasions is that it provides concrete evidence that one country's unilateral action (self-help) resulting in a violation of international law may likely encourage similar violations by other states. Contrary to expectations, to reiterate, the power reflex may prove detrimental to a major power's national interest in the long run, if its resultant breach of the international legal order should inspire counterviolations in its wake.[7]

The power politics dilemma, as just outlined, may seem intractable because of the built-in self-help attribute of the anarchic system we live in. But, as demonstrated, despite and perhaps because of anarchy, major powers have little to lose—in fact much to gain—from respecting community appraisal of the actions they are tempted to take unilaterally. In the Panama case (dubbed Operation Just Cause),[8] the United States could have gone to a forum such as the United Nations or even the Organization of American States (OAS) and sought community endorsement, very much as Washington did in getting Operation Desert Storm sanctified by the UN Security Council against Iraq. If indeed Washington was so sure of its "just cause," it need not have been afraid of community appraisal of its contemplated action (D'Amato 1990). The result would have been very different, in that the legitimacy of the U.S. action in Panama would have been established in the eyes of the world community. Both the United States and international law would have been better off in that event.

If time (and secrecy) was of the essence, then Washington should have voluntarily made a full disclosure of the facts to the world immediately after the invasion to get community understanding post facto. Prompt full disclosure would also have had the effect of showing that Washington had nothing to hide and that the operation was for a truly "just cause." The Bush administration neither went to an international forum ex ante nor voluntarily made full disclosure ex post for community scrutiny. The only explanation probably was that the administration was misguided by the Realist notion that observance of what would amount to the equivalent of "due process" under international law (community appraisal) and furtherance of U.S. national interests are opposed, as indeed they need not be.

Systemic Changes and International Law

Neorealists agree that an international system is defined by the power distribution across its units and that as the power distribution changes, so does the system. In this view, therefore, the nineteenth-century world represented a multipolar system, while the twentieth century saw the transformation of the world system from multipolarity (1900 to c. 1945) to bipolarity after the end of World War II (beginning c. 1950), and after 1991 to a different sort of multipolarity dominated by one superpower following the collapse of the Soviet Union. But neither the Neorealists nor the Realists before them seem to be aware, or to mind, that as the system transforms with a different power configuration, international law changes as well. I am referring to variations in both the role played by the law and the contents of the law, brought on by shifts in the power-defined rules of the political relations across the system. In the following sections, I give a few examples to illustrate what I mean by "changing contents" and then examine the varying roles the law played as the world system metamorphosed over time.

Changing Contents of International Law

I use the term *contents* broadly to include doctrines (e.g., open or closed sea) as well as norms of international law. I hope that the examples I offer are enough to illustrate the close linkage between changes in the system's power configuration and corresponding changes in the contents of the law at a given point, some with far-reaching effects in the international system.

Brierly (1963, 305) pointed out that under bulls of Pope Alexander VI in 1493, Spain and Portugal—probably the world's only modern naval powers at the time—claimed to divide the oceans between themselves. Their claims, and the underlying doctrine of closed sea, went unchallenged for a century, or as long as no other power could challenge the Spanish and the Portuguese at sea. Not until 1609 did Hugo Grotius publish his *Mare Liberum* (open sea doctrine) in justification of the Dutch resistance to the Portuguese and Spanish claims, maintaining that the sea could not be made the property of any state. The year 1609 happened to coincide with the dawn of a new era of the Netherlands' naval power (1609–1713), replacing the era dominated by Portugal and Spain (Modelski 1978; Rasler and Thompson 1989, 45–47). Although John Selden replied in 1635 with the *Mare Clausum* (closed sea doctrine), defending the ephemeral English position of the time, the world ever since Grotius came to embrace the doctrine of freedom of the high seas. The reason is the irreversible proliferation of naval powers since then. Just as they replaced the Spanish and the Portuguese, the Dutch were followed by Britain (1714–1945) and the United States (1816–), and others. Despite John Selden's espousal to the contrary, the British embraced the open-sea doctrine when they, after 1714, became the dominant naval power of the world (D'Amato 1994, 30). By the nineteenth century, there was a legion of European powers whose naval and merchant marine vessels were regularly plying the oceans.

Earlier we noted the change in the U.S. position from the classical absolute theory of sovereign immunity to the Cold War restrictive theory. Because the trend caught on in Europe and elsewhere among America's allies, in each case, the prevailing power configuration in the system anticipated corresponding changes in international law.

In a related area, the "law of neutrality," as it was known until World War I, had to be drastically altered as a result of two important changes bearing on the recalculations of power in the international system: the age of "total war" (Aron 1955) and the advent of modern air power. In the balance of power system of the nineteenth century, protection of the rights of neutral states and their nationals in times of war rested on the dual premise that the neutral states had no real stakes in the outcome of the war, and that protection of their interests would ensure their neutrality, so that they would not take sides between the opposing belligerents (Kaplan and Katzenbach 1961, 217–225). But the age of total war made this dual premise questionable at best.

More devastating to the political foundation of the "law of neutrality" was the advent of the modern air force. The introduction of the airplane in warfare both intensified the ferocity of air power and changed the strategic thinking associated with power calculations. Until World War I, it was possible for the law to require protection of neutral shipping. In that war, courts held that damage to neutral goods by belligerent bombing made the attacking nation liable for damages (Kaplan and Katzenbach 1961, 250). The importance of air power, beefed up by airborne bombers in World War II, made it impractical to enforce this part of the neutrality law. It was not realistic to demand precise aerial bombing such as strict respect for the rights of neutrals, especially neutral property within the territory of an enemy state at war, would require. Hence, the law's requirement for protection of neutral property within a belligerent's territory, rendered unrealistic by the introduction of modern technology into warfare, began its quiet but unavoidable exit.

Relevant to our interest here are two desiderata on what modern technology has done to the world's power calculations: first, in terms of what it means for the redrawing of the system's power configurations; and second, the concomitant shifts in certain norms circumscribing the conduct of relations among nations, including in wartime. But the sad thing is: except for a cursory concern for the former (Dupuy 1980; Schelling 1966; Wright 1949), there seems to be nothing in the Realist or Neorealist thinking on international relations that indicates an appreciation for the latter consideration.[9]

At issue is the close linkage between power configurations of the international system and the shape, and use, of its norms of behavior governing the system's units (states). The instances mentioned above—from the rise of the open-sea doctrine, the altered law of neutrality, to the changeover to the restrictive theory on foreign sovereign immunity—illustrate how norms of international conduct change over time under the impact of shifting power configurations. But as norms change, they in turn recondition international relations, that is, until another round of power reconfiguration precipitates corresponding changes anew in the system's norms of conduct.

Militating against the Neorealist fixation with power distribution as the determinant of system structure, Kocks (1994) proposes a "law-based approach," focused on "basic norms of international law" (p. 536), as an alternative criterion for defining the international system. I am not ready to go that far, but this discussion of the linkage between the two properties suggests that the system's norms of behavior should merit as much attention as the power configuration for defining system structure, in the interest of adequately understanding international relations. But Neorealists are fixated on only one of the two interrelated criteria.

Shifting Roles of International Law

The roles the law plays are a function of the political makeup of the varying structures of the international system. In the nineteenth century balance-of-power system, international law manifested different characteristics peculiar to its time. In that system, the nation-state achieved a status very different from the earlier subnational or feudal units with conflicting and overlapping loyalties. It also stood in distant distinction to the twentieth-century supranational entities, such as the two competing power blocs of Cold War vintage and the European Union (EU) emerging in the 1990s. The nation-state then was the focus of both internal solidary sentiments and interactions across national boundaries (Kaplan and Katzenbach 1961, chap. 2). Balance making (or shifting alliances) was necessary to ensure the security of each state. And this balancing dictate required a set of rules of conduct: (a) the maintenance of a fragile—as opposed to either grand or permanent—alliance system, so as not to threaten other states; (b) restraint in victory, so that a large enough number of states would be maintained to form a pool of potential coalition partners for the future; and (c) no tolerance of intervention in domestic politics of other states, to prevent one state from becoming too strong and to preserve systemic equilibrium. National sovereignty was hence an enforceable norm of international law because of the essential needs of the balance of power system (p. 33).

The only exception was in the hegemony of the European powers overseas, each vying with the other in their colonial empire-building scramble. Even there, they collaborated in maintaining their condominium in places like the Middle East (e.g., the so-called capitulations) and China (e.g., "extraterritorial rights"). And back in Europe they conducted their mutual relations within the bounds of the prevailing international law.

In the twentieth century, however, the permanent opposing alliances of the Cold War put new strains on international law. For one thing, interventionism was tolerated. Each bloc leader had an interest in intrabloc interference (e.g., the "Johnson Doctrine") and, reciprocally, had to tolerate similar interferences within the other bloc (e.g., the "Brezhnev Doctrine"). Supranational entities, such as the European Economic Community (EEC) and the Organization of Economic Cooperation and Development (OECD), posed problems for national sovereignty, eventually paving the way for its weakening as a cornerstone of traditional international law.

The Cold War was only one of the two epoch-making developments in the post-1945 world system that put new strains on international law. The other one was decolonization. At the same time, the world posed new demands on the law: protection against war, out of the world's reaction to the two world wars; abrogation of unequal treaties; and an end to racial discrimination. I deal with some of these issues in subsequent chapters, so I mention them here merely to highlight the interplay of the system's changing political parameters and its functioning norms of conduct.

The Cold War and International Law

Reisman (1990) notes that the Cold War "deformed" international law in a number of clearly identifiable ways:

1. Formal prohibitions on unilateral uses of force were skirted by exceptions like "wars of national liberation," which in turn generated and sustained counterexceptions, such as "freedom fights." (For instance, the

Reagan administration supported Jonas Savimbi's guerrilla forces fighting the socialist government in Angola.)

2. Symmetrical doctrines of selective intervention (à la Brezhnev or Reagan) were developed and vigorously applied by each of the protagonists.

3. The *jus in bellum* (law of war)—which historically had sought to reduce the savagery of war and to maintain a distinction between combatants and noncombatants—suffered a more serious blow from the advent of nuclear weapons during the Cold War than from the injuries suffered during the two world wars following the introduction of modern technology into warfare.

4. Espionage and covert actions were conducted almost with impunity. (Domestically, one might add, the blurring distinction between America's security and foreign policies resulted in the "privatization" of foreign policy under President Ronald Reagan, as demonstrated in the Iran-contra scandal.)

5. As between the two opposing blocs, the distinction between peace and war (each with its own legal regime) was rendered irrelevant. Neutrality too lost both its political and legal meaning.

International law, nevertheless, served a necessary function during the era of Cold War confrontation, which can be summarized in four respects: (1) It made possible a modus vivendi between the two opposing sides even during the darkest hours, such as in sustaining the necessary exchange and maintenance of diplomatic and consular agents in each other's capital. (2) It provided a legal framework within which agreements such as the Partial Nuclear Test Ban Treaty (1963), the SALT agreements (after 1972), and the INF treaty (1987) were negotiated, concluded, interpreted, and implemented. (3) International law set the outer limits for conflictual interactions between the two opposing sides both within and outside the United Nations. Even the Korean and Vietnam wars, which many considered as proxy wars for the two superpowers, were fought within the confines of the law of war defined by both custom and treaty. (4) Even with the two opposing alliances, NATO and the Warsaw Treaty Organization, international law prescribed the rules and procedures for the conduct of relations within each bloc and between the blocs. The Helsinki Accords of 1975 (Fry 1993), let us not forget, were bred of joint efforts by the two competing blocs and were conceived in the embryo of the law of treaties, in terms of how they were concluded and came into force. Further, in the event of disputes over the interpretation of treaty provisions, international law would have provided a set of guidelines for resolving them. The Soviet Union may, and did, claim that relations within the Soviet bloc were of a higher order, to be guided by what was known as the principle of "socialist internationalism," later known as "proletarian internationalism" (Ramundo 1967, 20; Hsiung 1972, 48–53). But never were the Soviets known to claim any rights for themselves outside the limits of international law. Even the Brezhnev Doctrine was couched in terms of the Warsaw Treaty. Any claim otherwise would not have been sustained under general international law, which took several centuries to build up to the point where it now commands the general support of nations.

This phenomenon remained woefully understudied throughout the Cold War, and the end of the Cold War is not going to reopen it for renewed scrutiny now. But it needs to be emphasized that under circumstances such as the Cold War, precisely because the opposing sides had so few values and views in common, international law performed an indispensable function, albeit a relatively narrow one, of providing a platform on which state-to-state relations could carry on despite the daily parade of conflicts. The same case can, with necessary adjustments, be made for Nazi Germany's relations with other countries during an earlier period of tension, until hot war broke out in 1939.

In the post–Cold War period, international law is destined to have a different role to play, the shape of which is still unclear. Speculations are that there will be less tolerance of interventionism, a greater role for non-state entities (including the United Nations), and more respect for human rights (Reisman 1990). One might add to this list the likely rise of an international law of peace, which conceivably will be built on the "international law of friendly relations" developed by the United Nations over the years. In this connection, international law will play a constructive role in the world's efforts to ban weapons of mass destruction and, conceivably, to ban or ameliorate what might be called "economic deprivation." The latter arises from the Third World's claim to a right to "sustained development" through rectifying the "unjust" distribution of wealth on the globe (UN Doc. C/CN.4/Sub.2/1987/23, p. 44; cited in Hsiung 1993a, 180).

Paradoxically, there were expectations of more, not fewer, interventions on behalf of human rights, not in communist countries as before but in the world at large (Donnelly 1992). The reason is that now without fear of a communist bloc counteraction, the curbs are removed from Western (especially U.S.) interventions for both human rights and humanitarian causes. This trend, ironically, surged only briefly. Both unilateral (U.S.) and UN humanitarian efforts seemed on the wane after discomfitures in Somalia and Rwanda. The trend bucked under both insurmountable local problems—such as were found in the two African nations—and severe budget constraints imposed by the Republican-controlled Congress since 1995 (*New York Times,* March 3, 1995, 3).

Conclusion

The interventionism and counterinterventionism created during the Cold War seemed to have left a legacy, however briefly, on the immediate post–Cold War period. The U.S. invasion of Panama may be considered an example of the remaining superpower's interventionist reflex acquired from the era just phased out. The Iraqi invasion, on the other hand, probably demonstrated a new phenomenon typical of the post–Cold War era, that of the perils of local bullies who surface in a power vacuum created by the disappearance of one of the two superpowers. In the case of the U.S. invasion, international law was unable, as in similar situations during the Cold War, to cope with the challenge presented by a superpower responding to a Cold War interventionist reflex, however anachronistic it may be in the new era. In the case of Iraq, the law had a rare chance of being pressed into service as the world community responded collectively (through the UN) to a local bully's threat, arising from a power vacuum situation. In either case, pure power politics will not be able to explain the complexities of a gray area that cuts across the subfields of international politics, law, and organization.

It is the purpose of this book to try to probe that gray area—to generate a better understanding of the complexities and totality of international relations. To borrow a metaphor from Krasner (1982, 509), the Neorealists see only the tectonic plates of power distribution and the occasional earthquakes in the system. They fail to see the "billiard balls and frequent collisions" that characterize international relations and the rules of the game circumscribing their incidence. Combining the three perspectives—international politics, law, and organization (more on this in Chapter 9)—would enable us to see both the tectonic plates and the billiard balls in action, and more. I hope to continue to demonstrate that the link from international politics to international law is a two-way street. Just as changes in the system's power configuration (international politics) result in corresponding changes in the rules of conduct (international law) among the system's units, the latter will in turn redefine international politics until another round of power shifts brings with it corresponding shifts in the system's rules of conduct.

Notes

1. I am relying heavily on Kenneth Waltz in this discussion of the Neorealist paradigm. Since the publication of Waltz's seminal *Theory of International Politics* (1979), as Buzan, Jones, and Little (1993, 1ff.) cogently observe, it has changed the theoretical orientation of the field of IR. The book has inspired important works

such as Gilpin (1981), Posen (1984), Walt (1987), Grieco (1990), and Cristensen and Snyder (1990). It has also brought about a critical literature, best exemplified in Keohane (1986), Spegele (1987), Walker (1987), and Wendt (1987). Although Neorealism and Structuralism are not necessarily coterminous, I am using the term *Neorealism* in such a way as to highlight the structural dimensions first propounded by its best known spokesperson, Kenneth Waltz.

2. To be fair, Neorealists are not so specifically negative about international law per se. But their dim view of international law can be deduced from their silence on the subject and, more important, their premises about self-help and power, leaving no room for international law. With regard to the latter, they have inherited the Morgenthalian "iron law" of power in international politics. I use *Morgenthalian* with reference to the Realist, and hence Neorealist, bifurcation of power and law, because not every modern Realist agreed on this point. Edward Hallett Carr (1939), for example, simply spoke of the overestimation of international law and legal institutions by IR scholars during the League of Nations years. Hedley Bull (1977), another great modern Realist, did not seem to have as low an opinion of international law when he spoke of an "ordered" international society and the need for "order" in world politics.

3. Although in journalistic parlance the term *world law* is used interchangeably with *international law,* the two are not the same, strictly speaking. World law denotes a body of norms regulating relations within a (hypothetical) system living under a functioning world government. Although world law is also envisioned in the Clark-Sohn proposals (1966), my thinking on this is probably closer to that of Falk (1975), who speaks of "world order" under a "central guidance system" (qua world government) whose "world assembly" presumably would make the rules that we call "world law" in this discussion. International law, on the other hand, is that body of norms governing relations between and among the coequal entities called states that make up the system that has no overaching authority over and above them.

4. When used without the structuralist connotations, I use the term *Realist* or *Realism* to indicate the original realist strand in Neorealism.

5. For all citations of cases, please see "International Law Cases Cited" at the end of this book.

6. Judicial decisions and teachings of the most highly qualified publicists may be used as "subsidiary" sources of international law. Cf. Article 38, ICJ Statute.

7. For a comparison with documentary sources of the various legal dimensions in Iraq's invasion of Kuwait and the U.S. invasion of Panama, see Ehrlich and O'Connell (1993, 1–108).

8. Legal scholars are divided on the defensibility of the U.S. invasion of Panama. For a debate, see "Agora: U.S. Forces in Panama: Defenders, Aggressors or Human Rights Activists?" in *AJIL* 84, 2 (1990): 494–524.

9. Critics might counter that the "regimes" school does address regime change. My reply is that (1) the regimes advocates are at best Neorealists of a revisionist variation; many are better classified as Neoliberal Institutionalists; and (2) the kind of change entertained by the regimes advocates in "regime change" are rather narrowly conceived and are unrelated to changes in systemic power realignment. Krasner (1982, 189f.), for example, defines regime change as "change . . . [involving] alterations of rules and decision-making procedures, but not of norms or principles."

2

THE SECURITY DILEMMA AND INTERNATIONAL LAW

The Security Dilemma and the Arms Race

In conditions of anarchy, states must rely on themselves to protect their own security and independence. However, in doing so, their search for security becomes a cause of insecurity for others. As each state arms itself against its neighbors, the neighbors respond by increasing their own armaments. Arms races take place as a result of the competitive arms buildup. This tends to make all states less secure, since it increases the level of potential threat to which all are exposed (Lieber 1988, 236f.). This security dilemma, as it is called (Herz 1950, 157–180; 1951, chap. 5), can be best summed up in two truisms: one state's security may mean another state's insecurity; and the state whose initial arms buildup at time-1 set off the competitive round of arms buildup may find itself, at time-n, less secure than before.

Examples of the security dilemma go back to the Peloponnesian War. For Thucydides (Hinley, 1951), the real cause of the Peloponnesian War was the rise of the power of Athens and the fear this evoked in the Spartans and their allies. In explaining British policy on naval disarmament in the interwar period (1918–1939) to the Japanese, Ramsey MacDonald said that "nobody wanted Japan to be insecure." But the problem was not with British desires but with the consequences of British policy, which was a form of self-help called for under conditions of anarchy (Jervis 1978, 170). In an earlier period, when Germany started building a powerful navy before World War I, Britain had objected that it (the German navy) could only be an offensive weapon aimed at Britain. As the British foreign secretary, Sir Edward Grey, put it, "If the German Fleet ever becomes superior to ours, the German Army can conquer this country" (p. 170). The other side of the coin is that whether Britain intended it or not, its navy had always constituted an important instrument of coercion threatening the security of Germany, among others. According to Luttwak (1981), there is in the security dilemma a "paradoxical logic," in that "states grow stronger only to become weaker."

In the post-1945 era, we saw a cutthroat nuclear arms race between the United States and the Soviet Union. McCormack (1989), in a book analyzing the rise and decline of U.S. hegemony, speaks of Washington's "atomic diplomacy" after World War II and its consequences. The United States, because it had unlocked the secret of atomic weapons, had every reason to be confident that power had shifted in its favor so that it was destined to lead in a war-shattered world. But, America's atomic diplomacy only "reinforced Russia's security fears, strengthened its resolve to control its East European buffer zone more tightly, undermined soft-liners on German policy, and led Soviet leaders to create a crash atomic bomb project of their own" (p. 45). By the early 1980s, while the Soviets had a clear numerical lead in a nuclear arms race whose enormous cost contributed to their eventual political demise, the United States likewise found its hegemony in decline (p. 216f.). McCormack's study ended before the Soviet disintegration in 1991, but the cutthroat nuclear arms competition equally brought untold scourge to both superpowers. The economic malaise and other woes the United States had brought on itself because of the nuclear arms race have survived the Soviet collapse and continued unabated well into the mid-1990s. Both superpowers were thus victims of a tragedy born of the security dilemma.

In game theory language, the security dilemma is an epitome of the Prisoner's Dilemma game (Rapoport and Chammah 1965, 33–50; Axelrod 1970, 60–70), which can be described in a few words: A lack of communication and of mutual trust between two prisoners, kept separately without communication, conspires to make "defection" (to squeal first, in exchange for amnesty) their own optimal strategy. The game theory matrix for the Prisoner's Dilemma is given below, with the numbers in the boxes being in the order of the actors' preferences.

PRISONER'S DILEMMA

		A: Cooperate	A: Defect
Cooperate	B	3 3	4 1
Defect	B	1 4	2 2

Although a better alternative would be for both to remain silent, the outcome is that both draw a light sentence (thus, suboptimal) as they each opt to confess against the other (hence, double defection). Anarchy in the international system is the equivalent of the lack of communication in the Prisoner's Dilemma game. Just as it has been shown that increase in communication tends to moderate a player's strategy (Rivera 1968, 375f.), international law mitigates the effects of anarchy and may therefore change each player's dominant strategy and elicit cooperation instead.

Mitigating Prisoner's Dilemma by International Law

Under anarchy, or in the absence of a central authority, nation-states cannot trust each other. In the conduct of their external relations, the only possible solutions to the Prisoner's Dilemma are through third-party intercession, collective action, and institutions.

To elaborate briefly, first, since states are sovereigns and hence enjoy juridical equality, no state can impose its will on any other state. Third-party intercession is the best substitute for the mediatory power of a central authority. Thus, international law provides for various modes of dispute settlement entailing the services of a third party, be it a mediator, an arbitrator or a tribunal (see Chapter 4), or the intervening role of an international organization such as the United Nations (see Chapter 10). Second, collective action results when states, as coequal sovereigns, join hands in the protection of their own interests or the community interests they support. Collective will thus transcends but encompasses the individual wills of nations. Collective action may take various forms, from balance of power and collective security (Chapter 3) to the regulation of both armaments and the use of force (Chapter 4). Third, institutions such as the UN, OECD, and WTO, built on the legal foundations of international law (Chapters 9 and 10), can act in behalf of the various coequal sovereigns, especially in cases where they are either divided by jealousy or caught in tangled battles over jurisdiction (Chapter 5). When all means of third-party intercession and collective action fail, there always remains the recourse to self-help, such as exercising the right of self-defense permissible under international law or, in extreme cases, individual or collective intervention, which international law purports to regulate (Chapter 3).

Working toward solutions through collective action and institutions, states may create "international regimes" such as the maritime regime supported by the law of the sea, the trade regime (GATT/WTO), the international finance regime under the Bretton Woods system, and security regimes (e.g., NATO) as established by treaty or practice. As we shall see, regimes have the function of ameliorating the effects of the Prisoner's Dilemma.

We live in an age that sees the rise of the community and the nation at the expense of the state (Gottlieb 1993). This, combined with the coincidence of divergent views of the industrial and developing nations, has occasioned the rise of a relatively new (post-1945) category of rights, known as human rights, self-determination, decolonization, "right to democracy," and even the right to "sustained development," as advocated with rising crescendo by the Third World states in the United Nations. The phenomenon has both changed the shape of international law and been contained within the outer limits set by the law (Chapters 7 and 8). The rise of community consciousness and the effects of the spread of industrialization also account for increased collective action in the area of environmental control. The resultant "international environmental law" can play a constructive role in defining rights and obligations over a problem that is sure to call for unrelenting collective action of states well into the next century (Chapters 9 and 10).

In the following sections, I analyze how international law mitigates the egoism-driven behavior of nations, and provide empirical evidence of how the problem of the security dilemma was mitigated over time, both bilaterally, in U.S.-Soviet relations, and multilaterally, through the CSCE (OSCE) process.

International Law and International Regimes

Before proceeding, I would like to suggest a distinction between *international law,* as it is used in this book, and *international regimes,* on which there is a growing literature (Krasner 1982; Young 1989; Rittberger 1990; Young and Osherenko 1993).

There is considerable overlap between the two. However, international law is both broader and narrower in meaning than international regimes. For one thing, regimes are more functionally specific. Even in the issue area of environmental control, for example, there are variable institutional arrangements for whales and whaling, transboundary air pollution control, and the control of chemicals that deplete ozone in the atmosphere (Young 1994, 44). In a way, international regimes are comparable to "particular international law," which is confined to either a specific geographical area (e.g., Latin America or Europe) or a specific issue area (e.g., human rights or outer space). In this sense, the two (regimes and particular international law) are almost coterminous. But *general* international law is much broader; it is in fact universal in its scope and application. One could nevertheless suggest that general international law can be a "nesting" of international regimes, in that the former provides an anchor for the latter, a perimeter within which international regimes operate.

On the other hand, international law is also narrower in a particular sense when compared with international regimes as defined in the regimes literature. A regime is said to contain not only "principles and norms," but also "rules and decision-making procedures" that are consistent with the same principles and norms (Krasner 1982, 187). As I use the term here, I do not see international law as necessarily comprising decision rules, unless the occasion implies otherwise.

There is also a divergency in perspective. As noted in Chapter 1, this discussion of international law always assumes an underpinning interplay of power politics and law, both in the formation of the norms and in their interpretation and application. On the other hand, the concept of international regimes and its most avid proponents do not seem to be as concerned with the power linkage to regimes in international relations. For instance, more recent studies of international regimes have provided little support for the theory of hegemonic stability, which has loomed as a central concern of those who stress power factors (Keohane 1984; Young and Osherenko 1993).

To me, regimes always have a legal dimension, as they are created by agreement or through state practice and operate within the confines of international law. But regimes proponents generally avoid any mention of international law. Here I may refer to "international law regimes," or "regimes under international law," for two reasons: to highlight the structures of arrangements—and the resultant modes of patterned behavior—defined by and operating under international law; and, more important, to focus on the particular part(s) of international law as it applies to the regimes in question. Besides, international law regimes denote an ongoing process in the formation and development of norms or principles in a given issue area. Some examples are: the law of the sea regimes, beginning with customary norms from traditional times and then in codified form under the 1958 conventions and culminating in the 1982 CLOS III; the nuclear arms control regime, whose landmarks ranged from the nuclear partial test ban treaty of 1963 to START II of 1992; and the CSCE regime, which commenced with the 1975 Helsinki Accords and continues within OSCE.

It is true that a relationship between nations can be defined by treaty, such as in the delineation of an international boundary, but a relationship so defined is not a regime. On the other hand, if a treaty should define a relationship between two or more neighboring countries over the control of river resources along their borders—such as the U.S.-Mexican Treaty on Utilization of Waters of Colorado and Tijuana Rivers and the Rio Grande (1944)—it does establish a regime. As a rule of thumb, a regime inaugurated under international law is not an executed agreement (one-shot deal), but creates an ongoing arrangement or structure of expectations. In addition, a regime may entail some form of institution to coordinate or oversee the arrangements. Hence, as regards the 1944 U.S.-Mexican treaty, the

International Boundary Commission was created to facilitate the carrying out of the principles contained in the treaty. But whether or not such a body exists is not always a good guide for identifying the existence of a regime. For example, we may speak of a "regime" on the prohibition of the use of force having been in existence since 1928, quite independent of either the League of Nations or the United Nations. The reason is that a number of treaties, such as the Kellog-Briand Pact (1928) and a few regional agreements (e.g., the Saavedra Lamas Treaty signed by Latin American states in 1933), together have sought to outlaw the use of force. Before the twentieth century, the complement of the norms forming the law of the sea existed only in customary international law. The absence of a treaty or institution, however, never stopped nations from recognizing the existence of a "maritime regime."

Despite these differences, there is a vast area of convergence between international law and international regimes. For one thing, the regimes literature makes a distinction between what is and is not a regime. All ad hoc, one-shot arrangements, based on short-term calculations, are not considered regimes (Krasner 1982, 187). This recalls our discussion in Chapter 1 about a state practice growing out of political expediency, as contrasted to a practice accepted as custom with the force of law (*Asylum* case). Second, international law shares a liberal-institutionalist assumption with international regimes, that the norms of conduct, created because of their perceived instrumental values, represent the will of an evolving community transcending interstate conflict. (I hasten to add a caveat: Unlike regimes as defined by their advocates, international law here is seen as the result of a law/politics interplay.) Third, because of its broad sweep, international law often subsumes international regimes and, more important, both are capable of mitigating the effects of the Prisoner's Dilemma (defection over cooperation) born of systemic anarchy. Analytically, the following reasons can be given.

First, international law eliminates what Stein (1990) calls a dilemma of choice (between cooperation and defection), as it either blocks out a particular choice—such as the Kellog-Briand Pact (1928) outlawing war as an "instrument of foreign policy"—or, alternatively, provides a framework for cooperation—such as the European Common Market established by the Treaty of Rome (1958). It is as though the lack of communication is remedied in the Prisoner's Dilemma game. The improved certainty is capable of transforming the anarchy-induced Prisoner's Dilemma into a Stag Hunt—in short, a double-cooperation game (cf. Hardin 1982, 157–172).

Second, the uniform provisions or symmetry[1] (Stein 1990, 191) in the payoff, prescribed by international law, tend to remove the "relative gains" barrier to cooperation, as it specifies the rules of the game (e.g., mutual obligations) and thus reduces uncertainty. Neorealists argue that states' preoccupation with the question "Who will gain more?" (hence, relative gains) inhibits cooperation (Waltz 1979, 105; Grieco 1990, 40–49). Under conditions of improved certainty under international law—such as in the specification of reciprocal obligations in the treatment of aliens and diplomatic and consular agents—concerns for prescribed gains and symmetry in the trade-off substitute for concerns for relative gains. In fact, states *cooperate* to create a common set of norms of behavior for their own good, either by treaty or through custom (i.e., repeated practice implying *opinio juris*). Hence, their urge for order leads them to collaboration in the creation of norms or regimes of international law in the interest of securing patterned behavior.

Third, regimes generated under international law seal a relationship of interdependence among the players (nations), such as between landlocked countries and transit states (discussed in Chapter 1), or as among members of the GATT/WTO. Hence, activity otherwise guided by calculations of egoistic interests (relative gains) becomes regime-guided activity (Krasner 1982, 187).

Last, regimes under international law convert international relations from a one-shot deal into an iterated game in which present loss can be traded for future gains. Hence, cooperation is more likely created under the "shadow of the future" (Oye 1985).[2]

Nuclear Arms Control and Peace Accords

Among the examples that can be used to illustrate the veracity of the assertions made in the preceding section, I would like to single out two: the nuclear arms control regime between the superpowers over three decades; and the Helsinki peace process following the accords of 1975 bearing its name. The two are strategically interrelated, as viewed in retrospect, one ultimately leading to the other. I review them briefly for the lessons they provide on international law as a mitigating force for the effects of the security dilemma. However, to understand the role of international law as a mitigating force, we have to address two prior points: systemic values and institutional learning.

Systemic values. Despite the Realist fixation with power as the sole determinant of international politics, I would like to call attention to a rival force, which, for lack of a better term, may be called "systemic values." These values derive from certain ideas or ideals whose time has come, having first originated from either domestic or international sources, but becoming universally embraced—at least by enough nations, including the major powers, to figure as a beacon for international endeavoring. Systemic values, used here, are of a different (in fact, higher) order from norms, which Talcott Parsons defined as "generalized formulations . . . of expectations of proper action by differentiated units in relatively specific situations" (cited in Kegley and Raymond 1994, 122). If norms can be viewed as "rules of the game," *systemic values* define what the game is for nations in their relations with each other at a given time. For instance, if in the eighteenth century the notion of the divine right to rule was an overriding systemic value, in the nineteenth century, it was the dictate of colonial empire building. By the same token, in the twentieth century, it is the right of self-determination with all its ramifications.

Kertesz (1967, 23) points out that the ideal of self-determination became an international slogan as a result of a propaganda contest between Lenin and Woodrow Wilson. The idea as first conceived had rather limited meanings. After World War II, self-determination, now coupled with "fundamental freedoms," became a lofty goal exalted in the United Nations Charter and held out for the world at large to attain.

By its design, self-determination was conceived as an effort to stem a possible resurgence of Nazi-type deprivations of basic human rights. But it was soon to become a legal and political weapon in the hands of subjugated peoples and their supporters, used in their fight for decolonization and independence (Hsiung 1993b). I return to this topic later, but I wish to stress here that the power of a systemic value whose time has come should be duly recognized, for it may redefine the game of nations. In Chapter 7 we shall see that when the United Nations passed the 1960 Declaration on the Granting of Independence to All Colonial Peoples, the Western colonial powers (UK, France, Portugal, etc.) did not even try to block it. Their collective acquiescence, even to their own peril, signified a sense of futility in trying to go against the tide of the moral forces in support of a systemic value (self-determination qua decolonization) that was so obviously irrepressible.

Thus, the universal acceptance of self-determination has, in less than five decades since the birth of the UN Charter, brought about the liquidation of the vast colonial empires of the West. The prevalence of self-determination was more recently borne out in the breakup of the Soviet Union and Yugoslavia.

Another impact of self-determination has been the rise since the 1950s of the principle of economic sovereignty, or sovereignty over natural resources (including oil) under one's own soil. Though this remains an understudied subject, I wish to note that, following the universal acceptance of economic sovereignty as a systemic value, and then as a principle of international law by the 1960s, the Western oil companies, known as the Seven Sisters, lost their oil-pricing power, a privilege they had arrogated to themselves since the nineteenth century (Szyliowicz and O'Neill 1975). Members of the Organization of Petroleum Exporting Countries (OPEC) took over oil pricing as well as sovereign rights over the oil extracted from under their soil, which resulted in the first energy crisis of 1973–1974. Many people have written about the energy crises, and even more have suffered from the energy problem. But few realize that the West's energy problem began with the rise of a systemic value known as "permanent sovereignty over natural resources," as confirmed and propagated by a UN resolution (GA Res. 1803 [1962]) that upheld an aspiration of the otherwise relatively powerless Third World nations. Economic sovereignty has since quietly changed the shape of things in the world.

The above, I hope, is enough to show the invisible power of what we call systemic values. Their power is of a different sort from what consumes the Realist's attention; but it is power nonetheless, as measured by the influence of those values on the course of events in the world system. Systemic values may begin as no more than a moral persuasive force, but when they are widely accepted by states, including the major ones, their power derives from the expectations they raise in the world community. Their sway depends on the extent of conviction with which they are held by strategic decisionmakers.

Institutional learning. The other point that needs to be made before proceeding regards institutional learning. Haas (1990) speaks of international institutions as "epistemic communities" (p. 40f.) and defines *learning* as "overcoming habitual behavior" (p. 222, n. 29). In the context of regimes under international law, learning may mean, among other things, the process by which norm-regulated behavior elevates to what Rosenau (1986, 864f.) calls "habit-driven" behavior. I use the term *learning* in two senses: National and international decisionmakers may learn that it is in their self-interest to rectify previous mistakes caused by egoistic calculations; and these decisionmakers may likewise learn to embrace a systemic value whose time has come. Stein (1994) suggests that "political learning" might more likely apply to a leader like Gorbachev, who had been an "uncommitted thinker" on previous Soviet security or other policies. I would add that a prerequisite for political learning is iteration of the game, such as international law can encourage.

Certain regimes of international law created at time-1 may be likely to rise to a higher plane at time-n, if doing so meets the expectations generated by a particular systemic value prevailing at the time (especially if it happens to have domestic backing). If the particular systemic value in question is incorporated into a treaty norm, its elevation to a "higher plane" may imply the making of a new treaty on a grander scale, such as in the natural progression from SALT I to SALT II, and from START I to START II, in the nuclear arms control regime.

Under these circumstances, international law may fulfill its potential of mitigating the egoism-driven effects of the Prisoner's Dilemma game, as manifested in the security dilemma phenomenon discussed at the beginning of this chapter.

We are now ready to look at the gradual but steady redirection of the cutthroat U.S.-Soviet nuclear arms race to an ever deepening arms control process. Once again, the purpose here is to review how regime making under international law created an iterated game and helped mitigate the egoism-driven behavior in U.S.-Soviet relationships.

The U.S.-Soviet nuclear arms control regime. The progress and success of the nuclear arms control process between the United States and the Soviet Union may have many reasons and angles to be explored. Some of these are the economic consequence of the arms race and public opinion at home, the skills of the negotiators, and the shifting power ratios between the two sides as measured by the sizes of their respective nuclear arsenals. One may treat the entire saga of U.S.-Soviet conflict as a series of "superpower games" (Brams 1985). But here our discussion will concentrate on the effects of iteration (i.e., the cumulative impact of earlier arms control agreements on subsequent strategic decisions), the factor of systemic values and institutional learning as defined above, and the phenomenon of egoism mitigation as a result of all these. Counting from the creation of the 1963 nuclear partial test ban treaty to START II, concluded in 1992, the twenty-nine-year process is typically an iterated game. The bilateral negotiations may have begun as a two-person, two-choice Prisoner's Dilemma (PD) game. The long process, however, changed it into an iterated PD. The game theory literature shows that when the number of iterations is high, intelligent players will (learn to) play a cooperative strategy (Luce and Raiffa 1957; Rapoport and Chammah 1965; Downs and Rocke 1990). Just as the earlier Hot Line Agreement (June 20, 1963) had served as a confidence-building measure for the Limited Test Ban Treaty (August 5, 1963), the latter in turn paved the way for subsequent agreements.

Including the 1963 partial nuclear test ban treaty, the long list of the bilateral agreements[3] making up a "regime of international law" between the two superpowers includes:

- The Limited [Nuclear] Test Ban Treaty (1963)
- The Accidents Measures Agreement (1971)
- The "Hot Line" Modernization Agreement (1971), which was an update of the 1963 "Hot Line" Agreement
- Strategic Arms Limitation Treaty (SALT I) of 1972, which was a package that included the Anti-Ballistic Missile (ABM) Treaty
- Prevention of Nuclear War Agreement (1973)
- ABM Protocol (1974), a revision of the 1972 ABM Treaty

- The Threshold Test Ban Treaty (1974)
- Underground Nuclear Explosions for Peaceful Purposes (PNE) of 1976
- SALT II (1979)
- The Intermediate Nuclear Force Treaty (INF) of 1987
- The Strategic Arms Reduction Treaty of 1991 (START I)
- START II (1992)

This list does not include multilateral treaties on nuclear arms control to which the United States and the Soviet Union were parties. One notable example is the Non-Proliferation Treaty (NPT) of 1968. But it is, by itself, an impressive list to convey a sense of a nuclear arms control "regime" under international law. Reviewing the history of bilateral treaty making for its own sake is not my intent; I only wish to point out a number of noteworthy features in the regime-building process:

1. Iteration (involving thousands of meetings and hundreds of proposals) seemed to create a momentum of its own, so much so that agreements of a lesser sort (e.g., "hot line" or partial test ban) eventually led to more agreements of broader significance, such as progression from mere test prohibition to strategic weapons limitation, and eventually to their reduction (cf. Jensen 1988). Under the INF and START treaties, actual nuclear weapons were dismantled.

2. In both the limitation and reduction agreements, equivalence rather than symmetry was the goal accepted by both sides, because their asymmetric weapons systems made it impractical to aim at exact symmetry. But a ratio between the targeted limitation or reduction and the actual size of each side's existing arsenal was taken into consideration. This ratio made both sides willing to accept parity (Jensen 1988, 177), even though at times it may mean uneven gains, in lieu of "relative gains," as Neorealists would insist.

3. Although the first important nuclear arms control instrument, the partial test ban treaty, was signed in 1963, the more substantive treaties on the limitation of strategic weapons were concluded only after 1971. The first treaty on nuclear reduction and dismantling was not reached until 1987. The momentum built by the earlier agreements, no doubt, raised expectations in many quarters. The cumulative effect of the earlier agreements was that they generated an atmosphere in which the craving for more-substantive arms control became a universally accepted systemic value.

It seems that after the arrival of the "age of détente" in 1968 (Bartlett 1994, 349–356), the world was ready for more-substantive arms control.

One indication was the launching of the peace movement, marked by the creation of such organizations as Greenpeace in Europe in 1971 and Ground Zero in the United States about the same time.

We have seen that central decisionmakers had a proclivity to "learn" lessons in hindsight that "defections" would not be self-rewarding in iterated PD games. Not surprisingly, by the early 1970s, it was already apparent to both superpowers that their cutthroat nuclear arms race only boomeranged. The world's peace movements after 1971 apparently lent further fillips to the systemic value of more-substantive arms control. By the mid-1980s, the economic woes at home drove both Reagan and Gorbachev to the realization that the escalating spiral of the security dilemma could only bring catastrophe to both countries. Hence, the decision to put a halt to the spiral came as a result of what we earlier called institutional learning.

If the post-1987 arms reduction move was a belated reversal of the giant wheel of the superpower arms race, the first important effort to mitigate the security dilemma spiral actually came as early as 1972. The ABM Treaty signed in that year provided a number of mutually agreed self-abnegation (MASA) measures. For example, both sides agreed not to deploy ABM systems for defense of an individual region "except as provided for in Art. III." Under that article, the parties pledged each to install only two ABM sites and, even so, only under a certain agreed ceiling of ABM systems or their components at each site. Another MASA measure was the specification of what was permissible in development or testing (Art. IV) and of what was not permissible (Art. V). While modernization was allowed (Art. VII), destruction of ABM systems or their components in excess of the allowable numbers was provided for (Art. VIII). Another MASA was the pledge not to transfer to other countries ABM systems or their components in excess of the preset limits (Art. IX). The treaty also provided for verification, though by "national means" at each party's disposal but "consistent with generally recognized principles of international law" (Art. XI). Article XIII sanctioned the creation of an institution, called the Standing Consultative Commission, to oversee the implementation of the treaty's provisions and to facilitate the exchange of information between the parties. There were provisions for iteration, such as the pledge that the two parties would continue on with "active negotiations for limitations on strategic weapons" (Art. XI).

This brief review of the ABM provisions is necessary to call attention to its three important features capable of mitigating the security dilemma entangling U.S.-Soviet relations: specification of the MASA measures to block out temptations to "defect"; pledges to commit each signatory to cooperate in certain specified ways; and provision for iteration, to make the ABM Treaty but a stepping stone to further agreements on a higher plane (limitation of offensive weapons). All these were designed to change the iterated Prisoner's Dilemma into an iterated Stag Hunt, or to convert a double-defection into a double-cooperation game. An immediate payoff of double cooperation was the agreement in a 1974 protocol to cut the ABM sites from two to only one on each side.

The Helsinki Accords and the CSCE process. A convergence of two opposing sets of goals, held by the two opposing blocs during the Cold War, coalesced to bring about the multilateral (thirty-five participants) negotiations that led to the Helsinki Accords of 1975. The negotiations had been pressed by the Soviet Union, which hoped to use the conference, to be known as the Conference on Security and Cooperation in Europe (CSCE), to enhance the legitimacy of Soviet control over Eastern Europe. But it became the device the West used to pressure the Soviet Union and the communist regimes in Eastern Europe to give greater respect to human rights (Fry 1993).

The Helsinki Accords had several elements. The first was a Declaration on the Principles Guiding Relations Between Participating States. The list included the basic traditional principles of international law incorporated into Article 2 of the United Nations Charter, thus creating what we call a "regime of international law." These principles are: respect for sovereign authority, refraining from the use of force, inviolability of frontiers, territorial integrity of states, peaceful settlement of disputes, and nonintervention in internal affairs. But the list also included respect for human rights and fundamental freedoms.

The Helsinki Accords contained three "baskets." Basket I dealt with security and disarmament and included provisions for prior notice of military maneuvers, exchanges of observers, and other confidence-building measures. Basket II focused on cooperation in economic matters, science, technology, and the environment. It identified ways to promote increased commercial exchanges between East and West. Basket III zeroed in on humanitarian and other fields and emphasized the free movement of peoples, ideas, and information. It included cultural and educational exchanges. The three baskets provided linkages of various issues that both sides had wanted.

The Helsinki regime, by its reaffirmation of the international law principles mentioned above, also resolved Stein's (1990) dilemma of choice, by blocking out the option to "defect." Most noticeable was the inclusion of the principles of "cooperation among states" and "fulfillment in good faith of obligations under international law" (Fry 1993, 175), signifying a commitment to cooperate. The clear specification of mutual obligations also increases transparency, making it easier to spot defection if it should take place.

The accords likewise provided for iteration, calling for periodic review meetings to continue the multilateral exchanges on European cooperation. The subsequent CSCE meetings in Belgrade, Madrid, Stockholm, Vienna, etc. at regular intervals continued the process that began at Helsinki. The iterated process provided a framework for consolidating détente, for enhancing confidence-building measures, and subsequently for helping manage the far-reaching political and strategic changes in Europe.

A significant spin-off from this process was the Charter of Paris for a New Europe (signed on November 22, 1990), which officially ended the Cold War, declaring: "The era of confrontation and division of Europe has ended" (Fry 1993, 359).

In retrospect, the CSCE process complemented the U.S-Soviet arms control process, in that the former helped extend the modus vivendi worked out by the latter to bring peace to Europe. A more cogent reminder was the conclusion, three days earlier (November 19), of a treaty limiting conventional forces in Europe (CFE) between members of NATO and the Warsaw Pact (*New York Times,* November 20, 1990, 1). It set limits on tanks, lesser armored combat vehicles, artillery pieces, armored helicopters, and fixed-wing combat aircraft (*Economist,* November 24, 1990, 50; *Congressional Quarterly Weekly Report,* November 24, 1990, 3931).

Critics may claim that both the Charter of Paris and the CFE treaty were made possible by the imminent crumbling of the Warsaw Pact and the weakening of the Soviet Union. Mikhail Gorbachev had no choice but to accept the agreements. But to refute this view, one need only ask why Gorbachev had refused to use the 400,000 Soviet troops still stationed in Eastern Europe the year before, when East European communist regimes were shaking loose from the Warsaw pact or just collapsing under the impact of the fall of the Berlin Wall. By contrast, Brezhnev had invaded Czechoslovakia to put a stop to Dubček's liberalization in 1968; Krushchev had intervened in the mid-1950s, responding to unrest in Hungary and other parts of Eastern Europe.

The answer is that it was Gorbachev who decided to unleash Eastern Europe. Time and again, he had made it known that he would not interfere in Eastern Europe's internal affairs, nor intervene by force in the event of its breakaway from the Soviet grip. He told President Reagan so in Washington at the signing of the INF Treaty in 1987, and again at their fourth summit meeting in Moscow in 1988. Before the Council of Europe in July 1989, Gorbachev explicitly renounced the Brezhnev Doctrine, under which the Soviet Union had claimed a special right to intervene in the Socialist Commonwealth, following the 1968 Soviet invasion of Czechoslovakia. Again, on October 25, 1989, Gorbachev reaffirmed to Finnish president Mauno Koivisto: "We have no right, moral or political, to interfere in events happening in [Eastern Europe]" (cited in Fry 1993, 166).

In his careful study of the Helsinki process, Fry (1993, 166) concluded that the "Helsinki process alone did not generate the cataclysmic changes in East European leadership and political and economic policies." "The impetus for these changes," he added, "came more directly from Mikhail Gorbachev himself."

I would carry this point one step further and note that the Helsinki regime had created a systemic value, as defined above, to the effect that it was wrong, and illegal under international law, to interfere in the internal affairs of other states in Europe—Socialist Commonwealth included—or to violate their territorial integrity by the use or threat of force, as was stipulated in Basket I of the Helsinki Final Act reached by the thirty-five participating parties in 1975, ten years before Gorbachev came to power in the Soviet Union.

Realists may insist that by the mid-1980s communism had run out of steam: the arms race and the long-flawed Stalinist economic system had impoverished the Soviet people. However, after everything has been said about the woes besetting the Soviet Union at the time Gorbachev assumed leadership, it remains true that during the mid-1980s the Soviet Union had neared a first-strike capability that made the U.S. ICBM retaliatory capability vulnerable. President Reagan's openly acknowledged "window of vulnerability" was a precise summation of the power ratio between the two superpowers at the time (Jensen 1988, 117). In the circumstances, any pure power theory does not seem to offer a plausible answer to why Gorbachev should decide to shift gears and opt for a conciliatory policy to the extent that would lead toward strategic reduction, beginning with the INF Treaty.

Political economists may offer a somewhat better explanation by looking at the Soviet economy, which seemed to begin to show trouble in the 1970s. Soviet economic growth rate had steadily declined through the 1970s, from the 8 percent annually in 1966 to 3.4 percent by 1981, though there was a recovery to 4.9 percent in 1986 (Gill and Law 1988, 323). Be that as it may, the economic reason still would not explain why Gorbachev's response should have been more political than economic. His reforms began with glasnost, or creating a more open society as if to conform to one crucial requirement (Basket III) in the Helsinki Accords. At Gorbachev's behest, the two most odious articles of the Soviet criminal code, under which most dissidents were sentenced, were repealed (Mullerson 1994, 163). If the intent of reform was to boost the Soviet economy, he did not have to do all that. In case anyone has any doubt on this point, just look at the East Asian high-performance economies (World Bank 1993). None of them had to democratize first to get to the economic success they are known for.

As noted above, Basket III of the Helsinki Final Act committed the signatories to cooperate in promoting human contacts and increasing exchange of information. This latter task required improving the circulation of and access to information and improving working conditions for journalists. As the former deputy foreign minister of Estonia (1991–1992), Mullerson (1994, 162) observed, the most successful part of Gorbachev's reforms was his glasnost, which, in Mullerson's words, "may be said to be tantamount to the freedom of the press." In addition to being party to the Helsinki Final Act, the Soviet Union in 1991 adhered to the Optional Protocol[4] to the 1966 International Covenant on Civil and Political Rights. The move put the Soviet Union under the jurisdiction of the Human Rights Committee established under the covenant. The committee has the right to receive petitions from individuals claiming to be the victims of any violations by their own government of the rights set forth in the covenant.

There is no ironclad proof that Gorbachev's reforms—glasnost, perestroika, and democratization—were inspired by the Helsinki regime. Even if Gorbachev had stepped forward to confirm this, many questions would remain unanswered. But let us, for heuristic reasons, assume that there is a link between the Helsinki regime and Gorbachev's reforms at home and a détente policy abroad, including the unleashing of Eastern Europe. And let us also assume that the link lies, harking back to the suggestion regarding systemic values, in the commitment Moscow made along with the other thirty-four participants to respect the provisions of the Helsinki Final Act and hence to live up to the expectations the treaty had raised.

Response to Skepticism

In adding a few points to the preceding line of inquiry, I hope not to harp on the link between the Helsinki regime and Gorbachev's reforms, but rather to offer further illumination on the nature of international law and, more specifically, to highlight the law's potential utility in the mitigation of the security dilemma problem raised at the beginning of this chapter.

First, critics may question: In view of the eventual outcome—collapse of communism in Europe, including the Soviet Union—how could it be possible that Gorbachev chose to embark on his reforms simply because he thought he had to comply with provisions of the Helsinki Accords, systemic value or no? The implicit answer favored by the critics was that he had no choice.

My answer to the latter point is that Gorbachev had at least one other choice, even assuming that the Soviet economy was in dire straits and had to be revamped. China after Mao had neither debunked communism nor embarked on anything approximating the proportions of either glasnost or perestroika. But since 1978, China's economic reform has registered an average annual growth of 10 percent or better. In more recent years it approached 15 percent, even as the world was in recession in the early 1990s. In terms of global trade, market size, and sheer economic bulk, China is becoming a fourth pole in a global system often described as tripolar (United States, Japan, and the European Union). Many Japanese, according to a 1995 Manichi Shimbun survey (*Christian Science Monitor* dispatch, January 19, 1995), now believe that China, rather than Japan, will be the most economically powerful country in the Pacific Century. But China's success, owing to its symbiosis of political conservatism and economic liberalism, has shown that this strategy would have been a safer alternative to Gorbachev's approach to reforming the dilapidated Soviet economy. Without intending necessarily to condone the Dengist brand of reform, I merely want to point out that it was not because he had no other choice that Gorbachev adopted the political liberalization route.

To return to the basic question regarding Gorbachev's chosen strategy vis-à-vis its outcome, I must agree with Stein (1990, 16) that in making strategic decisions states choose strategy, not outcome. This is not to deny the fact that in choosing a strategy states may compare the estimated outcomes. But as the Prisoner's Dilemma shows, the eventuality of a "suboptimal outcome" does not stop a player from taking what to him is his "dominant strategy."

This leads to a cognate point regarding international law. Realists may scoff at the law because of its lack of enforceability and may conclude that international law cannot possibly influence a state's policy or behavior in international relations. My answer is: International law's influence on states is due to the fact that oftentimes what matters to decisionmakers is not so much the outcome as what the law *prescribes*. Most analyses of Gorbachev's motivation for reform were, in fact, focused on its domestic sources. The point I am raising here will become more relevant if we search instead for its "international sources" (Deudney and Ikenberry 1992; Koslowski and Kratochwil 1994). To the extent that Gorbachev intended to roll back the West's "economic containment" (Stent 1987) to help salvage the Soviet economy, what better strategy would there be than to comply with the human rights regime created under the Helsinki Accords? With our eyes trained on this question, we would be turned to the real answer: Gorbachev's decision to launch glasnost was based on what he perceived, rightly or wrongly, to be his dominant strategy—considering his presumptive conviction regarding the systemic values created by and under the Helsinki regime. The question of outcome, paradoxically, becomes more salient only in retrospect. Thus viewed, international law's influence on decisionmaking may actually be greater than one might otherwise assume.

Second, Realist critics may ask a follow-up question, centered on the law's alleged ineffectualness due to its lack of enforcement. Even if decisionmakers should factor in, among other desiderata, what international law prescribes, the critics may ask: Wouldn't the law's ineffectualness debar it from being taken seriously at the stage of decisionmaking? My answer is a qualified yes. To get to the heart of the matter, we have to reexamine the nature of international law. As Nardin (1992, 19) cogently puts it, international law is a "rule-oriented," rather than "outcome-oriented," code of conduct. We can analyze this question at two levels. At one level, decisionmakers—to the extent that they consider strategy, not outcome—will consider among other factors what the rule-oriented code may prescribe on a given issue before coming to a definitive decision. At another level, while the alleged ineffectualness of international law may be a detracting factor, it remains true that should a country choose to bar international law considerations and, as a result, should violate the law, then it will find itself in a situation discussed under "unilateral action versus community scrutiny" in Chapter 1. The upshot is that an unprovoked violation is the best imprimatur to counterviolations or copycat violations. And it may even open the floodgate to retorsions, reprisals, or other forms of self-help by other states. Ultimately, the result may not be in the self-interest of the state that starts this chain of reactions by being the first to violate international law. Thus, its "rule-oriented" quality does not vitiate international law being a serious code of conduct that it is in a state's interest to follow.

One example for this complex chain reaction syndrome is Egypt's nationalization of the Suez Canal in July 1956 and the countermoves that followed. On July 26, President Nasser announced Egypt's nationalization of the Universal Company of the Suez Canal. The move was protested by Britain, France, and the United States, representing the shareholders in the company, users of the canal, and parties to the 1888 Constantinople convention governing the canal's status (Henkin 1968, 187). At the time, nationalization of this nature was of questionable legality. Many governments, including the ones that protested, considered the Egyptian move a breach of existing international law. On October 29, Israel moved into the Sinai Peninsula, a move members of the United Nations and most writers considered a violation of Article 2(4) of the UN Charter (hence, international law) (Henkin 1968, 196). When only Israel heeded their joint ultimatum calling for a cease-fire and mutual withdrawal of forces, Britain and France, on October 30, sent in troops to guard the canal (against Egyptian inroads). Most governments and most lawyers would likewise consider the joint British-French expedition a violation of Article 2(4) of the UN Charter, which explicitly prohibits the use or threat of force. Even though the British-French action proved to be futile attempts to shore up their sagging big-power status, the chain of events, accentuated by the Israeli and British-French use of force, clearly dealt a serious blow to the prestige of Nasser. The Israeli sally anticipated Israel's later annexation of Sinai and the Gaza Strip in 1967 (Safran 1969, 45–46; 332–349), a devastating loss to Egyptian interests. We see in this chain of events one violation (Egypt's nationalization measure) leading to counterviolations by Israel (occupation of the Sinai) and by the British and French (invasion of the canal). Nasser's loss of prestige and the Israeli move on Sinai were sad costs to Egypt's summary disregard of international law. The moral is that, contrary to Realist inclinations, it is often to a state's interest not to contravene international law without justifiable provocation.

Precisely for this reason, statesmen often had to bend their policy decisions so that the action flowing from them would not constitute an unprovoked breach of international law. Henkin (1968, 223) reminds us that in the Cuban missile crisis, various options were considered by President Kennedy's Ex-Com, including a bombing attack on Cuba. But Attorney General Robert Kennedy argued effectively that such an attack, especially without warning, would be another Pearl Harbor and would blacken the name of the United States. The argument was a turning point in that it redirected the deliberations to the quarantine option, which was finally adopted. Implicit in Robert Kennedy's argument, which carried the day, was exactly that international law *prescriptions* would make the bombing option unacceptable. While we are rarely privy to high-level policy deliberations in which international law prescriptions may or may not be weighed by decisionmakers, we do know that the whole area of the law on state responsibility and treatment of aliens is built on the principle of due diligence (see Chapter 5). International law, in short, prescribes a duty on the part of a host state only to pursue and apprehend the offender with *due diligence,* with a view to proper punishment for damage to an alien. The law does not require an ancillary duty to guarantee that justice is done (outcome).

Third, as regards security dilemma, it epitomizes a Prisoner's Dilemma game. If the combination of perception and choice of what appears to be the "dominant strategy" leads states to the security dilemma, then the key to its resolution lies in the restriction of the "dilemma of choice," so that the option to defect is closed out. As we have seen, international law regimes can help restrict the dilemma of choice. By summoning commitment to a prescribed recourse, international law regimes help block out the alternative route of defection for states that accept them. Reciprocity and symmetry in the trade-off of gains, such as international law regimes provide, will further increase the likelihood of double cooperation, because the specification of reciprocal duties and rights of states under the law reduces uncertainty and mitigates anxiety about "relative gains."

While the phenomenon of the security dilemma cannot be rooted out as long as systemic anarchy exists, international law regimes have the true potential of minimizing the severity of its adverse effects. We have seen this verified in the unfolding of both the U.S.-Soviet arms control regime and the Helsinki regime. What I have said of international law regimes is true of international law as a whole. I have used regimes to illustrate certain points merely because regimes are usually created and sustained by treaties or less formal agreements (not to mention those established through repeated practice) and hence are more readily visible. Much of general international law, on the other hand, is built on a large, amorphous corpus of customary norms, which are harder to pinpoint and explicate to the layperson. Nevertheless, in general international law, one finds the same elements that make regimes useful in mitigating the effects of Prisoner's Dilemma. These include iteration (recognized states in the world community are perpetual "subjects" of international law); transparency (by the clear specification of duties and rights of states); procedures by which remedies can be sought in the event of violations (i.e., defections); and a consensus sustaining a structure of common expectations without which there would be no assurance of minimal stability and predictability in international relations.

Notes

1. In arms control agreements, asymmetry in the weapons systems on both sides may require "equivalence" rather than symmetry in the prescribed reduction of weapons. Hence, a synonym for symmetry in this context is *equivalence*.

2. Nayar (1995, 70) notes that "the convergence among the conclusions of an increasing number of important studies relating to trade, shipping, and communications, apart from international aviation, raises serious questions about the concept of international regimes, so central to institutionalism and modified structural realism." Nayar, who looks in vain for the appearance of an arrangement that can be truly called a regime in international aviation, faults the concept of regimes for failing to take into account the brute power politics at work, even in an area like international aviation. My comment is twofold. One, aviation involves landing rights, a sensitive issue infringing on sovereignty. The South therefore could thwart the North in the latter's attempt to rely on market (rather than authoritative) allocation of resources in the development of an aviation regime (Krasner 1985, 11). Second, in view of the regime advocates' neglect of the importance of power, I stress throughout the book the law/politics interplay in the making and application of norms of international law.

3. For texts of these and other arms control agreements, see *Arms Control and Disarmament Agreements* (Washington, DC: Arms Control and Disarmament Agency, 1980, and 1996).

4. The United States did not ratify this protocol until the following year, in June 1992.

Part 2

Self-Help and Systemic Order

3

Self-Help and International Law

In the world we live in, which Neorealists define as an anarchic system (i.e., without a world government), self-help is the most reliable, though mostly unilateral, recourse open to states. In a broad sense, self-help may take different forms, including but not limited to arms buildup, balance of power, self-defense and collective security, and intervention.

This book examines how international law serves to mitigate the effects of anarchy, regulate efforts of self-help, or otherwise support the protection of national and international interests. Chapter 2 discusses how arms buildup, as a self-help by one state, easily turns into a competitive round of arms race between states; it especially notes how international law mitigates the effects of the security dilemma that the arms race entails. In this chapter, I address the other forms of self-help (balance of power, self-defense and collective security, and intervention) and the place of international law in relation thereto. Our concern here is ultimately how developments in the domain of international law have circumscribed the self-help discretion of states, offering food for thought for Neorealism.

Balance of Power and International Law

In the anarchic system, the worst fear of states is the eventuality that any one state or group of states should become too strong for one's own security. Throughout the history of the Westphalian system, the most frequent self-help response to the threat of what Morgenthau (1985, 222) calls a universal dominion is to form a winning coalition or countercoalition. Balance of power (qua diplomatic statecraft) has not only succeeded in countering attempts to gain universal dominion, from Louis XIV to Napoleon to a modern Hitler or Stalin. It has also proven to be a most effective means for preserving the existing order (i.e., equilibrium) against attempts to alter it unilaterally by an illegitimate use (or threat) of force or coercion, direct or indirect (Perkins 1981, 30). Each time, however, universal dominion was prevented only at the cost of warfare. A most recent instance was the frustration of Iraq's attempt to aggrandize power by annexing Kuwait in 1990, which was thwarted by a coalition of forces led by the United States, albeit armed with a mandate from the United Nations Security Council.

Balance of power finds a useful servant in international law, for the simple reason that the law sanctifies the very order of things that balance of power aims at preserving against change by force or threat of force. As President Harry Truman pronounced in his 1947 message on Greece and Turkey, "The world is not static and the status quo is not sacred. But we cannot allow changes in the status quo in violation of the Charter of the United Nations by such methods as coercion, or by such subterfuges as political infiltration" (Perkins 1981, 31).

Balance of power may not have prevented the partitions of Poland in the eighteenth century, but it is credited with having preserved the multistate system since the Thirty Years' War in 1648. Although balance of power may result in warfare, after each war the order constructed by the victorious and defeated powers (e.g., at the Congress of Vienna, 1815) generally reflects efforts to reestablish a balance within the framework of international law, usually in the form of a peace treaty.

Yet respect for international law is also enhanced in a balance of power system (qua system). As noted in Chapter 1, in agreement with Kaplan and Katzenbach (1961), sovereignty was an enforceable right under international law during the classic nineteenth-century balance of power system. In fact, that system depended on having a large enough pool of states from which potential coalition partners might be drawn in the balancing game. Hence, defeated essential actors must be allowed to reenter the world stage, neutral nations must be protected, and interventionism must be prohibited by collective action (that is, by balance of power qua diplomatic statecraft). Thus, international law has a better chance of being respected in a balance of power system. This logic prompted Perkins (1981, 27) to say: "Without some equilibrium (balance) of power there is little chance of [international] law." In monopolar or bipolar systems, by comparison, international law is often honored by its breach, for the simple reason that such systems lack the flexibility a balance of power system can provide.

Neorealists, who define the international system by reference to its inherent power configurations, rarely come to grips with the fact that those configurations are more often than not the result of a power-balancing schema cultivated by political engineering but ultimately codified by treaty. The role international law plays in promoting a balance of power structure may manifest itself in different ways, such as in the control of armaments (e.g., the Washington naval treaty of 1922), or in the mutual guarantee of boundary security (the Locarno pacts of 1925), or in the establishment of opposing alliance structures, from the Triple Entente v. Triple Alliance to the NATO v. Warsaw Pact competitions. The balance of power arrangements shored up by treaty, in these as in other cases, may or may not work, depending on the underlying political factors. But as long as these arrangements work as intended, international law serves a useful function in institutionalizing the inherent balancing design. On the other hand, when the shifting power alignments call for a new balance schema, the law performs a similar function. A handy example for both instances would be the post–World War II four-power agreements on Germany's partition and, subsequently, on German reunification.[1]

Self-Defense and Collective Security

For nearly 300 years since the birth of the modern multistate system, one frequent legitimate form of self-help at the disposal of states was open resort to war (use of force). This state of affairs remained until the movement to ban war bore fruit after 1928, beginning with the Kellog-Briand Pact concluded in that year. Only after the outlawry of war did the right of self-defense become the sole test for the lawful use of force in international law. This discussion therefore begins with a brief inquiry into the renunciation of war as an acceptable form of self-help.

The movement to outlaw war, a long-cherished dream of humankind, did not make substantive headway until after World War I. In that global conflict, the first taste of the scourge of modern full-scale warfare made war's outlawry an even more pressing task for all nations. As Mueller (1989, 53) cogently puts it, "A most powerful effect of World War I on the countries who fought it was an overwhelming—and so far, permanent—desire for international peace in the developed world." Hence, major war has become an "anachronism."

However, the League of Nations Covenant did not prohibit war outright. It merely made any war (or threat of war) a "matter of concern to the whole League" (Art. 11). By Article 10 of the Covenant, all members undertook to "respect and preserve against *external aggression* the territorial integrity and existing political independence of all members of the League" (italics added). Rather than banning war outright, the Covenant was more concerned with the prohibition and control of *illegitimate* uses of violence.

Despite Article 10, members of the League strictly limited the circumstances in which they would consider forcible action by a state as unlawful (i.e., in violation of the Covenant). This, paradoxically, left large areas of permissible hostility, extending to full-scale war, for which the League had no responsibility. Articles 12–15 of the Covenant left open a number of loopholes, or circumstances in which states remained free to take any action they wanted, including outright war (Jacob et al. 1972, 55):

- Should the Council fail to agree unanimously on a report (on how the League's members should act in the face of a breach of the peace)
- Should a majority of the Assembly (including states that were members of the Council) fail to reach agreement on what to do about a dispute
- Should the other party to a dispute not comply with the recommendation made by the Council or Assembly
- Should a League member be embroiled with a state outside the League
- Should three months have elapsed after the Council or Assembly issued a decision proposing a peaceful settlement
- Should the dispute be found by the Council to be solely within domestic jurisdiction

In any such event, from the League Covenant's point of view, resort to force by a disputant state would be an acceptable self-help.

Outlawing War: Limit to Self-Help Discretion

The Covenant, however, did take one positive step toward the disavowal of war as a legitimate self-help by states. Article 16 made resort to war by any member ipso facto an act of war on "all other members of the League." This stipulation would then call for various forms of sanctions, from economic to military, to be undertaken by member states at the Council's recommendation.[2]

The efforts to outlaw aggressive war were thus largely pursued outside the framework of the League, picking up from an unfinished task of the two Hague conferences at the turn of the century (1899 and 1907). However, after a few unrelated false starts elsewhere in the early 1920s, the conclusion of the Pact of Paris (also known as Kellog-Briand Pact) in 1928 represented humankind's first success in renouncing war as "an instrument of policy" in the relations among nations.[3] While the treaty's intended scope of application—whether the treaty renounces *all* wars—may be subject to debate,[4] it is clear in retrospect that the treaty's explicit limitation of the use of force to instances of self-defense ushered in a new era in international law.

An early instance showing the Kellog-Briand Pact's influence was the arrival of the Saavedra Lamas Treaty, a regional agreement signed by certain Latin American states in 1933—and by the United States in 1934—that condemns wars of aggression. The pact's long-range value lies in its role in spearheading the process toward a universal acceptance of the notion that the use of force, except in self-defense, is an illegal form of self-help. For our purpose, it bears noting that this is a landmark change brought about through international law. It represents a whacking chip into the self-help armor of states in the anarchic world.

Self-Defense

After World War II, the illegality of war—a notion first propagated by the Kellog-Briand Pact—became universally embraced as a systemic value, as we defined the term in Chapter 2. The United Nations Charter, adopted in 1945, distinguishes itself from the League Covenant, among other ways, in its explicit proscription of the use of force (Art. 2[4]). Self-defense is now made the only test of a legitimate use of force (Art. 51) as an exception to the general proscription. The latter article also makes self-defense a right to be individually and collectively exercised. Whereas individual self-defense may still be considered self-help narrowly defined, the right of collective self-defense denotes something else. Here we cross the bridge from the traditional self-help by individual states to collective security, which is, in Claude's words (1964, 224), the halfway house between international anarchy and world government.

Collective Security

The concept of collective security can be defined simply as one that calls for an "all against one" response to an illegal use of force—where "all" refers to all members of the community of nations, and "one" refers to the aggressor who pops up in our midst (Claude 1964, 224). A state is identified as the aggressor if it resorts to a use of force that may be self-help but not self-defense (e.g., to alter the status quo). In intent if not in form, collective security resembles balance of power as an approach to the maintenance of international security.

Like balance of power, collective security is a design providing the certainty of collective action to frustrate any attempt at supranational dominance. Its difference lies in two aspects: First, collective security aims at countering the *aggressive policy* of a state in the world system; balance of power, on the other hand, aims at containing the *overwhelming power* of a state in the system. Second, collective security as an organized approach to international peace and stability is often embodied in, and operationalized through, international institutions—either at the universal level, such as the League of Nations and its successor, the United Nations; or at the regional level, such as NATO, the OAS, etc. Balance of power, by contrast, may be less institutionalized, or may even be a "haphazard arrangement" (Claude 1962, 113), although a balance scheme may work through the medium of a formal alliance structure, in which case its difference with collective security may be blurring. The best answer I can think of is still Wright's (1955, 204) adage: The collective security system differs from balance of power "as art differs from nature."

Law of the UN Charter Revisited

The renunciation of war (use of force), along with its concomitant requirement for the peaceful settlement of disputes (see Chapter 4), naturally led to a corollary: the constraint on the self-help discretion of states. It only follows that the constraint requires a greater role of a third party—e.g., an international organization such as the United Nations—as the ultimate arbitrator of what is or is not self-defense. The United Nations Charter makes self-defense both an individual and collective right. The latter provides the juridical basis for collective security measures. Lest individual self-defense fail, collective security would lend the victim of aggression an institutional backup. Under this system, an attack on one is an attack on all members (recalling Article 16 of the League Covenant), hence calling for collective response.

The United Nations, as successor to the League, is a logical organization that gives institutional expression to the concept at the global level. Regional organizations such as NATO and OAS may likewise provide regional collective response should individual members need help to counter aggression.

All these developments are closely related in that, in addition to the self-defense restriction on the use of force, the institution of collective security offers another potential constraint on a state's self-help discretion. These are not just issues of international law, but are issues that concern how relations are conducted among the various sovereign states with their self-help discretion circumscribed. It is amazing that, despite all these obvious and crucial modifications, Neorealists continue to show an inured fixation on the allegedly unmitigated self-help as the most crucial derivative of the anarchic multistate system; they also demonstrate a sustained contempt for the place and reach of international law in the conduct of relations among the units (states) in the system.

Both self-defense and collective security—as precept and institution—have caused so much confusion; and self-defense more especially has been abused and appropriated even by perpetrators of aggression. It is therefore necessary to sort things out and to pinpoint their specific meanings in light of the provisions of the United Nations Charter.

Self-defense. Self-defense has a specific meaning and should not be confused with other forms of self-help that would properly fall under the categories of retorsions and reprisals or, in terms harking back to traditional international law, "hostile measures short of war." Let us first examine the language of the Charter in which the right of self-defense is defined:

> Article 51: Nothing in the present Charter shall impair the inherent right of individual or collective self-defense if an armed attack occurs against a Member of the United Nations, until the Security Council has taken measures necessary to maintain international peace and security. Measures taken by Members in exercise of this right of self-defense shall be immediately reported to the Security Council and shall not in any way affect the authority and responsibility of the Security Council under the present Charter to take at any time such action as it deems necessary in order to maintain or restore international peace and security.

In the first place, Article 51 of the Charter defines self-defense as an "inherent right," or something of a natural law nature that inheres in general international law, i.e., not to be taken away by anyone, certainly not by treaty, not even by the United Nations Charter.

Second, the right of self-defense is to be exercised "if an armed attack occurs." This precludes any act of self-defense that may be in anticipation of, or even simultaneous to, an armed attack. The kind of reaction taken by the United States in the Cuban missile crisis in 1962—i.e., a "quarantine" designed to forcibly stop further Soviet shipping of missiles to Cuba—was at best taken in anticipation of possible hostile action. In view of the restrictive view of self-defense in the Charter, the quarantine seemed to be more an act of reprisal[5] than one of self-defense, Washington's claim to the contrary notwithstanding. As Tucker (1972, 585) points out, the Soviet Union, in establishing missile bases in Cuba, with the latter's consent and cooperation, violated no express norm of international law. In the *Nicaragua v. the U.S.* case (*ICJ Reports* 14 [1986]:103–123), the International Court of Justice unmistakably applied the restrictive view of self-defense when it stated that the exercise of the right of individual self-defense "is subject to the State concerned *having been the victim* of an armed attack" (para. 195; emphasis added). On the meaning of armed attack, the court provided a specific definition: "An armed attack must be understood to include not merely action by regular armed forces across an international border, but also the sending by or on behalf of a State of armed bands, groups, irregulars or mercenaries, which carry out acts of armed force against another State of such gravity as amount to" (inter alia) an actual armed attack conducted by regular forces, "or its substantial involvement therein."

Third, according to the Charter design, an act of self-defense is a stopgap measure "until the Security Council takes measures." As we shall see, this reference to the Security Council is related to the Charter's design of a collective security system anchored in the Security Council. But on the question at hand, what legal effects does the "until the Security Council takes measures" clause have on a member state's right of self-defense? If the Security Council acts accordingly, does it suspend or even terminate a state's right of self-defense? The best answer I know is that since self-defense is an "inherent right," which nothing in the Charter can "impair" (Art. 51), the right cannot be abridged simply because the Security Council acts in the name of collective self-defense.

Fourth, should a state fail to act in self-defense in the face of an "armed attack," does the inaction vitiate the state's right of self-defense? Former UN Secretary-General Javier Pérez de Cuéllar seemed to think so, as he suggested that failure by Kuwait to act months after Iraq's armed invasion caused Kuwait's right of self-defense to "expire" (*Washington Post,* November 9, 1990, A30). But qualified international lawyers in their right mind would most likely rebut the expiration view. As self-defense is an "inherent right," it cannot "expire" simply because the injured sovereign state fails to exercise it. If anything, this would trigger the Charter-ordained collective security system into action, as it did in the Gulf (1990). In such a case, failure to resort to self-help (i.e., individual self-defense) by the injured state would be an occasion, and provide the legal basis, for what amounts to collective self-help (i.e., collective security).

Self-defense is most frequently misappropriated by states taking self-help measures (including reprisal) unrelated to self-defense as envisioned in Article 51 of the UN Charter. For instance, the United States called its mining of the Nicaragua Harbor in 1983–1984 an act of self-defense (see *Nicaragua v. the U.S., ICJ Reports* 14 [1986]:103–123). The court, nevertheless, rejected this claim, finding the United States in violation of international law instead. In this, as in the Cuban missile case before, more traditional-minded international lawyers probably would agree that Washington's actions amounted to acts of reprisal. But the reason for its invoking self-defense may have been that nothing in the UN Charter language upheld reprisal as a right. Despite the Charter's silence, the question of reprisals is an important one.

Reprisal is undeniably self-help in nature. Like self-defense, an act of reprisal must meet what Bowett (1972) calls certain "preconditions" before its use can find a reasonable justification. For example, the target state must be guilty of a prior international delinquency against the claimant state (Bowett 1972, 3). Reprisal is different from self-defense only in aim or purpose. It is punitive or deterrent in its goal (e.g., Israel's December 28, 1968, Beirut raid), whereas self-defense is permissible for the purpose of protecting the security of the state and the essential rights—in particular the rights of territorial integrity and political independence—on which that security depends (pp. 3, 10). The United Nations Security Council has, in general, taken a broader view of self-defense than of reprisal (p. 22). This may also have encouraged states to take the self-defense plea more frequently than that of reprisal. Nonetheless, acts of self-help tantamount to reprisals in the true sense of the word often have been tacitly accepted or tolerated in practice by the community of nations at large. Relevant examples are the French attack (launched from Algeria) on the Algerian rebel base in Tunisia in 1957; the British air attack on targets in Yemen in 1964; the U.S. rescue of the merchant ship *Mayaguez* after its capture by Cambodian forces in 1975; Israel's surgical strike at Iraqi nuclear reactors in 1981;[6] the Israeli air attack on PLO headquarters near Tunis in October 1985 (cf. von Glahn 1986, 566–576; 643–644); and the U.S. strikes against Libya in 1986.[7]

In fact, reacting to the undue frequency with which states misappropriated and even abused the pretext of self-defense, the Security Council later seemed to allow a partial rehabilitation of reprisals in its practice (Bowett 1972, 10–17; Tucker 1972, 595).

Collective security. Collective security finds its legal source in the same article of the UN Charter (Art. 51) that provides for Security Council follow-up action ("until the Security Council takes measures . . ."). Here is clear evidence that while self-defense is the sole exception to the prohibition of the use of force, its provision in Article 51 does not contradict the Charter's design of collective security. It is also evidence that, under the law of the United Nations Charter, member states' right to self-help is placed under a higher requirement—that of submission to the collective security system the Security Council is authorized to preside over. This Charter design stands in stark contrast to the harsh reality as it developed during the Cold War, which made a mockery of the UN collective security system as provided for in Articles 41–49.

A logical question to raise here is: Why the Security Council? Why does Article 51 require that individual member states report to the Security Council on measures they have taken in self-defense? An ancillary question is: Why is the Security Council, as the language of Articles 51–54 suggests, named the anchor of the collective security system under the Charter? The answer is in Article 24, which confers on the Security Council, among the United Nations' six principal organs, the "primary responsibility for the maintenance of international peace and security." But for our purpose here, the subjection of self-defense (self-help) to the scrutiny of collective action (i.e., collective security) should not be lost on those who argue that we live in an allegedly unmitigated self-help international system.

The Charter's inherent recognition of a special responsibility of the

Security Council reflects a realistic recognition of the importance of power. The Security Council, in which the Big Five victorious powers from World War II (Britain, China, France, the United States, and USSR/Russia) hold permanent seats, is the natural embodiment of that presumptive preponderant power that will be counted on in the collective security system of the United Nations. Hence, in international organization, no less than in international law, the power desideratum is, contrary to Realist conjectures, never out of sight.

Strictly speaking, the Security Council's power to take enforcement action should be differentiated from its role in collective security. A differentiation would help elucidate the true function of the latter. Enforcement action is provided for in Chapter VII of the Charter, that is, under Article 45, which has to be read in conjunction with Articles 39–49 and Article 25. The following loose paraphrase of these provisions provides the uninitiated with a view of the unrealized Charter *design* with regard to the Security Council's role in enforcement action, as contradistinguished from collective security.

- The Security Council has the power to determine the existence of any threat to the peace, breach of the peace, and act of aggression (Art. 39).
- Once it has so determined, the Security Council can decide to take either enforcement action or lesser measures (Arts. 41–42) falling under collective security.
- If it takes enforcement action, the Security Council may decide to activate those forces that member states, under standing agreements, would have made available on call to the Security Council (Art. 43).
- If the Security Council decides on fielding these forces in an action against the identified aggressor, the Council shall be aided by a Military Staff Committee (Art. 47) consisting of military representatives from the five permanent members, which shall in effect command these forces into combat.
- In an enforcement action called by the Security Council, all member states of the United Nations shall "join in affording mutual assistance" in support of the Council-ordered measures against the aggressor state (Art. 49).
- In the event lesser measures are taken, the operation is no longer an enforcement action but one of collective security. It will be less centralized and shall be carried out by responding member states with or without coordination by the Security Council (Arts. 41–42). Regardless of whether an enforcement action or lesser measures are called for by the Security Council, all member states agree to carry

out the Council's decisions "in accordance with the present Charter" (Art. 25).

This summary of the provisions in the Charter for enforcement action is provided for three reasons: First, critics—well intentioned but apparently underinformed—often criticize the United Nations for its lack of "teeth." This summary is a reminder that one should not impute the sad facts of reality (brought on by the Cold War) to a deficiency in Charter design. Second, if the Cold War suspended the Charter design from operation, the end of the Cold War may give it a renewed chance for the future. As stated in Chapter 1, international law is more a rules-oriented than an outcome-oriented system. The important thing here is that the UN Charter does have an enforcement action design (i.e., rules). The outcome intended by the rules may be frustrated by the circumstances of a particular time period, say, at time-1 (the Cold War era). One should not jump to the conclusion that it will likewise be frustrated at time-n. Besides, what matters for the present discussions is that rules, once unmistakably delineated, can serve to increase the transparency of "defection" and hence can have the effect of deterring or at least minimizing the instances of actual defection, as noted in Chapter 2.

A third reason for the summary is that it may offer a backdrop against which collective security—perhaps the second-best scenario under the Charter to deal with aggression—can be evaluated. Failing enforcement action, the Security Council in five decades has responded to the two most flagrant instances of brute aggression—Korea (1950) and Iraq (1990)—in the general context of the United Nations collective security system.

If the Security Council is to function as expected by the framers of the Charter, it must be veto-free, in that none of the five permanent members would withhold its "concurring vote" on substantive council decisions (Art. 27). This requirement equally applies to enforcement action and collective security, both under consideration here. But there are other prerequisites for enforcement action: (1) The Security Council must have the special agreements in place, under which the contracting member states "undertake to make available to the Security Council . . . armed forces, assistance, and facilities" that will be needed for carrying out an enforcement action (Art. 43). (2) Before these special agreements are possible, however, the Council's Military Staff Committee (MSC) must have a consensus regarding the requirements for the contingents to be made available by the contracting member states and placed at the disposal of the Council, including the troops' size, capabilities, and degree of combat readiness. (3) The MSC must also have consensus on details regarding logistics and the command structure, should the committee actually take charge and direct those forces into combat against the aggressor named by the Security Council in an enforcement action (Arts. 46–47). (4) The political climate in and out of the Security Council must be such as to sustain the kind of MSC consensus mentioned above.

Since in the Cold War years these conditions were nonexistent, the enforcement action mechanism, as spelled out in Articles 43–47 remained on paper. This was so, despite the fact that an MSC has been in existence throughout the period. Both the North Korean invasion of South Korea (1950) and the Iraqi invasion of Kuwait (1990) should have been cases to be dealt with by the Security Council under provisions for enforcement action, as just described. But, owing to the difficulties associated with all four prerequisites, both cases were treated by the Security Council as cases of collective security and handled in an improvised manner, albeit still within the frame of reference of Chapter VII of the Charter. In both instances, the Security Council's first act was to determine the existence of an act of aggression, in accordance with Article 39. All the ensuing Council resolutions flowed from this determination.

To be exact, the improvisation in both cases, based on Article 42, was nevertheless patterned after the Charter design of an enforcement action. For the dormancy of Article 43, which would have provided for contingents readily at its disposal, the Council called on members to contribute to an ad hoc ensemble of forces, to be commanded not by the MSC, but by one member state (the United States), which was so chosen because of both its willingness to lead and its logistical and firepower capabilities. Some important differences may be noted in how the Security Council acted on the two cases, however.

One major difference in the Iraqi case was the absence of a veto problem, which was due not to the absence of the Soviet delegate, as had been the case in the Council's deliberations over the Korean conflict some four decades earlier, but to the result of a Big Power consensus. A related difference was that the Council's Military Staff Committee was given a role to play (UNSC Res. 665, August 25, 1990) in coordinating the actions of member states responding to the Council's call for nonmilitary sanctions against Iraq under Resolution 661 (adopted August 6, 1990). Both developments unmistakably signaled the end of the Cold War.

Another major difference in the Iraqi case was that the Security Council had tried economic sanctions first (Res. 661 and 665), as provided for under Article 41 of the UN Charter. By dint of other resolutions, the Security Council also declared Iraq's annexation of Kuwait null and void (Res. 662, August 9, 1990); demanded the immediate release of nationals of third countries (Res. 664, August 18, 1990); ordered Iraq to desist from infringing on immunities and privileges of diplomatic premises and personnel (Res. 667, September 16, 1990); and called on Iraq to protect the safety, well-being, and demographic integrity of Kuwaiti nationals (Res. 674, October 19, 1990).

As a further difference, the Security Council adopted two resolutions (Res. 687, April 3, 1991; Res. 688, April 5, 1991) following a cease-fire on March 2, 1991, that laid down very harsh terms for Iraq to comply with.[8] The reason for this outcome was that the Iraqi cease-fire came as a result of Iraq's total defeat; and there was no division among the Council's permanent members. By contrast, the North Koreans had beaten the United Nations forces to the draw thirty-eight years earlier. The Korean armistice of 1953 came only after hard bargaining at the negotiating table.

What is the future of collective security? While the end of the Cold War made an unprecedented opening for a rare consensus on Iraq among the five permanent members of the Security Council in 1990–1991, there is yet a long way to go until the day when Articles 43–49 can be fully implemented, clearing the way for the Council's enforcement action mechanism to be fully operative when the occasion arises. Until then, the Charter's built-in collective security alternative will continue to be the world's best hope for a UN collective response to aggression.

Lessons Learned

From the preceding discussion of legally restricting the use of force to self-defense, some lessons can be drawn. First, the self-help discretion of states is no longer unmitigated as before. This important change in international law was made possible only after a prior change took place in the world's political conviction regarding wars. The prior change was the rise of a "systemic value" (see Chapter 2), in that an overwhelming majority of nation-states, including the major powers, came to accept the idea that the use of force for any other purpose than self-defense was unacceptable and must be resisted.

Another lesson is that the right of collective self-defense, undergirding the collective security system under the Charter, is a necessary companion to the right of individual self-defense. In case individual self-defense (or "self-help," pure and simple) should fail, the collective security system offers an institutional backup, as in the Iraqi case.

A third and related lesson is that while self-defense may connote a form of self-help—in fact, the only permissible self-help under contemporary international law—collective security is, strictly speaking, not exactly in the same category. It is self-help in more or less the same sense as balance of power (qua statecraft) is to be considered self-help. To the extent that collective security entails the interceding efforts by other states, often through an international organization involving a decisionmaking mode no longer within the control of one's own state (the "self" in self-help), the institution is, again to borrow Claude's (1964, 224) words, a modification of systemic anarchy. However temporary, the suspension of a state's self-defense initiative in favor of collective self-defense implies a substitution of "other help" (Mercer 1995) for self-help under international law. This calls for a modification of the Neorealist self-help derivative from systemic anarchy.

Intervention as Self-Help

The U.S. invasions of Grenada (1983) and Panama (1989) are among recent instances of armed intervention in the name of protecting national interests. What does international law have to say about interventions of this sort?

Contemporary international law unequivocally prohibits the use of interventions as self-help because they violate the sovereignty of other states. They also violate the stricture that the use of force is limited to bona fide self-defense. For proof of this point, one need only to look at the following evidences:

1. Article 2(4) of the UN Charter provides: "All member states shall refrain in their international relations from the threat or use of force against the territorial integrity or political independence of any state."
2. The charter of the OAS prohibits the use of force in language that is harsher and more categorical than that of the UN Charter. Article 18 of the OAS charter rejects a state's claim of the right to use force in another state's territory, or "*to intervene, directly or indirectly,* for any reason whatever, in the internal or external affairs of a state" (italics added).
3. The UN General Assembly Declaration on Principles of International Law Concerning Friendly Relations (Res. 2625/XXV, October 24, 1970) recognizes the principle of nonintervention after the fashion of Article 2(4) of the UN Charter.
4. The ICJ's decision in the *Corfu Channel* case recognized nonintervention as an operative principle, founded on respect for the sovereignty and political integrity of other nations.
5. The ICJ, in *Nicaragua v. the U.S.*, reiterated the court's rejection of intervention on grounds of law and policy.

Against this massive prohibition of interventions under international law, the question arises as to whether there are any exceptions. The answer is a conditional one. Certain specific conditions must be met to make an arguable case for excepting a state's coercive action from the blanket prohibition of interventions (as coercive self-help) under international law. Some examples are if the armed intervention is for legitimate self-defense; if it is to rectify mistreatment of the intervening state's citizens, but only after exhaustion of local remedies; if it is to suppress widespread violations of human rights—i.e., humanitarian intervention; or if it is in accordance with an existing treaty permitting such intervention (Joyner 1984, 133). Other circumstances in which an armed intervention may have an arguably defensible ground in international law are if the intervention is part of a collective action by an international organization (the OECS, for example) within the language of Articles 51–54 of the UN Charter; if it is at the invitation of the legitimate government; and if the intervention is for the abatement of an "intolerable international nuisance" (von Glahn 1992, 160ff.).

The Grenada Invasion

Nothing in the Grenada and Panama invasions would constitute a legitimate ground for exception from the legal prohibition of interventions. The Panama invasion was discussed in a different context in Chapter 1; the Grenada invasion will serve here as an example of an intervention seen as an act of self-help.

Facts. A coup on October 12, 1983, resulted in the breakdown of the central authority in Grenada. The dissident faction that overthrew Prime Minister Maurice Bishop sought a harder-line implementation of the "Leninist" restructuring of the Grenadian society. In the ensuing struggle, Bishop, three members of his cabinet, and some union leaders were murdered. At least eighteen people died (including women and children) when the coup forces opened fire on a crowd of Grenadians protesting their actions. Beginning on October 19, a draconian shoot-on-sight, twenty-four-hour curfew was imposed on the civilian population (*New York Times,* October 17, 1983, A1).

To rectify what the Reagan administration saw as an intolerable state of affairs, a multinational invasion was launched against Grenada. Led by 1,900 U.S. marines and army airborne Rangers, the invasion force also included 300 troops representing six eastern Caribbean (English-speaking) states: Jamaica, Barbados, Dominica, St. Lucia, Antigua, and St. Vincent. By October 30, the invasion had been completed and the island militarily secured (*New York Times,* October 30, 1983, A20).

The principal rationale, and legal defense, for the U.S. action was that it was a campaign to save 1,100 U.S. nationals residing in Grenada, including some students at the St. George's School of Medicine. Another aim was to "help in the restoration of democratic institutions."[9]

Questions in international law. Conceivable legal pretexts or justifications for the intervention would be protection of nationals (humanitarian intervention); collective defense through regional arrangements; and intervention by invitation of the legitimate host government.

First, if the intervention was for the protection of nationals, the United States would have to pass the test of necessity and proportionality, in the spirit of the classic *Caroline* case (Henkin et al. 1993, 872f.). Not only did Washington have to show that the necessity (of self-defense) was "instant, overwhelming, and leaving no choice of means, and no moment for deliberation," it would also have to show that the U.S.-led armed invasion and the consequential action, including the forcible removal of the coup leaders, was both necessary and proportionate to the threat of the chaos to the 1,100 U.S. nationals residing in Grenada.

Second, to justify the invasion as an act of collective self-defense through regional arrangements, the Reagan administration would have to overcome the prohibition of intervention built into the charters of the OAS and the OECS. The Rio Treaty (i.e., Inter-American Treaty of Reciprocal Assistance) would not enter into the picture, as the eastern Caribbean states were not parties to it. While the OECS is directed against "external aggression," the Grenada invasion was directed against an internal conflict. Several of the eastern Caribbean states, invoking Article 8 of the OECS charter, established a Defense and Security Committee to coordinate measures of collective self-defense. But, as Boyle (1985, 275) cogently points out, there were three insurmountable problems: Article 8 of its charter restricted OECS competence in such security matters to situations amounting to an "external aggression"; Article 8 provided no authority for OECS members to intervene in the domestic affairs of another OECS member state; and the organized invasion of Grenada was an enforcement action by a regional arrangement falling under the purview of Article 53 of the United Nations Charter. As such, Article 53 requires prior authorization by the UN Security Council, which was not sought. In addition, Beres (1987, 67) notes a further problem: While the United States was not a party to OECS, nowhere is there a provision in the OECS charter that would authorize an option by its members to invite external assistance in an intervention into the internal affairs of a member state (Grenada).

Third, a possible justification for the U.S. invasion was that it was by invitation, as indeed the deposed governor-general, Sir Paul Scoon, issued pleas for external assistance. But, again, two problems need to be resolved to uphold the "by invitation" claim: the governor-general's status—Sir Paul had already been deposed at the time he called for help; and, more important, the extent of the legal capacity of his office. As Vagts (1984, 171) points out, the governor-general was appointed by the queen of England. Whether he had the power to request help from a source other than the British government, in the name of Grenada, was not so certain. According to Sir Paul, it was not until the day after the U.S. invasion had begun (October 22, 1983) that he even considered external assistance to be necessary. Then what he asked for was not an invasion, but simply outside help (*Economist,* March 10, 1984, 32; Boyle 1985, 273).

Unlike in similar instances, there was a solid consensus among scholars of international law on the illegality of the U.S. invasion of Grenada.[10] The moral that emerges from the incident is twofold. First, Washington in self-defense resorted to the traditional right to protect nationals abroad and even to the dubious pretext of "restoring democracy" in Grenada. The deliberate eschewal of any reference to a right of intervention bespeaks an inherent recognition that intervention (as self-help) is not a right under contemporary international law. By the same token, the pains the Reagan administration took to avoid any mention of reprisal apparently grew out of a realization that contemporary international law, with its ban on the use of force for purposes other than self-defense, made reprisal a rickety peg on which to hang a case of self-help.

Second, the joint team Washington hastily assembled, which consisted of token troops from six eastern Caribbean states, may have been a futile fig leaf to conceal the illegality of the U.S.-led invasion. But the very fact that Washington found it necessary to dress up the armed intervention so that it would not appear to be a breach of international law indicates that legal constraints were part of the desiderata weighed by decisionmakers. This fact not only goes against the habitual Realist discount of international law in the complexities of international politics, but, more important, it challenges the very Neorealist formulation about self-help as a systemic derivative from the exigencies of brute power politics without regard to what international law may have to say.

Conclusion

This chapter has explored self-help in our anarchic system and the role of international law with regard to the various forms of self-help. We have seen how the outlawry of the use of force for all purposes other than self-defense has invariably affected the self-help discretion of states. Under the United Nations Charter, even the member states' right of individual self-defense (qua individual self-help) is subjected to a higher obligation to accept the Security Council's authority over collective security (qua collective self-help). Just as the constraint placed by international law on states' discretion in the use of force is a modification of the self-help system, the institution of collective security signifies a giant step forward from systemic anarchy. Viewed in the context of the advances made in contemporary international law, the only logical conclusion to draw is: Neither the anarchic characteristic of the Westphalian system nor the self-help attribute derived from systemic anarchy remains unmitigated and untouched by international law, Neorealist nonchalance notwithstanding.

Notes

1. Cf. Shafritz et al., (1993, 300f.). For text of the four-power agreement on German reunification, see Treaty on the Final Settlement with Respect to Germany, September 12, 1990, in *Survival* 32, 6:560ff.

2. For the full text of the League of Nations Covenant, see Manley O. Hudson, *International Legislation* 1 (1933).

3. Known by its formal name as General Treaty for the Renunciation of War, signed on August 27, 1928 (94 LNTS 57), the instrument became effective on July 24, 1929. It is still in force, and some new states, e.g., Barbados and Fiji, have adhered to it. As of 1993, sixty-six states were parties. See Henkin et al. (1993, 879).

4. Many international lawyers believe that the purpose of the treaty was to renounce war both as a tool of self-help to right an international wrong and as a rightful act of sovereignty to change existing rights. See Brierly (1963, 409); von Glahn (1992, 671). For a dissenting view, see Kaplan and Katzenbach (1961, 210).

5. A reprisal is an act of self-help on the part of the injured state, which has the effect of momentarily suspending, in the relations between two nations, the observance of certain rules of the law of nations. An act of reprisal would be illegal in the absence of a preliminary act contrary to the law of nations that precipitates the reprisal. See the arbitral award in the *Naulilaa* case, in *UN Rep. Int'l Arb. Awards* 2, 1011 (1949).

6. This is in spite of the fact that the UN Security Council did condemn Israel in a resolution passed on June 19, 1981, requiring the payment of "appropriate redress," which Israel refused.

7. The U.S. strikes against Libya, however, were condemned by the UN Security Council as "an act of armed aggression perpetrated . . . in flagrant violation of the Charter of the United Nations, international law, and norms of conduct." See "Reprisals," *AJIL* 80 (1986):165.

8. The two post-cease-fire Security Council resolutions laid down the following conditions for Iraq: (1) to respect Kuwait's boundary inviolability and agree to boundary demarcation with UN assistance; (2) to accept destruction of all chemical-biological weapons and all ballistic missiles above a certain range, and to accept on-site inspection for this purpose; (3) to agree not to develop nuclear weapons or weapons of mass destruction, and to accept IAEA on-site inspections; (4) to agree to create a fund (from proceeds from the sale of Iraqi oil on the world market) to pay compensation required by international law for claims arising from any direct loss or injury sustained by foreign nationals/companies because of the Iraqi invasion of Kuwait; (5) to accept the continuing UN-imposed ban on all imports of arms or technology for production of weapons of mass destruction; (6) to guarantee not to support international terrorism; and (7) to agree not to repress the civilian population in Iraq, including Kurdish-populated areas, and to redress (in cooperation with the UN) the urgent relief of refugees and displaced nationals within Iraq.

9. See text of Reagan's "Announcement of Invasion," in the *New York*

Times, October 26, 1983, A16; and "Legal Basis for the Invasion," *New York Times* October 27, 1983, A22.

10. The consensus can be seen in a sharply worded open letter, "International Lawlessness in Grenada," published in *American Journal of International Law* 78, 1 (1984):192–195.

4

War and Peace and International Law

In the Neorealist paradigm, systemic anarchy leaves the use of coercion or even violence as the ultimate arbiter of conflicts. Although we have seen in Chapter 3 how modern international law places constraint on states' discretion in the use of force, Neorealists may still think that the change is only in *modality* (as opposed to substance). Self-help, so they may argue, remains the same in substance, despite the formal outlawry of war and the introduction of institutions of collective security. This argument, we recognize, is consistent with the anarchic premise of Neorealism. In fact, it finds empirical support in the practice of many states whose actions flout the ban on war (use of force) and even thwart collective security mechanisms. On the other hand, Neorealists cannot deny the fact that control over, and prevention of, the resort to violence is in the self-interest of states (Kaplan and Katzenbach 1961, 198ff.). By the same token, Neorealists cannot deny that states in the anarchic system share a common urge for order.

States' urge for order is made all the more acute precisely because of systemic anarchy, or the lack of a world government to maintain order for states. This urge requires reduction in the incidence of conflict—or war prevention—in international relations; regulation of the use of force, i.e, in the conduct of war; and, as both a preventive and mitigative measure, arms control.

These three aspects are related in that they represent common endeavors to reduce the role of force in international relations; as Brown (1987, 144ff.) cogently points out, other means or contributing factors may include:

- Statesmanship of rational self-restraint, e.g., the Concert of Europe, the "Spirit of Locarno," the Kellog-Briand Pact outlawing war (as discussed in Chapter 3), and the Morgenthalean Rules of Diplomacy[1]
- International collective security (see also Chapter 3)

- Pacific settlement of disputes
- Conflict control

Along with dispute settlement, these measures testify to the constructive role international law plays in the control of force; they fall into a logical sequential relationship, as follows:

Step 1: Avoidance of conflict, by recourse to the peaceful settlement of disputes

Step 2: Regulation of armaments, aimed at mitigating harm in the event dispute settlement fails and armed conflict breaks out, as in the banning of dum-dum bullets; asphyxiating and other gases; and nuclear, chemical, or other weapons of mass destruction

Step 3: Regulation of the use of force, as in the provision of a set of criteria against which legitimate or illegitimate resort to force can be evaluated (*jus ad bellum*) and rules governing the actual conduct of war, against which violations, including crimes of war, such as wanton killing of innocent civilian populations, can be determined (*jus in bello*) (Gardam 1993, 391ff.)

These concerns fall under the rubric "war and peace." This chapter examines war and peace in the general context of what role international law plays in regulating international relations, both conflictual and cooperative. For obvious reasons, not all "war and peace" issues can be discussed in this book. The omission of the "law of war," for example, in no way reflects on its degree of importance as a code for belligerent behavior in international armed conflicts. However, I prefer to focus here on the larger question of the interplay of law and politics in international relations.

The norms developed in war prevention, the regulation of armaments, and the conduct of war testify to the dictum of *mutual restraint* by states, and their willingness to accept restraint, for the sake of ensuring a modicum of order and predictability in their mutual relations. The underlying dictum of mutuality is necessitated by the very condition of systemic anarchy. The lack of a supranational authority accentuates the sovereign coequality of nations, which militates against unilateralism either in the norms-making process or in the modes of dispute settlement. To the extent it is a unilateral reflex of individual states, self-help is therefore bound to be curbed under the force of international law. The norms that derive from mutual consent of states (*opinio juris*) because of a common need for order are thus consistent with and conducive to the national interests of states, whose conduct they purport to regulate. The Neorealist self-help imperative notwithstanding, states often choose to accept restraint out of enlightened self-interest. International law stands out as a useful and sensible instrument in war prevention and an indispensable guide for the conduct of armed conflict when war does break out.

War Prevention and International Law

As was implicitly shown in the three-step sequence, if major disputes can be settled by peaceful means, there will be no occasion to call into play the international law norms on the conduct of war; nor will the regulation of armaments be a relevant issue. By delineating rules and criteria for what is permissible behavior of states, international law has a much larger and more substantive role to play in war prevention than is evident to the uninitiated. Besides regulation of armaments and arms control, one might also consider the practical war-deflecting effects that could come from specifying a code of conduct for states that would cover the following areas:

Definition of the bases of jurisdiction. This would allow a state to know when it has the juridical competence to take charge or to act to espouse a cause either in its own right or in behalf of its nationals (see Chapter 5). This would be accomplished by reference to nationality, territoriality, passive personality, the protective principle, jurisdiction by agreement, or universal jurisdiction such as in case of piracy on the high seas (Schachter 1991b, 250ff.; Oliver 1991, 307ff.). Likewise, in the event of jurisdictional conflict, international law provides guidance for resolving the competing claims of jurisdiction (e.g., *Barcelona Traction* case), thus obviating the need to resort to coercion or violence.

Specification of the rights and duties of states. These include a state's sovereign rights of independence and the immunities and privileges accruing from its sovereignty. Conversely, they also include a state's duties, such as the duty not to infringe on other states' rights. Although these norms, as others, are often breached in the practice of states, an argument in their defense is that a clear delineation is more constructive than otherwise. By identifying what is permissible behavior of states, it increases the transparency of any defection when it occurs, thus providing a powerful deterrent to defections (i.e., violations of what is specified under international law).

Responsibility of states and treatment of aliens. Whereas injury to other states' interests, including those of their nationals, is sometimes unavoidable despite the best intentions, international law provides guidelines for determining what act or omission is attributable to a state, thus establishing its responsibility (*William Way Claim; Trail Smelter* case); what constitutes direct or indirect delinquency (*B. E. Chattin Claim*); and the obligation to pay compensation in the form of reparations (*Laura M.B. Janes Claim*) or, in rare instances, restitution (*Factory at Chorzow* case).

Territorial acquisition and sovereignty. Without question, territorial disputes account for many of the conflicts between states. By providing explicit guiding principles for determining the legitimate acquisition of title to territorial space, international law has obviated many would-be conflicts. International law also sets the rules on how to determine the superiority of certain claims over others in territorial disputes (e.g., *Island of Palmas* case). When competing territorial claims can thus be resolved by reference to a set of preestablished, unequivocal norms on what confers positive title, international law makes recourse to violence unnecessary and futile.

Maritime regimes. The sea has long been a highway for commerce and war as well as a provider of food and other resources. Despite earlier attempts by certain states to assert exclusive control (unilateralism) over vast maritime areas, modern international law recognizes that beyond a certain distance from the coast of a state the sea is free for reasonable use by all nations. This "freedom of the seas"[2] is subject to no restriction except that its exercise by one state must not interfere with the use of the sea by other states (Lissitzyn 1965, 18). As in other areas of international relations, exercise of the freedom of the seas follows the dictate of mutuality and reciprocity, as distinct from unilateralism inherent in the concept of self-help. The international maritime law (or law of the sea) also provides for rights and duties regarding the territorial sea, the continental shelf, jurisdiction over foreign vessels, etc. Conflicts are less likely to occur once the boundaries of rights and duties are clearly delineated.

The last commons. This term refers to Antarctica, outer space, the seabed and ocean floor, and the high seas. Two overriding concerns in this regard are who, if anyone, shall have access and claim to these vast areas, and what should be done to control pollution in them. Just as the commons are humankind's last frontier, international law norms in this respect are also the most recent addition, constituting an "evolving international environmental law" (Choucri 1995, 401). The standard treatment of the commons, which is to suspend or dispense with all sovereign claims (see Chapter 9), has removed a possible area of conflict from the agenda of nations in their mutual relations.

International law can play an important role in preventing or mitigating international conflict in the areas just described largely because it establishes mutual accountability in the behavior of nations in their mutual relations. By clearly demarcating the boundary lines of permissible behavior, international law establishes a structure of expectations where decisionmakers' views can converge. It helps foster self-restraint. This by itself may help ward off potential conflicts, because disputants know with no uncertainty where their own rights stop and where others' rights begin. This is not to turn a blind eye to the fact that powerful states, especially those without scruples, may prefer to transgress on other states' rights by resorting to coercion or violence. However, international law at least makes that eventuality much more cumbersome and transparent.

What if the function of international law as a depressant of the use of force should fail to prevent a potential conflict from coming to a head? The answer is that, short of a resort to the use of force, there is an intermediate measure, known as the pacific settlement of disputes, that may help defuse the issue or issues in contention and resolve the conflict before it boils over.

Pacific Settlement of Disputes

The following brief review of the evolution and essentials of dispute settlement measures is to provide a context for commenting on the linkage of law and politics in the area of the international law of peace.

First, international law, which consists essentially of substantive norms, allocating the rights and duties of states, does not require that states resolve their disputes by peaceful means, which is a procedural concern (Levi 1991, 271). A procedural exhortation, nonetheless, was issued at the 1899 Hague Conference, which resulted in the Convention for the Pacific Settlement of Disputes, updated in 1907. In addition to provisions on good offices, mediation, and inquiry, the convention contained a number of articles on international arbitration. Article 15 of the convention gave the objective of arbitration as "the settlement of differences between States by judges of their own choice, and on the basis of respect for law" (*Statutes at Large* 32:1799). But submission to arbitration, just as acceptance of any other mode of pacific settlement, was voluntary and on the individual states' own accord. It was left for the United Nations Charter to require that states "settle their international disputes by peaceful means in such a manner that international peace and security . . . are not endangered" (Art. 2[3]). In addition, Article 33(1) of the Charter suggests that parties to a dispute likely to endanger peace shall "first of all" seek a solution by negotiation, mediation, conciliation, arbitration, judicial settlement, resort to regional arrangements, or any other peaceful means of their own choice. The reference to the disputants' free choice of means confirms that neither general international law nor the UN Charter makes mandatory settlement of disputes by disinterested third parties. Let us take note of two distinct, though overlapping, lines of division: one between adjudicatory and nonadjudicatory means; and the other between those modes of settlement that do not require third-party decisions and those that do.

Of the various modes of pacific settlement enumerated in Article 33(1), only "judicial settlement," which in effect means submission to the International Court of Justice, is a full-dress settlement mechanism of the adjudicatory genre. It is one that entails third-party decisions. The only other modes that likewise require third-party decisions are arbitration and resort to regional arrangements, plus perhaps submission to the deliberative councils of international organizations (such as the UN Security Council or General Assembly), which is not mentioned in Article 33(1). Mediation and conciliation, as inquiry (fact finding) and offering of good offices, require the participation and even extensive assistance of third parties; but decisions are nevertheless left with the disputants themselves (Slomanson 1995, 326–329).

While third-party decisions are used only rarely, the *participation* of third parties, especially those trusted by the disputants, can be very instrumental. One good example is the role the United States played in the brokering of the Bosnia peace agreement of October 1995. In that instance of dispute settlement, the United States invited the heads of Serbia, Bosnia, and Croatia to a military base in Dayton, Ohio, where the three were cloistered in marathon negotiations until they reached an agreement (*New York Times,* November 1, 1995, 11). The U.S. involvement as a third party was further extended to the sending of 20,000 troops to join a NATO peacekeeping mission to monitor the implementation of the peace accord in the Balkans. But that assisting role does not change the fact that the disputants themselves made the binding decisions.

This contrasts with the procedures of arbitration and judicial settlement, in which decisions are made by disinterested third parties known as arbitrators or judges, who render binding awards on the disputants. In fact, arbitration, which anticipated judicial settlement in the evolution of the international law of peace, dates back to ancient Greece. As a procedure for dispute settlement, however, it fell into disuse until its revival in the nineteenth century, following the Jay Treaty (1794) and the Treaty of Ghent (1814)—especially after the example of Great Britain and the United States in submitting the *Alabama Claims* to arbitration in 1871 (Brierly 1963, 348; cf. Ralston 1929).

The foremost data collection on international arbitrations has been compiled by Stuyt (1990) of Nijmegen University in the Netherlands. His tally shows 180 cases of international arbitration between 1900 and 1945. During the next forty-five years (1945–1989) the number declined to a paltry forty-three. If the Cold War intervening in those years was the reason for the decline, the post–Cold War era may reasonably see a rise in the use of arbitration as a means of dispute settlement. In fact, the expectant mood has already resulted in a book, *The Flame Rekindled: New Hopes for International Arbitration* (Muller and Mijs 1994).

While not indulging in hope, I do wish to make two observations concerning international arbitration. The first concerns the virtue of standing or permanent arbitral tribunals—sustained by treaty or compromissory commitment in that states agree to arbitrate their disputes following preestablished procedures. If states chose arbitrators on an ad hoc basis, that is, *after* a dispute arose, the more powerful state might dictate the terms. Furthermore, states rarely consent to arbitrating their more sensitive problems except for a forced commitment that can be secured by prior agreement (Slomanson 1995, 355).

My second observation pertains to the composition of an international arbitral tribunal. Ever since the 1899 Hague Convention, which established the Permanent Court of Arbitration (PCA), the format adopted in the composition of a PCA tribunal has provided a model for all other arbitral tribunals. The PCA format (Brierly 1963, 350) has inspired the institution, in many subsequent instances, of a permanent panel (list) of potential arbitrators nominated by states parties to a treaty. When two states refer a dispute to arbitration, each disputant party will choose two names from the existing list. The four arbitrators so chosen will pick a fifth, who will be the president of the arbitral tribunal. In some other instances, the exact mix may vary. For example, as with the Law of the Sea Tribunal, instituted under the 1982 Convention of the Law of the Sea (CLOS III), each disputant chooses only one arbitrator from a preestablished list. The two arbitrators thus chosen then choose the three others (CLOS III, Annex vii, Art. 3). Nevertheless, this mix in the tribunal's composition, as well as the preparation of a preestablished list of potential arbitrators (Annex vii, Art. 2), preserves the PCA tradition in essence.

For its enduring appeal, the PCA formula combines both an element of control and a guarantee of third-party neutrality. In an anarchic world, states are encouraged to accept arbitration when they know they retain some measure of control, while conceding the same measure of control to the other disputant. Both also have a reciprocal obligation to accept a certain number of arbitrators not chosen by them, to ensure a necessary semblance of impartiality and objectivity. Hence, the arbitration rules developed by the UN Commission on International Trade Law (UNCITRAL) to govern the appointment of arbitrators consciously followed the PCA tradition.

Appropriately, when the Iran–United States Claims Tribunal, reputed to be the most important arbitral tribunal to date, was created in 1981, it followed the format of the PCA, except its membership increased from five to nine. And the tribunal was established with the cooperation of the PCA's International Bureau. The first and fourth presidents of the tribunal were members of the PCA (Muller and Mijs 1994, 1). Thus, the PCA-inspired practice has established a body of procedural norms for international arbitration.

Standing Arbitral Tribunals at a Glance

There are actual standing international tribunals whose task is to resolve cases submitted to them by states for arbitration in their respective areas of specialization. A cursory examination shows the following groupings of standing tribunals in a wide diversity of functional areas (cf. Slomanson 1995, 363f.):

Standing tribunals established by the United Nations to handle special cases. Other than the Iran–United States Claims Tribunal, there is, for example, the UN Compensation Commission (headquartered in Geneva), created by the Security Council to resolve individual claims against Iraq due to the latter's invasion of Kuwait. On the other hand, the Iran–United States Claims Tribunal (based at the Hague) has the mandate of entertaining claims filed by U.S. nationals against Iran, arising from the 1979–1980 hostage taking during the seizure of the U.S. Embassy in Tehran.

Standing tribunals for international business arbitration. One example is the Court of Arbitration of the International Chamber of Commerce (ICC), with its head office in Paris, which delegates arbitration requests to local experts on national committees in participating states. Usually these requests are for the arbitration of disputes over business between private persons or corporations. Three others worth mentioning are the Dispute Settlement Body of the World Trade Organization (WTO), the London Court of International Arbitration, and the Stockholm Chamber of Commerce Arbitration.

The International Center for the Settlement of Investment Disputes (ICSID). Part of the World Bank in Washington, D.C., the ICSID is a one-of-a-kind voluntary mechanism for settling disputes between governments and foreign investors.

The International Tribunal for the Law of the Sea. Established under Article 287 of the 1982 CLOS III Convention, and headquartered in Hamburg, the tribunal, following the tradition of the PCA, arbitrates disputes between states parties to the Convention on the Law of the Sea.

Administrative tribunals of international organizations. One such example is the UN Administrative Claims Tribunal, in New York, with the function of resolving claims between the United Nations and its employees. Another example is the International Labour Organisation (ILO) Administrative Tribunal, based in Geneva. Its generic function of settling disputes regarding international labor standards extends to various UN agency labor practices.

Chambers of the International Court of Justice (ICJ). These are panels composed of less than all the ICJ judges and constituted under Article 26 of the ICJ Statute, for the purpose of "dealing with particular categories of cases." These categories were originally conceived as labor, transit, and communication. However, after 1982, chambers of the ICJ also heard border disputes between the United States and Canada, Mali and Upper Volta (now Burkina Faso), and El Salvador and Honduras (Schwebel 1987). Although each chamber has to be appointed by the president of the ICJ at the specific request of states submitting their dispute to the court, they merit being listed as standing tribunals because the ICJ is a standing institution (Slomanson 1994, 366). One advantage of the chamber mode of dispute resolution is that the judges, usually three to five, may decide on a summary basis, dispensing with certain ICJ rules and procedures, thus reaching a decision with dispatch. Another advantage, which is more political in nature, is that since each chamber's membership does not duplicate that of the full court, states may not have to face judges who happen to hail from countries with whom they have poor relations (Slomanson 1995, 377).

One distinct feature about arbitration is that, like judicial settlement, the arbitral procedure calls for decisions by disinterested third parties (the arbitrators). Cynics may scoff at the usefulness of international arbitration on grounds of weak enforcement of arbitral awards. But the good news is that in the post–World War II era, nations are increasingly inclined to recognize and enforce international arbitral awards in their domestic judicial systems. An indication is the wide acceptance of the New York Convention on the Recognition and Enforcement of Foreign Arbitral Awards of 1958, which by 1996 was ratified by 107 states, including nearly all major commercial nations and China (*AWSJW,* January 2, 1996, 2).

Judicial Settlement by the International Court of Justice

Although arbitration and judicial settlement are similar in that both employ adjudicatory procedures, the two are different in most other respects (cf. Rosenne 1985, 7–10). Unlike in arbitration, disputants have no part in the choice of the judges (as distinct from arbitrators) in judicial settlement—for example, by the International Court of Justice. Only in the selection of the judges to form a less than full court chamber may a disputant party hope to be consulted by the court's president following a 1972 change in the ICJ's rules of procedure. But all other cases are considered by the full court's fifteen judges, in whose appointment the parties have no part, except during voting by the Security Council and the General Assembly to fill a vacancy on the court, as prescribed by Articles 8–13 of the statute.

In arbitration, the formal basis of decision (called an award) is respect for law (recalling Article 15 of the 1899 Hague Convention). The parties to an arbitration may actually choose the principles and procedures to be followed in arriving at an award, unless they prefer to follow those prescribed by the Hague Conventions. They may agree on the power and jurisdiction to be granted the arbitrator, the composition of the arbitral tribunal, the limits of the subject matter the tribunal may not overstep, the basis for the award, possibly the interpretation of the principles to be applied to the case, and the alternative awards the arbitrator may make. On the other hand, in the adjudicatory procedure by the ICJ, decisions—which are called judgments—are based on the rules of law (Levi 1991, 283). Most of the procedural details, such as power of the court, the basis for the decision, etc., are prescribed by law. Both arbitral awards and judicial decisions are binding on the parties, and both are final unless new facts can be produced that would decisively affect the decisions.

However, on the question of jurisdiction, the consent of the parties must be secured in both arbitration and judicial settlement. In arbitration, a *compromis,* which conveys a commitment on the part of the disputants, confers jurisdiction on an arbitral tribunal. In judicial settlement by the ICJ, the consent may take different forms, such as by special agreement; the parties' acceptance of the ICJ's compulsory jurisdiction according to Article 36 of the statute, which requires the filing of a formal declaration indicating acceptance; or the principle of *forum prorogatum,* where the defendant nation follows the plaintiff to the court to answer a complaint filed by the latter (such as in the *Asylum* and *Corfu Channel* cases).

The moral is that the requirement for state consent in the international adjudicatory procedures, including judicial settlement, stems ultimately from systemic anarchy. The decentralized nature of our Westphalian system calls for respect for the sovereign equality of states. This means that no authority, not even a judicial one, can impose its will (jurisdiction) on any state without its prior consent. Parenthetically, the idea of an international criminal court that can assert jurisdiction independent of the consent of a target party is a relatively recent development (see Chapter 10).[3]

Here lies both the virtue and weakness of the world's adjudicatory mechanisms. The virtue is that once a state has given its consent to adjudication, its willingness to be bound by the decision resulting from adjudication is foretold. It would work extra hardship for the state to go against its given word by spurning the final award later on. The weakness of the institution, on the other hand, is that states that have foresworn their determination not to bend to the will of law or reason will just not agree to accept the jurisdiction of the forum that is to adjudicate a dispute in which they are embroiled. In the case of the United States, for example, three days before Nicaragua was going to bring a complaint against it to the ICJ, Washington notified the court, on April 6, 1984, that the 1946 U.S. declaration accepting the court's compulsory jurisdiction "shall not apply to disputes with any Central American State" for a duration of two years.[4] The court, in handing down its 1984 decision ("Provisional Measures"), rejected the U.S. demurrer and ruled that Nicaragua's application was admissible. But pending the court's final judgment (Merits), which was not rendered until 1986, the United States withdrew its 1946 acceptance altogether on October 7, 1985. While withdrawing, the United States quipped that, of the five permanent members of the UN Security Council, only the United States and the United Kingdom had accepted the ICJ's compulsory jurisdiction

(Franck 1986, 48). (France, I might add, accepted the court's compulsory jurisdiction but withdrew in 1974.)

In a slightly earlier case in which the United States was the plaintiff seeking relief from the ICJ, Iran simply refused to appear (*U.S. Diplomatic and Consular Staff in Tehran,* 1979–1980). Iran's nonappearance, however, did not stop the court from ruling that it had jurisdiction in the case. Nor did it prevent the court from delivering its Order of Provisional Measures in late 1979 and its final judgment in May 1980. Iran refused to institute the interim measures of protection ordered by the court but released U.S. hostages in January 1981, or seven months after the ICJ handed down its judgment (Merits) in May 1980. Under the Declaration of Algeria by which Iran and the United States expressed their commitments to release of the hostages, withdrawal of sanctions, and settlement of claims, the United States agreed to withdraw all claims against Iran before the International Court of Justice (*ILM* 20 [1981]:223).

The same weakness in international adjudication stemming from the sovereignty of states, which may withhold their consent to the court's jurisdiction, also applies to the enforcement of its decisions. This is a natural, though deplorable, consequence of the principle according to which our Westphalian system is structured, which, to reiterate, is the principle of sovereign equality of states. International law can only be as effective as the political wills of nations allow it to be.

My intention here is not to praise or to indict the ICJ. But I do wish to point out that, considering the limiting circumstances (e.g., systemic anarchy, sovereignty of states, etc.) within which it has had to operate, the court has fared not as badly as some have suggested, especially if one looks at the aggregate data. First, according to one tally, between 1946 and July 1991, the court had eighty-six cases brought before it. All together, it rendered fifty-two judgments and twenty-one advisory opinions. It also issued 249 orders, mostly of a procedural nature but including some indicating provisional measures (Henkin et al. 1993, 806). According to another account, the court between 1948 and 1985 had rendered 115 decisions and advisory opinions (Franck 1986, 37). Still another source gave fifty-three contentious cases in the court's docket during the first forty years of its existence (1946–1986), whereas it also rendered eighteen advisory opinions (Slomanson 1995, 375). An official ICJ publication (ICJ 1992) contains eighty-nine entries, eighteen of which are advisory opinions and the remainder contentious cases. For the latter group, the court issued orders in fourteen cases and judgments in the remaining fifty-seven. No matter which set of data one looks at, the record does not match many people's worst impressions.

Second, the record is even more impressive in qualitative terms, when one considers the enormous contribution made by the court in the elucidation of the law (Higgins 1994, 202ff.). The court's decisions in such classic cases as the *Corfu Channel, Nottebohm, Barcelona Traction,* and *North Sea Continental Shelf* will have far-reaching effects in the interpretation of international law for decades to come. In addition, through its advisory opinions, the court either defused knotty political issues of the time (e.g., the *Western Sahara* case) or pointed to creative solutions to unique problems (e.g., *South-West Africa/Legal Consequences*) or unraveled the implied powers of organs of the United Nations (e.g., *Reparation; Certain Expenses; Competence of the General Assembly*).

Third, the utility of the court is not just in actual litigation in contentious cases. Often the filing of a complaint by one disputant state against another has the effect of encouraging settlement when deadlocked diplomatic negotiations are resumed. Nicaragua filed a transborder armed conflict claim against Honduras in 1988, for example. Although Honduras unsuccessfully attacked the court's jurisdiction, the parties then reached an out-of-court settlement. Nicaragua then withdrew the case from the court's docket.

Fourth, enforcement of ICJ's decisions is concededly weak. Again, if one takes an aggregate view, the list of cases in which a judgment was openly rejected by a delinquent state is not as long as might be expected. True, Albania refused to pay the compensation awarded to Great Britain in the *Corfu Channel* case. Iran failed to institute the interim measure of protection ordered in the *Anglo-Iranian Oil Company* and *U.S. Diplomatic and Consular Staff in Tehran* cases. But in the latter instance, Iran reached agreement with the United States shortly thereafter when the American hostages were released. The important thing is that, despite the notorious enforcement problem, very rarely have delinquent states openly denounced or reviled the court's judgment that found them delinquent. Theoretically, a state may, relying on Article 94(2) of the UN Charter, turn to the Security Council for assistance in instituting appropriate measures (e.g., sanctions) to ensure enforcement of an award it has won from the ICJ. So far, the article has been invoked only once, and inconclusively, before the Security Council (von Glahn 1992, 620). This recourse, nevertheless, has a great deal of potential for giving wider effect to judgments of the court in the future, especially now that the five permanent members on the Council can work together, as demonstrated in their unity in reacting to Iraq's invasion of Kuwait in 1990.

Finally, as of 1994, a total of fifty-eight countries had filed declarations accepting the ICJ's compulsory jurisdiction under the "optional clause" (Art. 36[2]) of the statute. Not counting the eleven that either expired or have been withdrawn, forty-seven such declarations are in force, including one by a nonmember of the United Nations (Switzerland). The one region in the world, Eastern Europe, where no one single country was known to have accepted the ICJ's compulsory jurisdiction (except as a carryover from the days of the Permanent Court of International Justice, the ICJ's predecessor), is now in a state of flux following the fall of the Berlin Wall in 1989. Admittedly, the number of countries that have accepted the court's compulsory jurisdiction is still meager. But the following points merit attention:

1. The "optional clause," by which states file their voluntary declaration of acceptance, is only one vehicle by which the court may acquire jurisdiction in a contentious case. A state that does not take the Article 36(2) option may still be answerable to the ICJ's jurisdiction, if it is a party to a treaty requiring that the signatories litigate their disputes in the ICJ. Thus, despite its withdrawal in 1985 of its 1946 declaration, the United States has been a defendant in a number of cases. In one, Libya accused the United States along with the United Kingdom of complicity in a conspiracy to avoid certain treaty obligations in relation to Libya's bombing of Pan Am flight 103 over Lockerbie, Scotland, in 1988. In another case, filed in 1993, Serbia similarly accused the United States of politicizing the Bosnia debate—by supposedly claiming that the Serbian military forces were perpetrating genocide in the former Yugoslavia (Slomanson 1995, p. 382).

2. The Court's jurisdiction may be established either by special (ad hoc) agreement or under the principle of forum prorogatum, as noted earlier.

3. In the more than seventy contentious cases presented to the ICJ since its inception in 1946, some states usually considered international outlaws—such as Libya, apartheid-era South Africa, and communist Bulgaria—have come before the ICJ either as plaintiff (Libya in two cases) or as respondent (Bulgaria and South Africa).

4. According to UN Secretary-General Boutros Boutros-Ghali (1992), one reason for limited utilization of the ICJ is the financial condition of the United Nations' smaller states. Many of them do not even have the resources to maintain a diplomatic presence in many countries. The same problem has historically limited their access to the ICJ as a dispute settlement center. As a partial remedy, he proposed the establishment of a UN Trust Fund to assist countries unable to afford the cost involved in bringing a dispute to the ICJ.

Considering the self-help impulse inherent in every state of our anarchic system, one has reasons to wonder why any nation would bother at all with an adjudicatory mechanism such as the ICJ. By definition, accepting adjudication means agreeing to accept the vagaries of a third party determining one's fate. In spirit and in essence, this goes against the unilateralist grain in the self-help impulse. Since sovereign states are absolutely under no obligation to accept third-party arbitration or judicial settlement, one would be at a loss to explain the number of nations (forty-seven) that submit themselves to the compulsory jurisdiction of the ICJ. Equally, at other times, states accept arbitration and let a third party (an arbitral tribunal) decide the outcome for them in disputes that may affect their vital interests.

Critics may deplore the underutilization of the judicial settlement process. But we can turn the question around and ask instead: Why would so many countries bother with the adjudicatory measures, knowing that they can always take the self-help option? According to the Realist view, the number should be zero. The answer, which can be very revealing of the utility of international law, is obviously that states find relying on disinterested third-party decisions preferable to the alternatives, which might mean stalemated nonsolution or forced resort to self-help.

One additional Neorealist contention is that anarchy inhibits cooperation between nations, because in a decentralized system members do not consider whether they can all benefit, but rather who is to gain more (Waltz 1979, 105; Grieco 1994, 40–49). A point rarely appreciated by the Neorealists is that the option of a third-party settlement mechanism mitigates the relative gains preoccupation of states in dispute. This can be easily demonstrated in the shift in the strategic calculations of decisionmakers. In direct negotiations when a dispute arises, states face a contest between A's terms and B's terms of settlement. But when a third-party mechanism option is used, the disputants' perceived choice is between having a third party–imposed solution (an award or judgment)—even if it is a less than fully satisfying one—and having a stalemated nonsolution. Assuming both disputants are similarly motivated to seek solution over nonsolution, they may find a saddle point where their procedural preferences converge.

To add another desideratum, if the relevant norms of the law are clearly on one side, and this is known beforehand, it is a zero-sum game. The other side will ultimately balk at accepting adjudication. Otherwise, and even when the gains may turn out to be uneven, both sides' preference for finding a solution, instead of a stalemate, will lead to their mutual acceptance of adjudication. Under the circumstances, even when one side may lose or gain less than expected from the outcome, it will have shown its rectitude for having committed itself to accepting a binding third-party decision. The loser government, besides, will find it easier to explain the outcome to its domestic constituency than if it had succumbed forthright to the demands of the opposing party through diplomacy. Furthermore, it will have the added advantage of having set an example for other states to follow in upholding the international law of peace in similar disputes. The relative gains consideration is thus drowned out in the midst of these additional strategic calculations. Since modern international law bans all uses of force except in self-defense, the fear of an act of self-help resulting in an "illegal war" (Schwarzenberger 1967, 194) is another reason states opt for adjudication and other means of pacific settlement of disputes rather than self-help, Neorealism's logical deduction from the systemic anarchy premise notwithstanding.

Conclusion

We have seen that states are at times more inclined to accept peaceful settlement of disputes (including third-party adjudication) than to resort to naked self-help. This inclination indicates a shift from a unilateralist reflex to one of mutual accommodation (such as resort to third-party dispute settlement signifies). While jurisdictional competence of international tribunals is essentially founded on consent, only in international arbitration is that consent by states given in relation to a particular dispute. In judicial settlement, the consent to jurisdiction of a forum, such as the ICJ or the European Court of Human Rights, is given in what Higgins (1994, 186) calls a "general way," so that it is a consent in principle rather than a consent in relation to a particular opponent or a particular case. Consent of this type amounts to a formal suspension of a state's right to resort to other options, including self-help. States that choose this option are apparently convinced that it is in their national interest to do so.

And, finally, we have seen that on a larger scale, compliance with the norms of the international law of peace growing out of mutual consent is likewise in nations' self-interest. The ultimate lesson for us is the reality that states may, as in the circumstances discussed, choose to suspend or forgo their right to self-help in favor of peaceful means of dispute settlement. Just as the outlawry of war has often foreclosed states' option for coercive, unilateral self-help, the option of noncoercive alternative settlement measures has made dormant the regulation of armaments and conduct of war regimes in ordinary times. The fact that states do avail themselves of pacific settlement of disputes, as an alternative to the use of unilateral self-help, confirms states' common urge for order, which international law is designed to satisfy in an anarchic international system. It also confirms that when noncoercive solutions are available within international law, states' first choice is not always to resort to self-help. Put another way, owing to the mediating role international law performs, the system of international relations witnesses a change from a competitive reliance on the unilateralist, Hobbesian self-help impulse to a reciprocal volition of mutual restraint. The change may not be readily perceptible to the casual observer, but it is a real and undeniable one.

Notes

1. The nine rules of diplomacy, as urged by Hans Morgenthau, are: (1) divest diplomacy of the crusading spirit; (2) restrict the definition of vital national interest; (3) look at the political scene from the point of view of other nations; (4) be willing to compromise on all interests that are not vital; (5) "give up the shadow of worthless rights for the substance of real advantage"; (6) "never put yourself in the position from which you cannot retreat without losing face, and from which you cannot advance without risk"; (7) "never allow a weak ally to make decisions for you"; (8) keep the armed forces an instrument of diplomacy, not its master; and (9) in formulating and conducting foreign policy, the government must not become the slave of public opinion. See Morgenthau, *Politics Among Nations,* 5th ed. (New York: Knopf, 1978), 550–560.

2. The "freedom of the seas" includes freedom of navigation, freedom to fish and exploit other resources above the bottom of the sea, freedom to conduct military maneuvers and weapons tests, and (in war) freedom to attack the enemy and interrupt his communications.

3. The idea of an international criminal court survived the Nuremberg and Tokyo trials at the end of World War II. There were many calls for the creation of an exclusively criminal international tribunal to try various types of international crimes, such as terrorism, hijacking, and war crimes. UN Security Council Resolution 827 of 1993 set the foundation for the United Nations International Tribunal for the Prosecution of Persons Responsible for Serious Violations of International Humanitarian Law Committed in the Territory of the Former Yugoslavia, usually known by its acronym, UNITY. This modern version of an international criminal court is mandated to bring to justice those who have committed crimes in the Bosnia arena since 1991. UNITY's jurisdiction will not be based on the consent of the individuals accused of war crimes or other offenses, but will be compulsory upon prima facie evidence that the accused have violated the rules of international humanitarian law applicable to armed conflict (Slomanson 1995, 387–388).

4. See ICJ decision 1984, in *Case Concerning the Military and Paramilitary Activities in and Against Nicaragua* (Nicaragua v. the United States); 1984 *ICJ Yearbook,* pp. 135–147, esp. paras. 12–16. For views supporting the court's jurisdiction, see William W. Bishop, Jr., "Nicaragua v. the United States," *AJIL* 79 (1985):373. See also Thomas Franck, "Icy Day at the ICJ," *AJIL* 79 (1985):379.

Part 3

Sovereignty and Its Restraint

5

Sovereignty, Jurisdiction, Immunity, and State Responsibility: Constraint of Anarchy

The lack of a central authority in the international system (or anarchy, in Neorealist parlance) necessarily leads to the juridical coequality of states, which are similarly sovereign in their own right. The Neorealist view holds that, in the anarchic and non-hierarchical system, "like units" (states) define themselves as the highest authority in all matters of government over their specified territory and people (cf. Waltz 1979, 95). Elsewhere, sovereignty is sometimes defined as that quality that "makes a territorial entity eligible to participate in international relations" (James 1986, 92). This *eligibility* to act on the international plane is to us a juridical competence, or jurisdiction, flowing from the very attribute and reality of sovereignty. As we shall see, the only exception is that international organizations, while not endowed with the sovereign quality of states, may have varying degrees of capacity to act.

Jurists tend to give rather narrow and technical meanings to the term *jurisdiction,* including a state's capacity under international law "to prescribe or enforce the rule of law" (American Law Institute's Restatement Second 1965; Levi 1991, 107). For our purpose here, jurisdiction is seen in much broader light, generally as an eligibility to act. It connotes a right by a state, under international law, to assert a claim or espouse a cause in behalf of itself or its national(s). The obverse side of this juridical capacity is state responsibility, as in the treatment of aliens and their interests. To facilitate their mutual relations, states routinely relinquish part of their sovereignty, on a reciprocal basis, in according other states (and those states' diplomatic and consular agents) immunity from the reach of their executive and judicial jurisdiction. Thus, sovereignty, jurisdiction, immunity, and state responsibility are interrelated. They are therefore discussed together in this chapter, especially in the context of the linkage of law and politics in international relations.

Sovereignty and Jurisdiction

States, as they interact in the anarchic system, need a body of norms governing the allocation of jurisdictional competence, so that they know when and how to act legitimately and when to yield to other states' jurisdictional rights. Equally, in the event of jurisdictional conflict, states also need a readily available body of norms that offer a guide for regulating and resolving such conflicts without resorting to self-help, and in a way that will not unduly infringe on their own sovereignty—that is, they need international law.

Although sovereignty and jurisdiction are closely related in practice, the two may not always coincide and may exist as two distinct concepts (Levi 1991, 108). The exercise of jurisdiction over no-man's-land may lead to establishing title to, hence sovereignty over, that land. In the Panama Canal Zone, until its retrocession by the end of 1999, the state of Panama is sovereign, but the United States has jurisdiction. In the *International Status of South-West Africa* case, the International Court of Justice (1950, 132) confirmed that the creation of mandated territories after World War I implied transfer of neither territory nor sovereignty to the mandatory power (South Africa), although the latter exercised jurisdiction. States may have jurisdiction, but not sovereignty, over zones contiguous to their territorial waters.

In practical terms, in a rare competition between sovereignty and jurisdiction, it can be argued that having jurisdiction is more decisive in determining an outcome. Some examples may illustrate this point. On the high seas, where no state has sovereignty, whichever state can establish its jurisdiction over a certain situation (e.g., a piracy, narcotics trafficking, a ship flying its flag) has the last say under international law.

To return to the Panama Canal Zone example, in the event of sabotage committed against canal facilities, the United States, which has jurisdiction but not sovereignty in the zone, plays a more decisive role in crime control than does Panama, which wields sovereignty. In the event of a murder committed on board a foreign ship docked in a U.S. port, it is the local court that has jurisdiction, although the state whose flag the vessel flies actually has sovereignty over the ship, as shown in *Wildenhus'* case. Of importance here is not the reason the port city should have jurisdiction (i.e., that the effect of the crime on board disturbed the tranquillity on shore), but rather that in the final analysis it is effective jurisdiction that matters more than remote sovereignty in the prosecution of the crime in question.

In the *Lotus* case (1927), a French ship collided with and sank a Turkish steamer on the high seas, causing the death of eight Turkish nationals. France claimed jurisdiction and assailed Turkey for instituting criminal proceedings against the French officer responsible after the ship reached the Turkish capital of Constantinople following the collision. The Permanent Court of International Justice (PCIJ) ruled that although the steamer *Lotus* had French nationality because of the flag it flew (thus France had sovereign rights over it), the French claim to exclusive jurisdiction was not supported by international law. Turkey had concurrent jurisdiction, the court pointed out, because of the nationality of the victims in an accident that took place on the high seas. More simply, the case involved the competition between a claim to jurisdiction backed by sovereign rights, and a claim of jurisdiction not so backed. The Permanent Court did not accept the superiority of the former claim.

International organizations constitute a class of entities that have the eligibility or capacity to act, although they possess no sovereignty. Their juridical competence, hence jurisdiction in the broad sense as used here, does not flow from sovereignty but from the instruments (treaties) contracted by member states agreeing to their creation. In an advisory opinion rendered in the *Reparation* case (1949), the International Court of Justice concluded that the United Nations, endowed with a large measure of international personality (though not sovereignty), had "the capacity to operate upon the international plane." This capacity, which extended to the exercise of functional protection of its agents (i.e., those individuals in the service of the UN), the court added, arose by necessary intendment of the UN Charter.

The same characterization applies to the International Civil Aviation Organization (ICAO), the International Labour Organisation (ILO), the International Maritime Organization (IMO), and other members of the United Nations family. In their respective functional areas, these agencies each have a jurisdictional right to act, often affecting the rights and duties of sovereign nation-states. For the ICAO, for example, that functional area is the development of the principles and techniques of international air aviation and air transport. It should be recalled that the ICAO was the first to be asked to look into the downing by the Soviet military of Korean Air Lines flight 007 in 1983. The jurisdiction of the ILO is in functions related to the improvement of labor's working and living conditions. The goal is to be achieved through the adoption of international labor conventions and recommendations, prepared by the ILO, that set minimum standards on wages, conditions of employment, etc. For its part, the IMO has a special responsibility (hence jurisdiction) for safety of life at sea and for the protection of the marine environment through prevention of pollution of the sea caused by ships and other craft. The IMO also deals with legal matters connected with, among other things, international shipping (NZMERAT 1991, 134, 138, 141).

The purpose of this discussion is to highlight an often neglected fact that nonstate actors like those described have jurisdictional rights without sovereign status. Neorealists consider state sovereignty as a product of systemic anarchy. Concededly, there is some awareness in the Neorealist literature that sovereignty may be mitigated by the mutual dependence of states (Waltz 1979, 96). The same literature, however, is silent on the question of certain international actors having jurisdictional capacity without sovereignty.

This is an unfortunate lacuna, because if the veracity and widening extent of this phenomenon should be taken into serious consideration, it may require a revision of the Neorealist thinking on anarchy. In the first place, consideration of the jurisdiction-without-sovereignty phenomenon may force the Neorealists to turn away from their state-centric preoccupation and to face squarely the proliferation and expanding activities of an array of nonstate actors, such as the global and regional international organizations. These entities increasingly intrude into the international system, competing with and even eclipsing nation-states as initiators and targets of international action. Undeniably, it is the Neorealists' fixation on sovereignty that accounts for their state-centric bias.

Second, a closer examination of the jurisdiction-without-sovereignty question shows that our Westphalian system is not as anarchic as the Neorealists make it out to be. We imply that the phenomenon in question is both more real and more important than is usually appreciated. It bears on our correct understanding and analysis of the international system we live in. For nation-states, eschewal of the issue of sovereignty will make them less jealous about guarding their rights against each other, hence more disposed toward cooperation. Indeed, there can be "concurrent jurisdiction," as the PCIJ suggested in the *Lotus* case. But there cannot be concurrent sovereignty shared by more than one state. Hence, the shift of focus from the desideratum of sovereignty to that of jurisdiction opens up the possibility of changing one's perception of international relations from a zero-sum to a non-zero-sum game. Furthermore, for nonsovereign corporate bodies, it has been proven that collective action of consequence, not requiring a central authority to act as an arbiter, is possible both among themselves and vis-à-vis nation-states. Exercise by these nonsovereign actors of their jurisdictional power nonetheless produces effects that reach to sovereign states. The absence of a central authority in no way thwarts the normal functioning of the likes of ICAO, ILO, and IMO. More than that, the GATT/WTO, another nonsovereign institution, is known to have effectively imposed international discipline over trade policies of sovereign states—and to have done so precisely in the absence of a higher central authority. Here lies one more evidence that overdramatizing the anarchic nature of the international system is misleading.

The bottom line is that preoccupation with state sovereignty, which in itself is a derivative of the postulate of systemic anarchy, inevitably blinds one to the extent of international collective action that either transcends state sovereignty or reduces its relevance. Neorealists' fixation with state practices associated with sovereignty confirms, tautologically, what they see as the hopelessly anarchic nature of the international system, which breeds sovereignty in the first place. But, as we have seen, the confirmation has no real value.

Competing Bases of Jurisdiction and Jurisdictional Conflict

This section addresses two large concerns: In conditions of anarchy, it is extremely important that states know under what circumstances they have the juridical competence, or jurisdiction, to act in furtherance of their interests or cherished values;[1] and in the event of a jurisdictional dispute, states need to know a way out that is both equitable and honorable. Therefore, what guidance international law offers on these two questions is very important in that it may help avert or resolve many an international conflict. In international relations, major fights do not result quite as often from reckless ventures or impulses of self-help by states as from jurisdictional conflict. What is intervention to one state may be to another state simply an attempt to protect self-interests or cherished values. Thus, the law must be clear and readily comprehensible to all nations as to who has the juridical competence or jurisdictional basis to act, and in what circumstances.

In the discussion that follows, I shall continue to use *jurisdiction* in its broader sense, except in contexts where narrower and more technical connotations of the term are called for.

Competing Bases of Jurisdiction

Other than by prior agreement between states, jurisdiction is usually determined in accordance with five general principles (bases):

- The *territorial principle,* determining jurisdiction by reference to the place where the offense or problem demanding attention takes place
- The *nationality principle,* determining jurisdiction by reference to the nationality or national character of the person, real or juridical, responsible for the offense
- The *protective principle,* determining jurisdiction by reference to the national interest injured by the offense
- The *universal principle,* determining jurisdiction by reference to the custody of the person committing the offense

- The *passive personality principle,* determining jurisdiction by reference to the nationality or national character of the person injured by the offense

Of the five principles, the territorial principle is regarded by most states and jurists as of primary importance and of fundamental character, although extraterritorial jurisdiction is often a vexing problem. The nationality principle is likewise universally accepted, despite differences in state practices as regards the extent to which it is used. The United States, as a whole, habitually takes a most liberal stand on the extraterritorial reach of its jurisdiction on the basis of the offender's nationality, as demonstrated in a number of civil and criminal cases, including *Blackmer v. U.S., Alcoa,* and *Flores.* The 1982 Convention on the Law of the Sea confers jurisdiction on the basis of nationality (Art. 97). The protective principle is today accepted by most states but, because of its perceived historical origin in the West's gunboat diplomacy, it is received with misgivings in many Third World nations. The principle of universal jurisdiction is by now everywhere accepted with regard to offenses such as piracy, slave trade, and illicit drug trafficking on the high seas (CLOS III, Arts. 99, 100–108). In fact, CLOS III makes it a duty for states that are parties to act in concert to control and suppress these offenses on the high seas (e.g., Art. 100), where no state has sovereignty or prior claim to jurisdiction.

The last principle, passive personality, is somewhat nebulous. The contention that the state whose national was the victim of an offense committed abroad had material jurisdiction, as part of the right of a state to protect its nationals, was upheld in the *Lotus* case. Presumably, this principle would be welcome to the lesser powers and hence anathema to the more powerful ones, as it would offer the former gratuitous protection in dealings with the latter. An indication of how the power disparity may affect a state's position in this regard may be found in the fact that the Turkish penal code based jurisdiction explicitly on the nationality of the victim (Art. 6). In the Mexican penal code, Article 186 provided that offenses committed abroad by a foreigner against a Mexican may be punished in Mexico if the offender was found within Mexican territory and not tried elsewhere (Bishop 1962, 459f.). In the *Cutting* case (1886), a U.S. newspaper publisher in El Paso, Texas, was tried and convicted of libel by a Mexican court. The victim of the alleged libel was a Mexican national; the accused, Mr. Cutting, the journalist, had resided in Mexico "off and on" for eighteen months (Dickinson 1929, 404).

In the wake of the *Lotus* case (1927), there were strong enough reactions that the doctrine of passive personality was in limbo. It was dropped as a basis of jurisdiction in the International Convention for the Unification of Certain Rules Relating to Penal Jurisdiction in Matters of Collisions, signed in Brussels in 1952. Likewise, it was missing from the 1958 Geneva Convention on the High Seas in provisions regarding jurisdiction relating to maritime collision. However, other treaties are not so consistent. Passive personality was accepted as an alternative basis of jurisdiction in the 1963 Convention on Offenses and Certain Other Acts Committed on Board Aircraft; in the 1973 Convention on the Prevention and Punishment of Crimes Against Internationally Protected Persons, Including Diplomatic Agents; in the International Convention Against the Taking of Hostages (1979); and in the European Convention on the Suppression of Terrorism (1976).

In contrast, the principle was not adopted in other treaties, such as the 1970 Convention for Suppression of Unlawful Seizure of Aircraft (Hijacking); and the Convention for the Suppression of Unlawful Acts (Sabotage) Against the Safety of Civil Aviation (1971). Besides, the CLOS III also omitted the passive personality principle. Echoing Article 11 of the 1958 Convention on the High Seas, the 1982 convention makes nationality the only basis of jurisdiction. Article 97 provides that, in a collision or any other incident on the high seas, only the state of which the person accused is a national, or the state whose flag the ship in question flies, shall have the jurisdiction for penal or disciplinary action.

Nor are state practices consistent. In the *Cutting* case, the U.S. position was negative, as Secretary of State Bayard declared in 1887: "To say that [an American citizen] may be tried in another country for his offense, simply because its object happens to be a citizen of that country, would be to assert that foreigners coming to the United States bring their penal law of the country from which they come, and thus subject citizens of the United States in their own country to an indefinite criminal responsibility. Such a pretension can never be admitted by this Government" (Moore 1906, vol. 2, 232–240). But in a number of recent cases, the United States insisted that it had jurisdiction to try an alien accused of killing a U.S. citizen abroad. In the *René Martin Verdugo–Urquidez* case (1985), a Mexican was tried and convicted by a U.S. court for killing a U.S. Drug Enforcement Agency (DEA) officer in that country. On demand, the Mexican police delivered him to the border to U.S. marshals waiting in Calexico, California (Lowenfeld 1990, 448). In the *Alvarez-Machain* case (1992), the U.S. Supreme Court, reversing a lower court ruling, upheld jurisdiction for the United States, despite the Mexican suspect's abduction (by DEA agents) from Mexico for the murder of a U.S. DEA agent there.

On the other hand, Mexico, which invoked its own penal code conferring jurisdiction on the basis of passive personality in the *Cutting* case above, was reported "mollified" over the U.S. Supreme Court's ruling (*New York Times,* June 18, 1992, 3). The *Alvarez-Machain* case was not exactly a U.S. duplication of the *Cutting* case 106 years earlier. In contrast to Mr.

Cutting's voluntary presence in Mexico, the more recent case involved forcible cross-boundary abduction, which did not just violate Mexican sovereignty in abstract, but also breached an outstanding extradition treaty. In the face of a storm of protest from Mexico, Argentina, and others in Latin America following the U.S. Supreme Court's ruling, the Bush administration had to offer reassurances that the United States would respect their sovereignty in spite of the ruling (*New York Times,* June 17, 1992, 8).

William D. Rogers, a former assistant secretary of state and a prominent international lawyer, commented that Washington's behavior in Mexico was the opposite of its behavior in the effort to oust Iraq after its invasion of Kuwait. But the fact of the matter is that the United States has a long-standing practice of extraterritorial abductions on a number of grounds, including passive personality. Other grounds are narcotics trafficking and terrorism. In a 1988 case, known as *Matta-Ballesteros,* a Honduras national was forcibly abducted by U.S. agents from his home in Honduras and brought to the United States for trial on narcotics charges (Lowenfeld 1990, 446). In the same year, Fawas Yunis, a Lebanese wanted for hijacking and destruction of a Jordanian airliner bound from Beirut to Amman, was lured to a yacht on the high seas. From there he was overpowered and arrested by FBI agents and brought back to Washington, D.C. He was tried and convicted for violation of provisions of the U.S. criminal code (*Fawas Yunis*).

All these cross-boundary abductions were made following a series of laws enacted by Congress in the 1980s criminalizing certain activities committed outside U.S. territory, even by non–U.S. nationals. These legislations were based in part on the doctrines of passive personality and universal jurisdiction (cf. Lowenfeld 1989, 880ff.). But under international law, none of the legitimate bases of jurisdiction would sanctify the use of extraterritorial abductions. The juridical tenet *male captus bene detentus* (a person improperly seized may nevertheless properly be detained) is a domestic precept (Henkin 1989, 305). In U.S. domestic law, it is confirmed by the Ker-Frisbie doctrine (Lowenfeld 1990, 460–465). This rule, nevertheless, has been applied by the courts of a number of states, including Canada, France, Germany, England, and Israel (see cases cited in Halberstam 1992, 738, n. 14).

Neorealists may see these acts involving extraterritorial abduction as smacking of self-help by brute force and typical of an anarchic system of sovereign states without effective law enforcement. But in the final analysis, such acts are a jurisdictional-conflict question. The rationale for the United States taking the unusual initiative—employing aggressive means of gaining custody of the suspect—to assert jurisdiction in each case was anticipated and illustrated in an earlier cognate case, *Flores* (1933). Mr. Flores, a citizen of the United States, was charged with murdering a fellow countryman on board a U.S. ship at anchor in a port in the Belgian Congo, some 250 miles inland from the mouth of the Congo River, or a place subject to the sovereignty of the kingdom of Belgium. After committing the crime, Flores was forcibly brought into the port of Philadelphia. The district court sustained a demurrer to the indictment and discharged the prisoner. But the U.S. Supreme Court reversed the ruling on the ground that the offense fell sufficiently within the admiralty and maritime jurisdiction of the United States. Casting a long-lasting influence, the Supreme Court pointed to and justified a practical way out of a jurisdictional conflict due to the alternate application of the territorial (for Belgium) and nationality (for the United States) principles. Both the United States and Belgium would have jurisdiction over Flores but on different grounds; hence they would have concurrent jurisdiction. After noting that there was no agreement among nations or writers on international law as to which sovereign should yield to the other when both try to assert jurisdiction, the court stated that "in the absence of any controlling treaty provision, and any *assertion of jurisdiction by the territorial sovereign* [emphasis added], it is the duty of the courts of the United States" to prosecute Flores according to U.S. statutes, "interpreted in the light of recognized principles of international law."

Although the more recent cases were different with respect to the nationality of the abductees (they were all foreign nationals), the United States nevertheless could claim jurisdiction alternatively on the basis of passive personality (when U.S. agents were killed) or universal jurisdiction (in the event of terrorism or drug trafficking). A controlling similarity in all these cases was that, as in the *Flores* case, no territorial sovereign was known to assert its concurrent jurisdiction. The United States, in a way, exercised jurisdiction by default. One might argue that the Mexican government's protest in the *Alvarez-Machain* case was lodged post facto and did not change its failure, for whatever reason, to assert its territorial jurisdiction. One other major difference in the more recent cases was probably the excessive coercion used. But that is a question of degree, not of sort. If the by-default thesis can stand up, the U.S. resort to extraterritorial abductions, as cited, is not due to systemic anarchy, with reference to which Neorealists would usually define the imperative of self-help. The reason is that normal and easier relief was obtainable, especially in the *Alvarez-Machain* case, because the United States had a treaty right to request the suspect's extradition from Mexico.

Except for the pretext of exercising jurisdiction by default, the United States in all the above cases of abduction was clearly on shaky legal grounds. The State Department's legal adviser, Abraham Sofaer, clearly admitted so. Testifying before Congress in 1989, Sofaer invoked a 1937 statement by a former legal adviser (Hackworth): "It is a fundamental principle of the law of nations that a sovereign state is supreme within its own territorial domain and that it and its nationals are entitled to use and enjoy their territory and property without interference from an outside source."[2] Glennon (1992, 747) called this norm a "bedrock of customary international law," which is enshrined in the United Nations and OAS charters. In the *Alvarez-Machain* case, the Supreme Court makes much of the absence of any explicit prohibition of abduction in the U.S.-Mexican Extradition Treaty. In addition to being a fallacious inferential reasoning, the court's argument raised a red herring deflecting the crucial issue of U.S. violation of Mexican sovereignty. By comparison, the Supreme Court's argument in the earlier *Flores* case—"in the absence of assertion of jurisdiction by the territorial sovereign"—was more palatable. Besides, in the more recent case, the Supreme Court did not heed to its predecessor in the 1933 case that U.S. laws should be "interpreted in the light of the recognized principles of international law."

Extraterritorial abduction is a poor way to resolve a jurisdictional conflict. International law provides more amicable solutions, as we shall see. Resorting to abduction the way the United States did in the cases cited is not compelled by a lacuna in international law. It is plain flouting of the law, very much resembling domestic scofflaws violating domestic law for whatever reason. The Neorealist self-help explanation is not adequate, since the inveterate habit of scofflaws, domestic or international, has little to do with whether there is law enforcement or not. When other forms of relief (see next section) are available, compulsive law breaking has little to do with systemic anarchy. Calling volitional circumvention of the law mere self-help, despite available relief, is to give deliberate law breaking a dignity it does not deserve. Nor does it convincingly establish a case for the self-help system.

Jurisdictional Conflict and Resolution

Given the multiple, hence potentially conflicting, bases of jurisdiction listed in the preceding section, it is almost certain that there will be frequent conflicts over state jurisdiction—legislative, executive, and adjudicatory. Suppose, in a hypothetical case, a Canadian injured a Frenchman in the United States while engaging in a conspiracy to counterfeit British currency. This tangle of events could trigger the territorial jurisdiction of the United States, the nationality jurisdiction of Canada, the protective jurisdiction of the United Kingdom, and the passive personality jurisdiction of France. As Janis (1993, 330) notes, a typical resolution of a conflict of this sort depends on cooperation between the nation-states involved and on the restraint and sense of accommodation displayed by domestic courts. Potential and actual conflicts among the jurisdictional reaches of national legal systems are often avoided or moderated simply by a certain deference one nation's courts show the courts and laws of another state. That certain amount of deference is known as "comity," as defined in *Hilton v. Guyot* (1895). Contrary to the Neorealist view that anarchy impedes cooperation because of the relative gains question, states prefer to cooperate or show restraint when they are aware that the alternative conflictual outcome is worse than uneven gains or nonsolution to a conflict.

In a slightly simpler real-world case in 1970, Belgium sought relief from the International Court of Justice in behalf of its nationals, who were shareholders, for reparations allegedly due them by Spain for certain actions resulting in damages to a company incorporated in Canada (*Barcelona Traction*). The case involved three states in a conflict of jurisdiction situation: Which state—Belgium, Spain, or Canada—actually had jurisdiction or the right to assert protection? In searching for a solution, the court decided that Belgium lacked *jus standi* to exercise diplomatic protection of Belgian shareholders in a Canadian company with respect to measures taken against it by the government in Spain. Only Canada had the protective right or jurisdiction to act, the court ruled. The ultimate inherent lessons are that questions of jurisdictional conflict can be settled by adjudicatory means; and, even more important, that there is a body of established norms by which these questions can be decided. There is no reason why any nation, even the United States, should need to resort to unilateral action in the event of a real or potential conflict regarding jurisdiction.

In practice, one common solution to jurisdictional conflict is to recognize international legal limits to state jurisdiction rather than to rely on unilateral action. Although the precise extent of those limits is debatable, the general consensus is that, as demonstrated in the 1937 Hackworth statement cited by Sofaer before Congress in 1989, no state has the right to extend its legislative, executive, or judicial power into the territory of another state except with the consent of the latter.

The care with which this golden rule of international law is taken into account in state practices is in part expressed in the regime of extradition. Two criteria are instructive: First, no state is required to surrender a fugitive sought by another state without an extradition treaty (*Factor v. Laubenheimer*). Second, the offense giving rise to extradition must be included specifically in the treaty or be regarded as a crime in both contracting parties (the rule of double criminality).[3]

The law governing extradition, in laying down these two criteria, does so to ensure that jurisdictional rights of both countries are protected: the state harboring the fugitive (it has territorial jurisdiction) and the requesting state (its jurisdictional claim is based on nationality, passive personality, or the protective principle). In *Alvarez-Machain,* the United States willfully abandoned the available legitimate relief obtainable through an existing bilateral extradition treaty. An excuse may be that Mexico was unwilling to surrender one of its own nationals, if asked. But an alternative relief would have been referral of the case to a mixed arbitral tribunal, consisting of U.S. and Mexican members. Washington's option to rely on unilateral action, i.e., extraterritorial abduction, which in itself violated Mexico's territorial sovereignty, was no ordinary self-help, in the Neorealist sense of the term. It was deliberate hooky playing with international law. Theoretically, under the reciprocity rule governing relations of nations, Mexico and other states would have a legitimate ground for carrying out the same type of illegal abductions against the United States. But the mere fact that neither Mexico nor any other state chose to do so should not be taken solely as the result of their inability to match Washington's power and guile; but it should be a sober reminder that not all states are equally given to the self-help impulse that the Neorealists define as typical of state behavior in an anarchic system.[4]

According to Waltz (1979, 111), "A self-help situation is one of high risk . . . of war in a world of free states." In Neorealist thinking self-help generates a competitive system, possibly leading to a conflictual system. It should be reiterated that no state, not even Mexico, was prodded into a competitive round of extraterritorial abductions (or their equivalents) after the fashion of the United States, despite the string of cases cited. If power disparity should be the reason, one may legitimately raise the question whether any other powerful country, such as France, England, Germany, or Russia, had similarly indulged in extraterritorial abductions while at the peak of its power as the hegemonic leader of its time. If not, the bottom line is that power alone cannot explain the recent rash of U.S. abductionism. Another noteworthy element is the incidence of the chorus of protest from Latin American and other nations, which amounts to a community-wide appraisal of the United States' unilateral acts. This lesson should not be lost, because it shows something that the Neorealist thesis of self-help, dictated by systemic anarchy and relying solely on one's power, cannot convincingly explain.

A tantalizing question is which state should yield its jurisdictional right when two states have concurrent jurisdiction on different grounds. In the *Lotus* case, when France and Turkey had concurrent jurisdiction, the gratuitous coincidence of the French steamer turning up at Constantinople, following the collision on the high seas, gave Turkey a first chance to assert jurisdiction, superseding France's challenge. The *Barcelona Traction* case shows how the ICJ established a hierarchy of the three competing bases of jurisdictional claims by as many parties to the dispute. Another solution is offered by the doctrine of *forum non conveniens,* which is a commonsensical principle that permits a court (presumably also an executive authority) at its discretion to refuse to undertake a case properly within its jurisdiction

(Janis 1993, 336). This is a clear indication of the kind of restraint exercised by domestic courts or executive authorities in Mexico and other states. Thus, in addition to other means of resolving jurisdictional disputes, the doctrine of *forum non conveniens* offers a procedural fuse to ensure that the proverbial house (of international relations) will not burn down because of an electric overload (jurisdictional conflict). Besides, states can always avert getting into jurisdictional fights by concluding judicial cooperation treaties, such as the Hague Convention on the Taking of Evidence (TIAS, No. 7444).

All this is enough to demonstrate that international law offers the possibility of orderly conduct among states in the face of systemic anarchy.

Immunity to Sovereign Jurisdiction

Despite the inviolability of sovereignty, states voluntarily surrender or suspend part of their sovereignty as a matter of routine in their mutual relations. For example, foreign sovereigns and their designated agents (e.g., diplomats and consular officers) are made immune from the jurisdictional reach of foreign municipal (domestic) courts or administrative powers. The doctrinal justification for the immunity of states is their sovereign independence and the "common interest impelling [states] to mutual intercourse" (*Schooner Exchange* case). The current doctrine for the immunities and privileges of diplomatic and consular agents, on the other hand, is functional: it allows them to effectively perform their respective functions in the territory of a foreign state. In the preamble of both the 1961 Vienna Convention on Diplomatic Relations (500 UNTS 95) and the 1962 Vienna Convention on Consular Relations (596 UNTS 261), it is explicitly stated that the purpose of diplomatic and consular privileges and immunities is "not to benefit the individuals but to ensure the efficient performance of the functions" of the respective diplomatic and consular missions on behalf of their own states. In both conventions, the diplomatic and consular functions are then clearly defined.

The granting of immunities to both foreign sovereigns and their diplomatic-consular agents amounts to a curtailment of the host state's sovereignty, made necessary by the reciprocal need for normal relations of nations. What is more noteworthy is that such self-imposed curtailment of sovereignty is voluntary on the part of sovereign states despite systemic anarchy. This amounts to a theoretical challenge to Waltz's (1979, 91) famous statement that "no state intends to participate in the formation of a structure by which it and others will be *constrained*" (emphasis added).

In the context of the interplay of law and politics in international relations, there are two divergent trends in the granting of immunities. One is a steady trend toward a restrictive theory with regard to the immunity of states. The other is a contrary trend toward the unbridled protection of the immunity of diplomatic and consular agents. These trends owe their origins to two different political desiderata.

Until 1926, state practice showed a common proclivity to grant unrestricted, or absolute, immunity to foreign states, as can be seen in the outcome of the *Berrizi Brothers Company* case (1926). In that case, the U.S. Supreme Court rejected the argument, accepted in a prior stage of the case by the district court, that Italy was not entitled to immunity in an in rem proceeding brought to enforce a claim for cargo damage against a merchant vessel owned and operated by Italy.

In the same year, however, the conclusion of the Brussels Convention on the Unification of Certain Rules Relating to Immunity of State-Owned Vessels (176 LNTS 199) signaled a first important step away from the classical absolute theory. Under this new convention, immunity for government-owned vessels was waived. Although the convention was in force only among its signatories, the United States, while not a signatory, later announced and has since followed a policy of not claiming immunity for its publicly owned or operated merchant vessels. The timing of the 1926 Brussels convention apparently had something to do with the rise of the modern trading state engaged in commercial activities since the birth of the Soviet state in 1917. As the Cold War broke out in the post–World War II era, more countries opted for the restrictive theory, which made a distinction between public acts (*jure imperii*) and private acts (*jure gestionis*) of states: only the former enjoy immunity. The United States in 1952 formally announced, via the so-called Tate Letter (Department of State *Bulletin* 26:984) that henceforth it would follow the restrictive theory of sovereign immunity in the consideration of requests of foreign governments for a grant of sovereign immunity. As regarded ships, the restrictive view was adopted in two multilateral treaties concluded in 1958: the Geneva Convention on the Regime of the High Seas (Art. 9) and the Geneva Convention on the Territorial Sea and Contiguous Zone (Arts. 21 and 22).

What constitutes *acta jure gestionis* is not determined by international law, but is subject to definition by states in their domestic laws. In this country, Section 1603(d) of the U.S. Foreign Sovereign Immunity Act (1976), which denies immunity to the commercial acts of foreign states, defines "commercial activity" by reference to the nature, rather than purpose, of the course of conduct or a particular transaction or act. Congress, by a legislative act, therefore reversed the Supreme Court ruling in the *Berrizi Brothers Company* case: "We know of no international usage which regards the maintenance and advancement of the economic welfare of a people in time of peace as any less a *public purpose* than the maintenance and training of a naval force" (emphasis added). This can be understood only as a political reaction to the perceived problem of the spread of socialism in the world, in that an increasing number of states were found engaged in state-sponsored commercial activities.

The opposite trend, toward expanding the immunities and privileges enjoyed by diplomatic and consular agents, found wholesale codification in the two Vienna conventions signed in 1961 and 1962. Both conventions went beyond guarantees under traditional customary law. In the 1961 convention, diplomats enjoy inviolability of person and of mission, as under traditional law. But, going beyond traditional law, the inviolability of the premises of a mission is extended to allow no exception, not even during a fire, unless the head of mission gives consent before agents of the receiving state (e.g., local police or firefighters) can gain entry (Art. 22[1]). Diplomats are immune from jurisdiction, both civil and criminal, of the receiving state (Art. 31). In time-honored state practice before, diplomats were exempt from criminal, but not civil, jurisdiction of the receiving state. Under the new convention, immunity was extended to civil matters as well, so that now diplomats are immune even from the traditional requirement to appear as a witness in court (Art. 31[2]). Whereas fiscal and customs privileges were a courtesy under customary law, the 1961 convention makes tax exemption a mandatory privilege for both a diplomatic mission and individual diplomats (Arts. 23 and 34).

While state immunity is limited to public acts (*jure imperii*), the immunities granted to diplomats under the 1961 convention seem not to have any such rigid restriction. The blanket extension, under Article 31, of diplomatic immunities from both civil and criminal jurisdiction makes only three very narrow qualifying exceptions: in the case of actions relating to private properties owned by diplomats in their *personal* capacity; actions relating to succession in which agents are involved in their *personal* capacity; and any professional or commercial activity undertaken by diplomatic agents *outside* their official functions.

Comparing the norms governing state immunity and those codified in the 1961 Vienna convention on diplomatic immunities, Cahier (1969, 28) drew the unavoidable conclusion that diplomats today seem to enjoy more immunity in a foreign country than do the states they represent. This seems to have since been borne out in scattered judicial decisions by domestic courts.

The main reason behind this unusual discrepancy and the continuing trend even beyond the early 1960s lies in the changing environment of international relations since the end of World War II. While more new states sprang into existence and an ever increasing number of embassies were established in the capitals of the world, there was simultaneously a "blurring" of diplomatic traditions, resulting in what McClanahan (1989, 142) calls "declining standards of diplomatic courtesy." Besides the many communist states at the time, there were new revolutionary regimes as well. Supporters of the Cultural Revolution in China and Colonel Qaddafi's Libya, for example, were not known to be the greatest believers in the protection of diplomatic privileges and immunities. Instances of diplomats being attacked by terrorists were frequently reported. The 1961 Convention on Diplomatic Relations was, in this light, a response to a perceived urgent need for offering greater protection to diplomatic personnel in an increasingly hostile international environment.

Even after the two Vienna conventions, some serious violations of diplomatic immunities in state practices continued to haunt the diplomatic community. In June 1967, for instance, three Guinean diplomats, including the country's foreign minister and its permanent representative to the United Nations, were arrested in Côte d'Ivoire during a stopover, as they were returning home from a special session of the General Assembly. The third Guinean was an official of the Universal Postal Union; his family was traveling on the same plane and was also arrested. The detention, Ivorian officials claimed, was a retaliation against earlier Guinean detention of nationals and residents of Côte d'Ivoire. The diplomats were not released until three months later, on September 22, after prolonged efforts by U.N. Secretary-General U Thant to obtain their freedom.[5]

This and other instances of infringement of diplomatic immunities (McClanahan 1989, 146–149) called for tighter protection, including that of state officials on ad hoc missions and their families. A result was the 1973 Convention on the Prevention and Punishment of Crimes Against Internationally Protected Persons, Including Diplomatic Agents (TIAS, No. 8532). *Internationally protected persons* in this treaty is a loose term defined broadly to include heads of state and government, foreign ministers, and officials of international organizations. The convention defines the crimes to be prevented and punished (Art. 2: murder, kidnapping, attack, etc.), the bases of jurisdiction, and the obligations of states parties to cooperate in the prevention and prosecution or extradition of the alleged offender after his or her apprehension. More relevant to our discussion here is Article 8, which makes offenses against "internationally protected persons," as defined in the convention, extraditable crimes even in the absence of an extradition treaty or, more important, even if an existing extradition treaty should not include any such offense named in Article 2 of the convention (hence, not extraditable under general international law). The provision is important because in effect it amounts to an imposition on the sovereign wills of states parties to the present convention. The usual rationale for the inclusion or noninclusion of a particular extraditable offense in an extradition treaty is precisely that such decision reflects the sovereign wills of the signatories. But this is circumvented by the constraint of the 1973 convention. That it is possible for states parties to the new treaty to accept such a constraint on their sovereignty is remarkable. The development offers a challenge to a basic Neorealist assumption that states in an anarchic system are unlikely to voluntarily accept any such constraint (Waltz 1979, 91).

State Responsibility

State responsibility is the obverse side of state sovereignty, by virtue of which states are entitled to an important number of international legal rights. By the same token, states are concomitantly obliged by international legal duties. Foremost among them is the duty to conserve international peace and to accept by recognized pacific methods settlement of differences that may arise with other states. Requirements for these and other duties are both inherent in customary international law and codified in such treaties as the 1934 Montevideo Convention of Rights and Duties of States, the UN Charter, and the OAS charter. Provisions in these documents are by and large evidence of existing norms in international custom.

Because the responsibility of states is an extensive topic, I address here only the question of state responsibility that arises from a *delinquency,* which could be either direct or indirect. It is direct if it arises from injury to a foreign state per se, such as from a treaty violation; it is indirect if injury is caused to a foreign state's citizen, juridical person, or entity possessing its nationality. Delinquency is defined as the consequence of either an act or omission (e.g., the *Corfu Channel* case) that violates any of the substantive principles of international law, with injurious effects to another state.

In the anarchic system, wherein only states are subjects of international law, only the *injured* state can assert a claim against the offending state for damages owed either to itself (in case of a direct delinquency) or to its national (if indirect delinquency)—that is, provided an "act of state" attributable to a specific state has created an international delinquency according to international law standards. Because of the principle of sovereign coequality, a foreign national can ask for protection by his or her home state *only if* local remedies have been exhausted (the *Interhandel* case); and the individual has the nationality of the protecting state (*Nottebohm* case). Once a state has taken up the case of its national(s), the state is juridically pursuing the case as if it were its own, quite apart from the individual(s) (cf. *Mavromatis* case).

It is amazing that in an anarchic world international law offers such a complement of norms and procedures for identifying what is an "act of state"; defining what constitutes a wrongful conduct by state agents attributable to a state (as applied in the *William Way Claim* case), or a state's failure to act or exercise due diligence in the protection of an alien (*Laura Janes Claim*), which creates a delinquency; and defining what is denial of justice (*B. E. Chattin Claim*). The law in this area has been established through custom supported by widely accepted state practices (*opinio juris*).

The development of the law of state responsibility for injury to aliens was anticipated probably as early as in ancient Greece (Thucydides' *Peloponnesian War*). Modern advocacy was found in Emerich de Vattel, one of the foremost eighteenth-century commentators, who wrote in his book *Law of Nations* that "whoever ill-treats a [foreign] citizen injures the State, which must protect the citizen." This branch of state responsibility was drawn from the internal tort law as customarily applied by many states. Violations that may trigger state responsibility for injury to aliens may include nonwealth injuries, denial of justice, confiscation of property, and deprivation of livelihood (cf. Slomanson 1995, 179).

Because of the spread of socialism in the twentieth century, confiscation of alien property became a major problem, both legal and political, in international relations. The law on expropriations underwent three unsuccessful waves of challenge, the first mounted by the arrival of the Soviet Union and the Soviet bloc states (Katzarov 1964, 34ff.). Despite the initial resistance by the Soviet Union to the requirement under international law for adequate, prompt, and effective compensation, the Litvinov Settlement of 1933, which offered a lump-sum settlement, became the model for future settlement with other communist regimes in nationalization cases involving the properties of U.S. citizens. In 1948, for instance, an agreement of this nature was reached with Yugoslavia (Re 1966, 4). The International Claims Settlement Act was enacted by Congress to implement this agreement by establishing a commission—the Federal Claims Settlement Commission—to adjudicate claims filed by American claimants. Later the act was amended to extend the program to settlement with Cuba and China (Hsiung 1972, 139f.).

The second wave of challenge to international law on expropriations came from Latin American states. The U.S. formulation of the prompt, adequate, and effective compensation requirement in case of foreign expropriation of U.S. properties was formulated by Secretary Cordell Hull in response to Mexican expropriation decrees in 1938 (Hackworth 1940–1944, vol. 3, 655–665). The third wave of challenge was mounted by the Third World, beginning with the 1960s. In 1974, on the occasion of the establishment of the New International Economic Order, the UN General Assembly passed the Charter of Economic Rights and Duties of States. Instead of the adequate, prompt, and effective compensation required by international law, in case of expropriations (nationalization), the charter would substitute only "appropriate compensation," to be determined according to domestic law, not international law. This development, and the fact that it did not pass empirical tests in cases like *Texaco v. Libyan Arab Republic,* were noted in a different context in Chapter 1.

Despite these three waves of challenge to international law on expropriation, the question was not whether an expropriating nation should be obliged to pay a compensation. From our discussion, it is clear that even the Soviet bloc countries agreed to pay a lump-sum settlement. And the Charter of Economic Rights and Duties of States, passed under Third World aegis, did not demur on the issue of compensation per se. The disagreement was on how much compensation should be paid, how it was to be determined, and according to whose law.

Conclusion

In this chapter, we have seen that while states are clothed with sovereignty, their mutual need for normal relations with each other impels them reciprocally to accept constraint on their sovereignty. This constraint is seen in the extension of immunity to foreign states and their agents, in the requirements of the law on state responsibility (e.g., compensation paid for expropriation of foreign property), and in the way states resolve jurisdictional conflict (e.g., via comity and *forum non conveniens*). Although violations of state sovereignty do happen, as in the United States' habitual exercise of extraterritorial jurisdiction, few states are likewise driven to a competitive reliance on self-help, as Neorealists would predict.

We have also touched on the jurisdiction-without-sovereignty phenomenon created by, and endemic to, the proliferation and active participation of international organizations. We have noted that the Neorealists' preoccupation with sovereignty is responsible for their finding on systemic anarchy and for their state-centric bias. There is an inherent tautology in Neorealist thinking in this respect. Since state sovereignty is exclusive, and since states guard their sovereign rights jealously, the Neorealist fixation on sovereignty inevitably leads them to their pessimism about a system without central authority, which breeds state sovereignty in the first place. We have also argued that if one's attention is directed to the prevalence of autonomous and collective action by international organizations, made possible despite the absence of a central authority by the phenomenon of jurisdictional capacity without sovereignty, one's perspective would probably be very different on the postulate of anarchy and the self-help system.

The preceding section noted that the Soviet bloc and Third World states, as well as certain Latin American states, have insisted on a right to "nationalize" foreign property. Nevertheless, they disagreed with the West on how compensation was to be defined and measured. None of the challenging groups rejected the idea of paying compensation for expropriated foreign property, and in most cases, nationalizing states did pay. To the extent that agreeing to the obligation of paying a compensation, however defined and measured, is a sign of accepting a responsibility toward aliens and their properties, which signifies a disposition toward accepting constraint on state sovereignty, the obvious conclusion is that even the blocs of nations most hostile to the West find room for accepting international law. In this light, the Neorealist argument about states' rejection of constraint because of anarchy is too sweeping and hence less than convincing.

Notes

1. As Mandelbaum (1996, 17) cogently argues, historically the foreign policy of the United States has centered on U.S. interests, defined as developments that could affect the lives of U.S. citizens. Instead, President Clinton's interventions in Somalia, Haiti, and Bosnia were "intended to promote American values."

2. *FBI Authority to Seize Suspects Abroad: Hearing Before the Subcommittee on Civil and Constitutional Rights, House Committee on Judiciary,* 101st Cong., 1st Sess. 31 (1989). For comments, see Glennon (1992, 747).

3. Art. 2(1) of the European Convention on Extradition (1957), Council of Europe, European Treaty Series, No. 24, provides: "Extradition shall be granted in respect of offenses punishable under the laws of the requesting Party and of the requested Party."

4. Prompted by the U.S. Supreme Court decision in the *Alvarez-Machain* case, twenty-one states of the Ibero-American Conference proposed that the UN General Assembly request an advisory opinion from the ICJ concerning the legality of extraterritorial arrests and apprehensions of criminal suspects. See Virginia Morris and M. Christiane Bourloyannis, "The Work of the Sixth Committee at the 47th Session of the UN General Assembly," *AJIL* 87 (1993):322.

5. See 1968 *Annual Report of the Secretary-General on the Work of the Organization,* UN General Assembly, *Official Records* (23rd Sess.), Supp. No. 1 (A/7201), 207–208.

6

HUMAN RIGHTS AND INTERNATIONAL LAW: STATE SOVEREIGNTY IN CHECK

From the standpoint of positivist (i.e., state-centric) international law, *human rights* connotes the protection of aliens in their own country against their own government. An inherent conflict with the sovereignty of a home state, therefore, lies in any external advocacy of human rights for its citizenry.[1] Hence, the rise of an international human rights law is an unmistakable sign of state sovereignty in check, under a relentlessly changing structure of the world community.

Under traditional international law, only states are subjects of international law. Individuals, who are objects of international law, are bound by certain duties, such as not to engage in piracy, narcotics trafficking, slave trade, etc. They do not enjoy procedural rights, however: Individuals cannot bring a case to an international tribunal; nor can they espouse a claim against a foreign state. This is not surprising, because traditional international law is (a) a law regulating relations between states, and (b) a law concerned with the protection by a state of its own nationals abroad, not of aliens in their own country.

Rise of Human Rights

The subject of human rights may seem to the uninitiated to have always been a concern in International Relations.[2] The truth is that it did not enter into the IR vocabulary until World War II. A good indication for this is that the Covenant of the League of Nations was silent on the question of human rights. Only Article 23 perfunctorily acknowledged a responsibility of member states to enhance the social welfare of their citizens in certain areas. This is not to deny the fact that the League, nevertheless, was forced to face two related issues: rights of minority groups and rights of refugees (e.g., White Russians, Armenians, Assyrians from Turkey).

Human rights emerged after 1945 as a result of (1) Nazi atrocities during World War II, which were shocking to the human conscience—although world reaction to German and Japanese atrocities varied; and (2) cumulative change concerning the issue of individual rights in international law, beginning with the mid–nineteenth century through the first half of the twentieth century. The nineteenth-century movements to protect individuals, such as victims of war and slavery, succeeded in winning state endorsements of their concerns. Somewhat later movements were also relatively successful in focusing attention on the protection of laborers, refugees, minorities, and others (Forsythe 1991, 35).

Concessions on the part of states in granting rights (though not necessarily what we would call human rights today) to individuals created two effects: The status of individuals as being capable of receiving certain substantive rights was recognized under international law; and while individuals were still denied procedural rights, such as a *locus standi* before an international tribunal, they came to be endowed, per some treaties, with certain substantive rights. For example, the Hague Conventions at the turn of the twentieth century and the Geneva Conventions of 1949—for the protection of victims of war—offered certain rights to individuals. As a result of these treaties, POWs, civilians in a war zone or an occupied territory, or sick and wounded combatants were all given substantive rights under international law.

Jurisdictional Hindrance to the Espousal of Human Rights by Individuals

The classical doctrine regarding espousal of the rights of individuals was formulated in the *Mavromatis Palestine Concessions* case (PCIJ 1924). The Permanent Court of International Justice ruled: "It is an elementary principle of international law that a State is entitled to protect its subjects, when injured by acts contrary to international law by another State, from whom they have been unable to obtain satisfaction through the ordinary channels. By taking up the case of one of its subjects, and by resorting to diplomatic action or international judicial proceedings on his behalf, a State is in reality asserting its own rights—its rights to ensure, in the person of its subjects, respect for the rules of international law" (*PCIJ Reports,* Ser. A, No. 2, 12). Hence, Article 34 of the ICJ Statute states: "Only states may be parties in cases before the Court."[3]

There is considerable tension between theory and state practice with respect to individuals' rights in international law. Positivist (state-centric) international law since the nineteenth century rejects individuals as subjects of public international law. Scattered legal practice, on the other hand, never entirely abandoned the more inclusive doctrine of the law of nations formulated in the seventeenth and eighteenth centuries in Europe (Janis 1988, 170). In the *Paquette Habana* case (1900), for instance, the U.S. Supreme Court allowed foreign individuals to sue and receive compensation from the U.S. government for its alleged violations of the customary international law of the sea.

A body of state practice emerged in the nineteenth century, establishing customary norms of international law that provided for compensation for the expropriation of alien-owned property. Advocates of individual rights could point to the fact that state compensations were paid to individuals whose property had been affected, not to their state. But opponents may counter that it was because of the private nature of the property being affected that compensations were made to the individual owners. In lump-sum compensations, such as those made under the Litvinov Assignment (by the newly recognized Soviet government in 1933), the assignment was made directly to the United States, not to individuals. It was the U.S. government that had to allocate the appropriate amounts of compensation to be paid to individual American claimants whose properties had been expropriated in the Soviet Union. It was due to this fact that the United States won the *Pink* case (1942), in which the United States was able to recover the surplus assets held by the New York Office of the Soviet-expropriated First Russian Insurance Company.

The bottom line is that individuals may enjoy certain substantive rights (e.g., the right to compensation in case of expropriation), but they do not enjoy procedural rights; and their states must espouse their claim internationally. The rise of individuals' procedural rights is a slow process, thanks to the human rights movement following World War II.

International Human Rights Law

The making of an international human rights law and the emergence of a number of human rights organizations entailed, and brought about, a qualitative change in positivist jurisprudential notions about the relationship between individuals and international law (Janis 1988, 174). International human rights law posits the direct application of international law to individuals and in some instances even gives individuals direct access to international machinery (e.g., per the European Convention on Human Rights). These developments demonstrate that individuals, despite strict positivist doctrine, are now, at least in Western democracies, elevated to a position where they may in special circumstances be considered *subjects* of public international law.

As Nazi atrocities raised the question of human rights to the human conscience, the subsequent Nuremberg Trials established forcefully that the norms of international law should and do apply to individuals. It was Nazi individuals, not faceless entities, that committed those crimes. Nuremberg not only confirmed and fleshed out the notion of individual responsibility, but also, equally important, pointed to the conceptual separability of individuals from their state. And it was driven home to the world that human rights protection was too important a matter to be left entirely to states.

This is the position in the Preamble and Article 55 of the United Nations Charter. The Preamble declares: "We the peoples of the United Nations [are] determined [among other things] to reaffirm faith in fundamental human rights." Article 55-c provides: "The United Nations shall promote universal respect for, and observance of, human rights and fundamental freedoms for all without distinction as to race, sex, language, and religion."

A rationale for the inclusion of human rights and self-determination in the UN Charter was the belief that it would enhance the chances of peace, for two reasons: first, rivalry between colonial powers were a source of war; and, second, subjugation of colonial peoples could also be a source of revolutionary reaction leading to war among metropolitan powers (Claude 1964, 319).

The UN and Human Rights

The United Nations' role in the development of human rights began with the formulation and crystallization of a set of definable principles and standards, something approximating an international bill of human rights. This was created by way of the following documents:

- Universal Declaration of Human Rights (1948)
- Genocide Convention (1948)
- International Covenant on Civil and Political Rights (1966)
- International Covenant on Social, Economic, and Cultural Rights (1966)

The Universal Declaration was the first to postulate for all nations such precepts as "life, liberty, and the security of person," "equal protection of the law," the right to trial, the right to "own property," and the "freedom of thought, conscience, and religion" (UN Doc. A/810, December 10, 1948, 71). In adopting this declaration, the UN General Assembly was persuaded that the lessons of Nuremberg should not be forgotten, and that human rights should be guaranteed by explicit provisions of international law. The other three documents—the Genocide Convention and the two covenants—codified in treaty form the thirty rights principles contained in the Universal Declaration. The four documents constitute what is unofficially known as an international bill of human rights. All other human rights treaties and declarations can be said to be either based on or developed from this core of rights principles. The following are some of the many other human rights documents the United Nations has issued over the years:

- 1951 Convention Relating to Refugees
- 1952 Convention on the Political Rights of Women
- 1959 Declaration on the Rights of the Child
- 1963 Declaration on the Elimination of All Forms of Racial Discrimination
- 1969 International Convention on the Elimination of All Forms of Racial Discrimination
- 1971 Declaration on Mentally Retarded Persons
- 1975 Declaration on Protection of All Persons from Being Subjected to Torture and Other Cruel, Inhuman, or Degrading Treatment or Punishment
- 1981 Declaration on the Elimination of All Forms of Intolerance and of Discrimination Based on Religion or Belief
- 1981 Convention on the Elimination of All Forms of Discrimination Against Women
- 1987 Convention Against Torture and Other Cruel, Inhuman, or Degrading Treatment or Punishment
- 1990 Convention on the Rights of the Child
- 1990 International Convention on the Protection of the Rights of All Migrant Workers and Members of Their Families

Development of Human Rights Law

Codification through treaty making is only the most visible part of the United Nations' involvement in the promotion of human rights. It also plays a monitoring role in more ways than one, usually through a committee specifically created for the implementation of a human rights convention in force. For example, a UN Human Rights Committee began to function in 1977, after the UN Covenant on Civil and Political Rights entered into force the year before. This committee is empowered to consider reports on measures adopted and progress made in achieving the rights enshrined in the covenant. In practice, the committee also functions to clarify obligations under the covenant. A similar function has been performed by the Committee on Economic, Social, and Cultural Rights, which has under it a Sessional Working Group whose task it is to assist the Economic and Social Council (ECOSOC) in the consideration of reports submitted by states parties to the Covenant on Economic, Social, and Cultural Rights (NZMERAT 1991, 39).

Under ECOSOC, the Commission on Human Rights, established in 1946, was directed to prepare recommendations and reports regarding an international bill of rights, international declarations or conventions on civil liberties, the status of women, freedom of information and similar matters, the protection of minorities, the prevention of discrimination on the basis of race, sex, language, or religion, etc. (NZMERAT 1991, 61). Some of the major conventions came as a result of the commission's spadework. The commission utilizes an established procedure—known as the 1503 procedure—to list states (thirty of them in 1978–1986) manifesting a persistent pattern of gross violations of internationally recognized human rights (Tolley 1986, chap. 6).

Over a decade, the United Nations human rights program has developed an impressive array of new enforcement machinery that has changed fundamentally what the world organization can and does accomplish to aid individual victims of human rights violations. The new human rights mechanisms, developed without fanfare, include the following:

- A variety of specialized "theme mechanisms" (a working group and several independent rapporteurs) to take effective action (often on an emergency basis) wherever individuals are encountering such severe human rights problems as disappearances, summary executions, torture, religious intolerance, and (recently) arbitrary detention
- Numerous "special rapporteurs" (or representatives) to examine conditions in individual countries, e.g., Afghanistan, El Salvador, Iran, and Romania (on the list for some time); and Iraq, occupied Kuwait, and Cuba (added in 1991)
- An expansion of the activities of committees that monitor compliance with human rights treaties, several of which have new optional complaint mechanisms through which individuals can seek redress when human rights are violated
- Substantial expansion of the Advisory Services program, which offers "technical assistance" in human rights
- An initiative to expand UN public information on human rights in a new world campaign designed to advance awareness of rights and of the UN machinery through which individuals can claim their rights (Issues 46 1991, 172)

The human rights movement has produced three genres (generations) of rights: individual rights—such as the right to life; group rights—such as right of self-determination (see Chapter 7); and collective economic rights—such as the right to adequate food (E/CN.4/Sub. 2/1987/23) and to development (GA Res. 41/128).[4] In the exercise of the right of self-determination, more than seventy former colonies have gained statehood in the past five decades. While there is no dispute on the right of self-determination, these new nations are now pushing in the United Nations for a third generation of human rights: a collective right to economic development of nations. The 1986 UN Declaration of the Right to Development (GA Res. 41/128, 41) declares the right to development to be "an inalienable human right" of every human being and all peoples. It remains to be seen how this right to development, dressed up as an inalienable human right, is going to be enforced.

Common Versus Dual Standards in State Practice

The conflict over whether there can be uniform common standards is a long-running problem. One concrete case, showing non-Western nations' resentment of Western standards being used in judging their human rights records, was the outrage provoked by the inclusion of a human rights index in the *Human Development Report* issued by the United Nations Development Programme (UNDP) in 1991. The index ranked countries according to criteria used in a 1985 study by Charles Humana. Led by Malaysia, a coalition of Third World states in the General Assembly reacted violently to the index, which in their view was culturally biased, outdated, and inaccurate. The index, they said, had little to do with how a country meets its people's basic needs, which the annual *Human Development Report* purports to measure.[5]

Essentially, the instance dramatizes the non-Western world's objection to being judged according to the West's definition of human rights. This concern about the West's pushing its allegedly idiosyncratic standards on all non-Western nations seems to be widely shared. It underscored the consensus of the forty-nine Asian states signing the Bangkok Declaration of 1993. While reaffirming the importance of human rights, the declaration stressed "the universality, objectivity, and *non-selectivity* of all human rights" (Art. 7). It also highlighted the "need to avoid the application of *double standards* in the implementation of human rights and its politicization" (emphasis added).

Besides disagreements over what human rights standards should be among nations, a serious though underdiscussed problem is that of double standards. One example is the wide discrepancy between the different branches of government in Washington in their attitudes toward human rights. The Department of State has, since the Carter administration, made human rights watch a part of its routine in the conduct of foreign relations (Mower 1987). U.S. foreign aid is even conditioned on the recipient's human rights practice, as determined by the State Department's own human rights office (Cohen 1982). On the other hand, the U.S. ratification record of human rights treaties is bewilderingly dismal.

More than thirty treaties were drafted, nineteen adopted, under the auspices of the UN General Assembly to provide international protection for one or more aspects of the rights set forth in the 1948 Declaration of Human Rights. The United States signed ten and, with Senate advice and consent, has ratified only six, all since 1986. These are: the 1948 Genocide Convention, which the Senate approved thirty-eight years late, in 1986; the 1966 International Covenant on Civil and Political Rights, along with its Optional Protocol I, which was ratified only in June 1992; the Convention on the Abolition of Slavery, Slave Trade, and Institutions and Practices Similar to Slavery, in 1992; the Convention Against Torture, ratified in 1994; the Convention on the Elimination of All Forms of Racial Discrimination, in 1994; and the Convention on the Elimination of All Forms of Discrimination Against Women, in 1995.[6]

This small number of ratifications is matched only by the weighty package of reservations, understandings, and declarations (RUDs) the United States invariably attached to each ratification. Henkin (1995, 341) has disaggregated and analyzed the five major principles underscoring these usual packages of RUDs. A crucial result is, in his words, "rejecting higher international standards" (p. 342). For example, in ratifying the International Covenant on Civil and Political Rights, the United States refused to accept a provision prohibiting capital punishment for crimes committed by persons under eighteen years of age. In ratifying the torture convention, the United States in effect reserved the right to inflict inhuman or degrading treatment (when it is not punishment for crime),[7] and criminal punishment when it is inhuman and degrading—but not "cruel and unusual."[8]

The double standards problem actually runs deeper than the discrepancy in attitude between the different branches of government in Washington. For instance, Congress was fond of picking on China for, among other things, its use of prison labor. China is not a country particularly known in the West for its protection of human rights. But, of all things, why is prison labor singled out? Concededly, the congressional concern can be justified by the provisions in Section 307 of the Smoot-Hawley Tariff Act of 1930, which prohibits the import of goods produced in whole or in part by forced, slave, or prison labor. Yet, as a *Businessweek* report (Bernstein 1992, 41) shows, "there is prison labor in America, too!"

The report says that as many as 5,000 convicts are hired in twenty-one states in the United States to manufacture goods or otherwise provide services (such as packaging) for private companies under contract. In fact, this figure is low as compared to that provided by the American Institute of Criminal Justice. In an unpublished survey, the institute reported that 10 percent of America's inmate population, or about 30,000 prisoners, were employed in state prison industries (cited in Funcke, Wayson, and Miller 1982, 5). By comparison, 90 percent of a much smaller inmate population in the United States in 1885, or 38,000 prisoners, were similarly employed in prison labor industries then.

Numbers aside, at issue here is that whatever laws exist to regulate convict labor in the United States exist only at the state (not federal) level. In many states, prison industries are not banned, and there is no federal law that explicitly prohibits the use of prison labor. On the contrary, the U.S. Prisoner Rehabilitation Act of 1965 permits employment of prisoners with work release status by firms whose products enter interstate commerce. Benefits were extended by Executive Order 11755 (1974) to state prisoners with work release status in federally funded projects (Funcke, Wayson, and Miller 1982, 3). Whatever restrictions existed under earlier laws—the Hawes-Cooper Act of 1929 and the Ashurst-Sumner Act of 1935—that may limit or forbid the interstate transport of inmate-made goods were lifted in 1979 (Bernstein 1992, 42).

Section 307 of the Smoot-Hawley Act controls only imports; it does not prohibit the export of inmate-made products from the United States. Besides, there are loopholes in the law. For example, exceptions to the already one-way ban are allowed if the hired prison labor is "voluntary" and if the compensation is not below the wage paid to nonconvicts (Zimmerman 1992, 42).

Since it chose not to become a party to the Convention on the Abolition of Forced or Compulsory Labor, the United States is under no international obligation to undo the discrepancies in the standards it applies to foreign countries. There are safeguards for foreign imports into America being investigated on suspicion of being convict products. Nonetheless, the lack of a ban on prison labor within the United States itself, while certain imports are banned on suspicion of having been made by prison labor, does present an inconsistency giving rise to a prima facie case of double standards with regard to human rights.

The inconsistency is a natural product of an overriding concern in Congress that the artificially low price of imports made by prison or forced labor will unduly harm U.S. domestic products and workers. The primary purpose of Section 307 is to offer protection to domestic producers and workers, especially the latter. Typically, the AFL-CIO was the voice behind the congressional protest against the alleged Chinese use of prison labor in certain imports to America. Thus, a labor protection issue conveniently became a human rights issue. Nevertheless, Beijing had to sign a special agreement with Washington aimed explicitly at keeping out Chinese products made by prison labor, allowing U.S. diplomats to inspect Chinese institutions in disputed areas (*New York Times,* August 8, 1992, 3). The crux of the matter is that Congress was in fact concerned with the onslaught of low-cost Chinese imports, allegedly causing unemployment in this country (CBR 1992, 14).

The problem surrounding the maintenance of consistent standards regarding human rights is not limited to the United States. Another example is the United Kingdom, which, unlike the United States, is a party to many of the UN-sponsored human rights conventions and to the European Convention on the Protection of Human Rights. Like the United States, the UK accepted the Universal Declaration of Human Rights (1948). Yet domestically, at least twice recently the British judicial system wrongly jailed ten of its innocent subjects. In 1989, a British court of appeal freed three persons who had been wrongly jailed for fourteen years since 1975 for Irish Republican Army bombings in Guildford and Woolwich. Two years later, a British appeals court freed another six men, known as the Birmingham Six, who had been wrongly convicted in 1974 for the IRA bombings of two Birmingham pubs, in which twenty-one people were killed and 160 injured (*New York Times,* March 17, 1991, 3).

On another front, the UK, despite its high-sounding paeans to human rights in Hong Kong in anticipation of the crown colony's 1997 reversion to China, was reportedly rallying support in the Council of Europe for a revision of the European Convention on Human Rights, with a view to curtailing the European Court's power. The reason was reportedly the UK's resentment that the court had handed down thirty-eight awards against Britain, out of a record seventy-eight human rights cases brought against it under provisions of the convention (Yu Yiping 1996).

In Canada, a commission of Ontario jurists and civic officials produced statistical evidence to substantiate previous suspicions of racial bias in the country's criminal justice system. From 1986 to 1993, it was found, the number of blacks imprisoned in Ontario increased by 204 percent compared with a 23 percent increase for whites. Analysis of police and bail court decisions showed that the proportion of accused whites released by the police (29 percent) was significantly greater than for accused blacks (18 percent) (*New York Times,* January 28, 1996, 3). The point is that data like these are treated in the West as a matter of racism, whereas if anything similar should happen in a non-Western country, it would probably be headlined in the Western media as human rights abuse.

Enforcement Problems

The anarchic world we live in makes state sovereignty sacrosanct (see Chapter 5). Here lies the root of the enforcement problem. The term *enforcement* is used here to include monitoring, listing of human rights violations, and possibly rectifications sought through external pressure. In our anarchic system, there can be two forms of enforcement internationally: by an international agency such as the United Nations, or by individual states engaging in something analogous to a citizen's arrest. But collective monitoring or enforcement is subject to prior consent by sovereign states. Under some conventions, states parties are obliged to be accountable for their domestic human rights practices to an international body, such as the UN Commission on Human Rights, special committees established to implement the provisions of certain human rights conventions, or any similar mechanism. For example, a committee was established under the terms of the Optional Protocol I to the 1966 Covenant on Civil and Political Rights. Individuals who claim to be victims of human rights violations at home may appeal to this committee (Art. 1). And Article 4(2) of the protocol requires that the state being complained against "shall submit to the Committee written explanations or statements clarifying the matter and the remedy, if any, that may have been taken by that State" within six months after receiving a filed complaint forwarded by the committee.

Under the Convention on the Elimination of All Forms of Racial Discrimination (1969), a special committee is mandated to hear complaints from individuals against their governments. The committee has the power to appoint an ad hoc conciliation commission (Art. 12) to resolve the cases of complaint. Still another convention, the Torture Convention, likewise provides for a complaint mechanism in the form of the Committee Against Torture performing a similar function (Art. 17).

In these cases, states parties may be required to provide certain information or to correct certain established abuses in cases brought by private citizens who are victims of the alleged violations. Parenthetically, that individuals may in some of these cases enjoy the right of espousing their own cause before an international body is a giant step toward private citizens' acquiring procedural rights under public international law. But enforcement, in the strict sense of the word, runs against certain difficulties, as demonstrated by the experience of the monitoring mechanism under Optional Protocol I to the 1966 covenant: First, individuals may bring complaints against a state only if they are "subject to its jurisdiction" (Art. 1), meaning they must have the nationality of that state. Second, the alleged victim must have exhausted all local remedies (Arts. 2 and 5-b). Third, the complaint filed by a victim must not be anonymous communication (Art. 3).

Under other treaties, such as the Racial Discrimination Convention, a third state may bring a complaint on human rights abuses by a named state. Under the European and Latin American conventions on human rights, individual persons may also file complaints against governments before a commission. However, the biggest loophole, insurmountable under the aegis of state sovereignty, is that the state being named must be a party to the relevant convention. Thus, by choosing not to ratify the conventions, a country like the United States is absolutely above international accountability. For instance, the treatment of American Indians is at best a case of "partial justice" (Schattuck and Norgren 1991). Even if it were an egregious case of human rights abuses, the United States would remain above reproach—unless one could convincingly prove that the abused norms are part of customary international law, which exist independently of the conventions not ratified by the United States.

The alternative form of enforcement, by individual states doing a "citizen's arrest," is not free from its share of the problems, albeit of a totally different sort. U.S. invasions of Grenada (1983) and Panama (1990) were discussed before in different contexts. While they are only peripherally human rights cases, they do point up the danger of similar unilateral acts by individual states that, when struck by an inexplicable sense of mission, may intervene in the name of a self-defined just cause—which could conceivably be human rights protection—on behalf of individuals who may be legitimate victims in another sovereign country (cf. Beres 1987, 52).

The double standards mentioned earlier may likewise be found in the area of international human rights monitoring. The United States, for one, has always relished accusations of reported human rights abuses in other places, such as Tibet or pre-1987 Taiwan. Reportedly, these concerns even led to flights of fancy about supporting an independent breakaway Tibet or separatist Taiwan as an ultimate solution to the problem. These may be legitimate concerns, at least well intentioned. But Washington is less than consistent on similar matters closer to home. A United Nations body—the Special Committee on the Situation with Regard to the Implementation of the Declaration of Independence to Colonial Countries and Peoples—routinely inquired into Puerto Rico's "human right" of self-determination. Inquiries of this sort were rebuffed by Washington as presumptuous interference, and it summarily severed its relations with the committee in 1992.[9] This means that the United States is now under no obligation to make reports or otherwise account for what is happening to or in Puerto Rico. Under positivist international law, Washington has a legitimate concern that external interest in Puerto Rico's separatist independence not become interference in U.S. domestic affairs, which would be a breach of U.S. sovereignty. To be consistent, Washington should know that all external (including U.S.) supporters of Tibet's and Taiwan's separatist independence must pass the same test of respect for national sovereignty and abstention from interfering into another state's internal affairs.

Efficacy of International Law

The discussion thus far merely illustrates the conflict between two perspectives: the perspective of human rights as a *community* concern, versus the *state-centric* perspective that holds state sovereignty as impervious to any supranational authority and hence to the imposition of any standards from an external source. The tension is not new: it is reflected in the very coexistence of Articles 2(5) and 2(7) in the United Nations Charter. From a larger and community-oriented standpoint, Article 2(5) requires that member states "shall give the United Nations every assistance in any action it takes in accordance with the present Charter, and shall refrain from giving assistance to any state against which the United Nations is taking preventive or enforcement action." By implication, community interests would reign supreme over those of individual states. But two paragraphs later, state centricism raises its head again. Thus, Article 2(7) states: "Nothing in the present Charter shall authorize the United Nations to intervene in matters which are essentially within the domestic jurisdiction of any state."

Realists may be torn between their habitual state-centric preoccupation and an occasional concern for human rights as a community issue, although I do not know many realists, classical or structural, who are bleeding-heart human rights advocates. But because of their power inclinations, realists may choose to blame the conflict just described on the imperfections of international law. I am prepared, however, to argue that general international law has a solution to the problem, but it is the intrusion of politics that has made the conflict an intractable one. General international law purports to play only a minimal role, that of defining what is to be regulated by international law and what by municipal law. For instance, on the question of jurisdiction over persons, international law leaves much to the domestic law of states. Under general international law, a sovereign state has the supreme authority over all persons or property located within its territory. Among other things, the Right of Territorial Supremacy means that the state determines who are its citizens and regulates their rights and duties accordingly (cf. Lauterpacht 1955, 286). It may even include the control (authority) over citizens who journey beyond the territorial boundary of the home state. The minimal standards required by international law, such as those requiring "equal treatment" for aliens and norms for determining which shall prevail in the event of a competition of nationality claims variably based on place of birth (jus soli) and on citizenship of parents (jus sanguinis), are instrumental in and by themselves, but not in conflict with municipal laws.

But the intrusion of politics into the realm of international law causes all the conflict. As seen before, "human rights" and "fundamental freedoms" were first conceived by Western states as a political weapon against Nazism, to prevent its possible resurgence. The international protection of human rights was given the sanctity of international law, first as part of the UN Charter and then as the subject matter regulated by an array of multilateral treaties. The internationalization of human rights (Forsythe 1991), though not without its intrinsic value, was a political act in the final analysis. As we shall see in Chapter 7, the making of "self-determination" into a human right was also a political act, though this time by the anticolonial, non-Western elites backed ideologically by the Soviet Union. Making human rights into a political tool resulted in tension between the authority of international law and that of domestic law over the question of state sovereignty, and the trivialization of international law itself.

Western nations may scoff at the developing nations for trivializing international law by trying, among other things, to create by artificial means a New International Economic Order (as in 1974 via the United Nations) or by foisting on the world their pretensions to things like the "right to subsistence" or "right to development." On the other hand, the developing nations may, with equal conceit and vehemence, retort that it was the Western powers that had tried to impose political servitude on international law first. In view of the sequence of events, it would be hard to refute this claim by the developing nations. Their political use of international law, in their pursuit of such "human rights" as the right to development, following upon the right to decolonization, came only after the West's attempt to fashion human rights into a powerful political weapon to use against dictatorial regimes. During the course of the Cold War, much political mileage was made of human rights against communist regimes. After the end of the Cold War, while the West may find the weapon's usefulness waning,[10] the nations of the South are actively extending the political battle to new grounds, over collective economic rights.[11] As this third genre of human rights is most likely to be a dragnet of international conflict in the future, let us look briefly at its rise and implications.

Right to Development as a Possible Conflict Nexus

In its crusade in the United Nations, the South strategically identifies its "economic subjugation" by the predatory West, as well as the world's "unjust" distribution of wealth, as the source of the South's miseries (C/CN.4/Sub.2/1987/23, p. 44). Tactically, the South insists that all human rights are "indivisible" and defines development as an "inalienable human right" (GA Res. 41/128, Arts. 6[2], 9[1], 1[1]). By this linkage, the South deftly places its claims to the right of development on a par with the West's concerns about individual rights, such as the right to liberty and to the security of person. This position of the South is called an "alternative" approach to human rights (GA Res. 39/145), thus potentially upstaging the traditional Western concerns that individuals' rights be asserted against their governments.

The South's alternative approach, in effect, redirects the human rights fight to the poor nations' demand that the West has a responsibility to help them realize their right to economic well-being. A number of United Nations documents declared it a "primary responsibility" of states to create international, as well domestic, conditions "favorable to the realization of the right to development" (e.g., GA Res. 41/128: Arts. 3[1], 4). It is apparent to which states this "primary responsibility" is attributed.

In the assertion of its collective economic rights, the South claimed that developing countries are "entitled" to assistance from the richer West. It identified a possible source of such assistance, which would be the funds to be freed up from "general and complete disarmament" (GA Res. 41/128, Art. 3). The reference to the West's diversion of resources to the pursuit of cutthroat arms races with the [former] Soviet bloc was transparent. Furthermore, the South urged that all states should ratify the many existing human rights conventions. The allusion to the United States was also transparent.

In holding out its alternative approach to human rights, the South singled out each nation's right "to choose freely its own socio-economic and political system, and to exercise full sovereignty over its wealth and natural resources." In a General Assembly resolution, reference was made specifically to Article 1(2) and Article 25 of the International Covenant on Economic, Social, and Cultural Rights. And all member states (clearly a reference to the West) were called upon to respect this right of the developing nations to choose their own domestic system (GA Res. 39/145, Art. 11). Obviously this expressed a central grievance of the developing nations that the West often tries to dictate to them on their domestic system.

In a similar vein, the 1993 Bangkok Declaration (A/CONF.157/ASRM/8), which reaffirmed the right of development of nations (Art. 17) and emphasized the "non-selectivity of all human rights" (Art. 7), also proclaimed the right of "all countries, big and small, to determine their political systems."

The West, for its part, rejects the notion of collective rights for states or peoples. Typically, countries like the United States define human rights in terms of the rights of individuals and oppose even the possibility that civil or political liberties of individuals could be delayed to accommodate the social or economic development of the state (Issues 40 1985, 109).

In contrast, the former Soviet Union and other left-leaning states staunchly supported the "right to development." They backed the notion that compensation should be sought by the developing countries for past colonization, which to them represented "acts of aggression" (Commission on Human Rights Res. 1985/43). Despite the West's objection, the Declaration on the Right to Development was swiftly adopted by the General Assembly (GA Res. 41/128, December 4, 1986).

The divisions of opinion during the debates on the adoption of the declaration are a preview of the potential conflicts between the South and the

West yet to come. The crux of the contention is whether collective economic rights of states or peoples should be accepted as legitimate rights on a par with traditional human rights (such as the right to life and liberty). The South insists that they are. Chief Moshood Kashimawo Abiola of Nigeria, for example, was reported to have a single consuming compassion: "to have white people in Europe, the United States, and the Mideast repay Africa for the damage done by the slave trade" (*New York Times,* August 18, 1992, 2).

A way out of this malaise would seem to depend on an intensification of interdependence of the industrialized and the underdeveloped worlds. Take the migrant worker's plight, for example. If interdependence (i.e., mutual vulnerability) is high, both the nations that receive migrant workers and the nations that send migrant workers will have a convergent interest in the protection of those workers. The same may be true in other areas. The dictate of geoeconomics, in other words, may determine the future directions of the third wave of human rights—collective economic rights of nations—and how they will be received by the industrial nations (Hsiung 1993b, 180–185). But conflict could erupt on the different priorities that both groups (West and South) would assign to the different genres of human rights concerned. In agreement with the other developing nations, China is known to consider the "right to subsistence and development" the first and foremost of the human rights of nations.[12] The Bangkok Declaration of 1993, signed by forty-nine Asian countries, also reaffirms the "right to development, as established in the Declaration of the Right to Development, as a universal and inalienable right and an integral part of fundamental human rights, which must be realized through international cooperation, respect for fundamental human rights, establishment of a monitoring mechanism, and the creation of essential international conditions for the realization of such right" (Art. 17).

While it remains to be seen how these third-genre rights advanced by the South are to be realized, one thing is clear: Following the formulation of the right to development as an "inalienable human right," all developing nations can now invoke it against the West in demands that foreign aid should not be conditioned on the recipient state's human rights record and that "human rights" (those of the first genre) must not be used as a pretext for meddling into the internal affairs of other nations.[13] One notable development in recent years is that the South has learned to become more vocal and united in its effort to combat what its members believe to be the West's inertness to their alternative views on human rights. The South's newfound influence can be seen in the final language written into the Vienna Declaration on Human Rights, culminating the work of the much-heralded UN Conference on Human Rights, held in Vienna on June 14–25, 1993. The Vienna Declaration, representing the voice of the 167 states that attended the conference, is in fact a demonstration of governments' preference for technical assistance programs rather than tougher measures designed to ensure accountability for human rights violations as they occur. It reaffirms the universal, indivisible, interdependent and interrelated nature of human rights, as the South is wont to claim. In addition, it also contains a reference to the significance of regional particularities and requires that due attention be paid to historical, cultural, and religious backgrounds.[14]

I consider this document an authoritative affirmation that what we have called the third genre of human rights, as promoted by the developing nations, is now incorporated into the growing corpus of human rights law, on an equal footing with the individualistic human rights (first genre) promoted by the West since the end of World War II.

Conclusion

The first conclusion one can draw from the above discussion is that the international extolment of human rights has shaken and changed positivist (state-centered) international law. But we should not neglect the different political masters that groups of nations have used the human rights tool to serve.

Second, in a political sense, the emergence of a human rights law denotes the rise of world community over state sovereignty, though over the dissent of some states. One legitimate question now is whether the erosion of state sovereignty has any redeeming features. A positive answer to the skeptics is that a state's legitimacy, hence its internal security, probably increases as its government adheres to, and can live up to, a body of internationally set human rights standards. The socializing effects of the emergent human rights law are eufunctional because such law sensitizes states to the need to protect certain rights defined by international, not municipal, law and to the question of ultimate state accountability to these objective standards. As we have seen, even those states that are most vehemently opposed to the West's political use of human rights do not question their existence, only the substantive meanings they are to be given.

In this connection, the results of a cursory survey to determine how many states have voluntarily accepted three sample human rights conventions that provide monitoring and enforcement mechanisms were a bit surprising: sixty-six states, among those that are parties to the International Covenant on Civil and Political Rights (1966), also opted to ratify the companion Optional Protocol I, which provides for a monitoring mechanism; 174 states, including China, Cuba, and Libya, ratified the International Convention on the Elimination of All Forms of Racial Discrimination

(1969); and seventy states became parties to the Convention Against Torture (1987), including China and Libya. In fact, Libya ratified all three conventions. The cutoff date for all three lists was 1977.[15]

This tally, admittedly, does not tell us much about the extent of enforcement, since there is no known direct correlation between the number of states ratifying a human rights convention and the enforcement record of its provisions. Nor does it tell whether a ratifying state is necessarily more disposed to showing a better human rights record measured by the provisions of the ratified convention than if it had not ratified the treaty. It nevertheless raises two interesting points. One is that to get around the sovereignty hurdle, a better approach is probably to shift our focus from enforcement to compliance, or self-implementation of the provisions of a ratified convention (Forsythe 1991, 45). Emphasis on compliance would be more realistic, since it would not entail the imposition of the will of an external authority, hence no invasion of state sovereignty.

The other point is that, despite the uncertainty about a possible linkage between ratifications and enforcement, it is amazing that so many states voluntarily accepted the human rights conventions under scrutiny. It can be safely assumed that these states did so with the full knowledge that ratification meant acceptance of the regime created by each convention and, ultimately, acceptance of constraint on their sovereignty. This point becomes all the more compelling when one realizes that all these states would have been fully within their sovereign rights not to accept any of the human rights conventions. The question is: Why would they bother in the first place? It would make no sense if anyone says that these states ratified the conventions just to break them.

If we focus on motivation rather than outcome, we realize that nonratification simply results in a bad reputation for the recalcitrant state; the United States is a ready example. But ratification creates an obligation, and noncompliance with the terms of a treaty one has ratified would create a "scofflaw" stigma much more undesirable than just a bad reputation. Hence, ratifying a human rights convention that provides for an enforcement mechanism is, in the final analysis, an act implying a readiness to countenance constraint on one's sovereignty. That being the case, the amazing fact is that so many states have chosen to accept such an onerous consequence and often in more than one instance!

A typical realist view on this is probably that ratification by so many countries is meaningless, as they include even Libya, Cuba, and China; it simply serves to cheapen those conventions so ratified. But I submit that if we pose a prior motivation question—*why* did so many states opt to ratify in the first place?—our perspective might be different. Neorealists hold the view that in an anarchic system, states will not accept even nominal constraint on their sovereignty; that so many have done so is indeed impressive, in that it defies a Realist explanation.

The reason for the seemingly counterintuitive behavior of these states is actually simple when one considers the alternatives. To codify human rights norms in treaty form is to establish a guide for order, and to do so by multilateral decision involving the input of states that become parties to the instrument they negotiated. The alternatives would be either uncertainty due to legal lacunae or, worse, the arbitrariness of unilaterally imposed standards by one's critics, which are most likely the more powerful states. To simplify, the choice is really down to order or anarchy. So many of the states apparently chose order, even if it should entail constraint on their sovereignty. The implicit moral here is that there are ways to mitigate systemic anarchy, even at the price of risking constraint of one's sovereignty. Many states, as we have just seen, are willing to pay the price for their choice of order over anarchy.

My claim regarding the human rights law is threefold. First, the rise of the modern human rights law is a good indication of state sovereignty in check. Second, the foothold that the concept of human rights has gained in the consciousness, and conscience, of the world's nations is an unmistakable sign of the rise of a crucial *systemic value* (as we defined the term in Chapter 2) whose time has come. The remaining disputes are over the specific meanings of the concept, not over the concept itself, which seems to have developed a life of its own. And third, the universal embrace by nations of the human rights concept, as typified by their ratification of the various conventions noted above, is concrete evidence that nations, in their dealings with one another, prefer certainty to uncertainty, and collective standards setting to unilateral judgmentalism, just as they prefer order to anarchy, as defined in this book. The bottom line is that all the development surrounding the emergence of a human rights law, especially the acceptance by states of constraint on their sovereignty, cannot be explained by any theory narrowly focused on power alone.

Notes

1. Paragraph 5 of the Bangkok Declaration, adopted by forty-nine Asian states on March 29, 1993, which called for a "just and balanced approach" to human rights, emphasized "the principles of respect for national sovereignty and territorial integrity as well as non-interference in the internal affairs of States, and the non-use of human rights as an instrument of political pressure." See UN Doc. A/CONF.157/ASRM/8 (1993), p. 4.

2. As throughout this book, International Relations capitalized denotes the field of study concerning the relations of nations.

3. For this section, see discussion in Janis (1988, 170ff.).

4. See a comparative discussion of the three genres (generations) of human rights in Hsiung (1993b, 171f.).

5. *Asian Wall Street Journal Weekly,* April 27, 1992, p. 5.

6. This is partly based on my own queries to the State Department, and partly on Henkin (1995, 341). The Henkin account missed the third one listed here; hence, he gave a total of five, instead of six, ratifications by the United States.

7. Cf. U.S. Supreme Court ruling in Ingraham v. Wright, 430 U.S. 651 (1977): Corporal punishment of schoolchildren is not "punishment" within the meaning of the Eighth Amendment.

8. See Rhodes v. Chapman, 452 U.S. 337 (1981). The reservation also refers to the Fifth and Fourteenth Amendments. Henkin (1995, 342) comments that "perhaps some treatment or punishment, although not barred as cruel and unusual by the Eighth Amendment, might be deemed to deprive a person of life, liberty or property without due process of law."

9. "U.S. Suspends Cooperation with Decolonization Committee," *United Nations Chronicle,* June 1992, p. 79.

10. A U.S.-sponsored resolution to take on China for its human rights violations was defeated in the fifty-three-member UN Commission on Human Rights, sitting in Geneva, March 8, 1995, by a 21-20 vote with twelve abstentions. See NCNA dispatch from Geneva, carried in *Qiao Bao* (China Press, New York), March 9, 1995, p. 1.

11. Mindful of the end of the Cold War, I am using the term *South* in lieu of *Third World.*

12. The view was expressed by Professor Wenzong Liu of the Institute of International Law, College of Diplomacy, Beijing, in an interview with Xinhua News Agency; dispatch carried in *Qiao Bao* (China Press, New York), January 23, 1995, p. 2.

13. For example, see China's statement to the UN Commission on Human Rights, January 8, 1996; NCNA dispatch carried in *Qiao Bao* (China Press, New York), January 9, 1996, p. 1.

14. Cf. Michael H. Posner, "Reflections on the Vienna Conference," *ASIL Newsletter,* September-October 1993, pp. 19–21. See also "Vienna Declaration and Programme of Action Set Goals for 21st Century," *UN Chronicle,* September 1993, pp. 54–61.

15. The tallying is based mainly on information available in the supplement to Henkin 1993.

Part 4

The Rise of Community Interests

7

SELF-DETERMINATION, DECOLONIZATION, AND THE COLLAPSE OF EMPIRES

In Chapter 2, we looked at certain "systemic values" that may, when their time has come, shape the course of development in the anarchic international system, perhaps as extensively as does the dynamics of the system's power balance. In the Neorealist paradigm, only power counts insofar as it is the backbone of self-help and insofar as its configuration defines the idiosyncratic structure of the international system at a given time (Waltz 1979, 97f.). But, as I have argued, in addition to the physical power of states, the moral force of certain systemic values may be another factor that helps shape the system, by (re)defining the goals that states pursue with all their might and energy, such as in empire building or adjusting to empire-breaking movements of the time. For the twentieth century, we named "self-determination" as the all-consuming moral force that may be compared with the competitive drive for colonial empire building in the nineteenth century. The comparison is apt in terms of its influence on the overriding pursuit of states and consequently in the reshaping of the international system as that pursuit led to shifts in the system's power distribution.

This chapter looks into how the clarion call of self-determination has feuled the post–World War II movement of decolonization and, more recently, fired the centrifugal (secessionist) drives that brought down the Soviet empire and spawned the turmoil in the former Yugoslavia.

The significance of this subject will come into sharper focus as we mull over the merciless outcome of decolonization. In a few short decades, the West's colonial empires built over at least a century and a half were toppled. And following that, the communist empire the Soviets had toiled to build and hold together since Stalin was brought down like a house of cards. Certainly there were other causes in both these great historical movements, but the call of national self-determination clearly provided the initial impetus and ultimately the justification. Self-determination has become a "human right" of nations and peoples in contemporary international law, as we shall see.

Neorealism fails to cope with its significance because self-determination deals with nationhood and nationalism, for which the Neorealist literature, and much of the contemporary IR field as a whole, has shown a nearly total neglect (Lapid 1991, 2). Here, because of the all-consuming nature of the movements fired by national self-determination, we are entering into an area where, in the pedagogical sense, international politics, international law, and international organization intersect.

The United Nations played an indispensable role in making self-determination (SD) into a human right and then serving as both a forum and stage on which most of the SD-motivated struggles were fought out. Convinced that only within politically independent units could the human being achieve self-respect and that only territorially separate states could provide the framework for development, the majority of the United Nations membership strove to loosen colonial ties around the world after World War II. In retrospect, the UN's efforts were tantamount to extending democracy to the international scale (Jacob, Atherton, and Wallenstein 1972, 505). Appropriately, the inclusivist force that self-determination has become (Franck 1992, 59) made it possible for the doctrine to be later invoked by the disfranchized peoples (and republics) in the former Soviet Union, in their post-Brezhnev revolt, as they asserted their right to democratic participation and, failing that, to secession (Müllerson 1994, 93).

Origins of Self-Determination

The idea of self-determination, which may be a logical extension of Western ideology, was advanced most vigorously by Russia in the nineteenth century, presumably to foster its imperial designs. During World War I, self-determination became a tool of allied psychological warfare. Then, in 1917, to facilitate the Bolshevik cause, Lenin advocated the principles of nonannexation and self-determination for all peoples. Finally, it was legitimatized in President Woodrow Wilson's Fourteen Points and the subsequent Treaty of Versailles (Kertesz 1967, 23).

In its original framework, the principle applied primarily to Central Europe. It guided in establishing successor states to the Austro-Hungarian monarchy and the cordon sanitaire along the Soviet borders. Versailles significantly extended its range of potential application, as the League of Nations created mandates from certain territories detached from the defeated powers to be administered by Britain, France, and Italy (Jacob, Atherton, and Wallenstein 1972, 507). The latter, as mandatory powers, accepted some international responsibility to guide some of these ex-enemy territories toward independence.

By the time of the UN Conference on International Organizations (UNCIO) in San Francisco in 1945, the consensus behind the idea of "sacred trust" contained in the League of Nations Covenant (Art. 22) had eroded. But self-determination managed to be included in the UN Charter, although in the Charter language it is couched not as a right, but as a principle. Article 1 declares: "The Purposes of the United Nations are . . . to develop friendly relations among nations based on respect for the *principle* of equal rights and self-determination of peoples" (emphasis added). As a "principle," it suggests that states should not—as the Germans and the Japanese had recently done—subject peoples to an alien rule against their wishes (Jacob, Atherton, and Wallenstein 1972, 526).

But the major coup was not to come until 1960, when a resolution of the General Assembly transformed self-determination into a foremost human right, with its far-reaching effects. To comprehend the events leading up to that coup, one must keep in mind the political context provided by the end of World War II and the creation of the United Nations. First, actively engaged in the drafting of the Charter were a number of non-European countries overtly hostile to the prewar colonial system. Among the fifty-one founding members of the United Nations, twenty-seven had either newly won their independence or were about to do so after some form of colonial rule (e.g., India, Lebanon, and the Philippines). The Soviet Union, prompted by ideological reasons of its own, was a most fervent and staunch supporter of this group of new nations that empathetically sought to remove the colonial yoke from the world's remaining subjugated peoples. A third critical change in the political environment was that World War II had weakened the colonial masters' hold on their overseas colonies. In these territories, nascent revolutionary movements were feverishly trying to overthrow the struggling colonial regimes. An example was the Dutch East Indies, where the future Indonesia was to emerge from the ashes of the Dutch colonial empire ruined by an indigenous nationalist conflagration.

To the vast colonial problem, the UN Charter provides a two-pronged approach: (a) the trusteeship system, and (b) some form of accountability to UN supervision by colonial powers for the "non-self-governing territories" they administer. The decolonization effort of the United Nations derives from the Charter principle of "equal rights and self-determination" (Art. 1[2]), as well as from three chapters in the Charter (XI, XII, and XIII) devoted to the interests of dependent peoples. Since 1960, the United Nations has also been guided by the General Assembly's Declaration on the

Granting of Independence to Colonial Countries and Peoples (GA Res. 1514[XV]), by which a speedy end of colonialism was proclaimed an urgent goal of the world organization.

Although they were at first two separate issues, self-determination and human rights were finally lumped together to form part of Article 1 of the UN Charter, enunciating the purposes of the new world organization. They share a conceptual commonality in two aspects: First, just as in the case of human rights, the promotion of self-determination was considered necessary to prevent another conflagration like World War II. An underlying notion, which dates back to the drafters of the League Covenant, was that competitive struggle by states for colonies was a cause of international conflicts (Claude 1964, 319). Hence, to promote peace, colonies must be helped on the road to self-government. Second, self-determination, which fully matured into a right of subjugated peoples after 1960, is a right to be asserted by people against their governing authorities, after the fashion of human rights. The growth of self-determination from a "principle," as first enunciated in the UN Charter, into a "human right" per the 1960 declaration followed a logical progression.

Self-Determination Defined as a Fundamental Human Right

Interestingly, just as the West was enthusiastic about the promotion of human rights in behalf of individuals (what in Chapter 6 we called the first genre in the development of human rights), the Soviet Union was the prime mover behind making self-determination into a collective "human right" of subjugated nations and peoples (the second genre in our classification). Against the changing political backdrop in the United Nations, the Soviet Union seized the initiative in 1960, after an additional number of former colonies had gained statehood and joined their ranks in the United Nations (e.g., Singapore, Malaysia, Cameroon, Senegal, and Congo). In that year alone, seventeen newly independent states, sixteen from Africa, were welcomed into the world organization. On September 23, the Soviet Union requested that an additional item, a "declaration on granting of independence to colonial countries and peoples," be added to the agenda of the General Assembly's fifteenth session (UN Doc. A/4502, September 23, 1960). This was the session—with Nikita Khrushchev as head of the Soviet Council of Ministers in attendance—when member states heard the Soviets urge for the removal of the multitude of injustices flowing from the Western colonial system. The Soviet declaration also went on to proclaim that all colonial countries "must be granted forthwith complete independence" and that all foreign bases in other countries must be eliminated (Kay 1972, 149).

However, in the end it was the draft of the Afro-Asian group, rather than the more radical Soviet draft, that was adopted. Unlike the Soviet draft, which was both anticolonial and anti-West, the Afro-Asian text was anticolonial but avoided explicit attacks on the West, eschewing mention of any specific Western power by name. Instead of proclaiming "the following demands," as the Soviet draft would have it, the final text adopted simply "declares" (Kay 1972, 150f.). Adopted as GA Res. 1514 (XV) of December 14, 1960, the declaration (full text in Brownlie 1995, 307–309) defines the denial of self-determination as the "subjection of peoples to alien subjugation, domination, and exploitation." This denial constitutes a "denial of human rights . . . contrary to the Charter of the United Nations" (para. 1). It also stipulates that "all peoples have the right to self-determination; by virtue of that *right* they freely determine their political status and freely pursue their economic, social, and cultural development" (para. 2, emphasis added). This characterization set a precedent for future human rights documents on the question of self-determination. For instance, both the two 1966 human rights covenants—one on civil and political rights, and the other on social, economic, and cultural rights—declare in their identical Article 1: "All peoples have the right of self-determination."

The mainstream view among international lawyers and political scientists is that the 1960 declaration offered an "authoritative interpretation" of the UN Charter (Brownlie 1995, 305). But I would offer a revisionist view, that the declaration in effect amended the UN Charter, though without going through the formal amendment procedures specified in Article 108 of the Charter. The veracity of this argument becomes clear when one reviews the Charter's intent on the future of the "non-self-governing territories."

Three out of the nineteen chapters of the Charter are explicitly concerned with the welfare and advancement—but not independence—of non-self-governing peoples. One of the major advances of the Charter over all previous international arrangements is its "Declaration Regarding Non-Self-Governing Territories." The original United Kingdom proposal was to annex the declaration to the Charter. But, at the UNCIO in San Francisco, in 1945, this declaration was made a chapter (now Chapter XI) of the Charter. The rationale for this was that rivalry between colonial powers would be a source of revolutionary reaction leading to war (Claude 1964, 319); hence it must be addressed squarely by the new world organization.

Member states are under an obligation within the UN system to help "develop self-government," not independence, of the non-self-governing peoples (Art. 73[b]). Under Article 76(b), one of the goals of the Trusteeship Council is to promote, on behalf of the residents of the trust territories, the "progressive development towards self-government or independence." Note here that the word *independence,* coming after the words *self-government* and *or,* is almost an afterthought. In any event, this provision applies only to trust territories, not to colonies not placed under trusteeship. Furthermore, the trusteeship system was established to supervise *progress* toward self-government or independence. Emphasis was not to be on conditions in these territories, but rather on progress being made toward obtaining the goals set forth (Jacob, Atherton, and Wallenstein 1972, 513). And the trusteeship approach was to be applicable only to ex-enemy territories (from both world wars). States with their own colonial areas were not under any specific obligation, under the Charter design, to place their colonies under a system of international supervision, other than transmitting "for information purposes" to the secretary-general "statistical and other information of a technical nature relating to economic, social, and educational conditions" of these colonies (Art. 73[e] of the UN Charter).

General Assembly Declaration on the Granting of Independence

The Declaration on the Granting of Independence (GA Res. 1514 [XV]) changed all this. First, it transformed self-determination into a legal precept and an "inalienable human right." Second, in lieu of progressive development toward self-government, the declaration "solemnly proclaims the necessity of bringing to a *speedy and unconditional end* colonialism in all its forms and manifestations" (emphasis added). On both counts, it amended the UN Charter. On another front, the declaration initiated an even more serious de facto amendment. It concerned the power vested in a special committee—known as the Committee of Twenty-Four—created pursuant to General Assembly Resolution 1654 (XVI) of November 27, 1961, to implement the 1960 declaration on decolonization. The committee was given the power to "inform" the Security Council of any developments in dependent territories that might threaten international peace and security. Presumably, these developments could include any measure by an administering authority to retard or thwart the speedy progress toward independence of a dependent territory it administers. According to Article 39 of the UN Charter, only the Security Council has the power to determine if "any threat to the peace" exists and if so to "decide what measures shall be taken . . . to maintain or restore international peace and security." General Assembly Resolution 1654 confers on the Committee of Twenty-Four a similar power to determine the existence of a threat to international peace and security that should be brought to the Security Council's attention. Only a fine line separates *informing* and *determining*. The committee would not be able to "inform" the Security Council of anything unless it had first made a determination that there was a threat to peace and security within the meanings of Resolution 1654 and Article 39 of the Charter. In this sense, Resolution

1654, which was the functional equivalent of an "enabling legislation" to the Declaration on the Granting of Independence, had the effect of amending Article 39 of the Charter, although without the legal garb of an amendment.

The Charter's formal amendment procedures, under Article 108, require ratification by not only two-thirds of the UN membership, but also all the permanent members of the Security Council. If the amendment package—on self-determination and decolonization—had been presented through the normal amendment procedures, it most probably would have failed. Recall that in 1960, the nine abstentions in the 40-0 vote for the adoption of the Declaration on the Granting of Independence included those cast by France, the United Kingdom, and the United States. Any one of these three permanent members of the Security Council could have vetoed the declaration if it had been treated as a formal Charter amendment. There is no question that both the Declaration on the Granting of Independence and its "enabling legislation," Resolution 1654 (XVI), amended the UN Charter through less than conventional means.

Regardless of whether this had been an unintentional or a deliberate maneuver, the upshot was that more than eighty previously dependent territories (including those under trusteeship) became independent, and the decolonization process became largely complete by the early 1990s.[1] The number of people living under colonial rule has dwindled from 750 million in 1945—or one-third of the world's population then—to 1.5 million in 1995. And by 1994, when Palao (formerly part of Micronesia) became independent, all the original eleven trust territories had crossed the threshold of statehood, thanks to the process of self-determination (*UN Chronicle* 32, 3:10). To a large extent, the independence of the former Soviet republics also followed the path of self-determination. The structure of the international system, in the sense used in Neorealism, has changed accordingly.

To this day, no member state or commentator is known to have raised an issue about the apparent procedural irregularity in the de facto amendment of the UN Charter in the manner just described. This historic episode is worth reconsidering for several reasons:

1. The events surrounding the adoption of the Declaration on the Granting of Independence and the subsequent process of decolonization are a best testimony that physical power of nations is not the only determinant of critical changes in the international system, including those that may reshape its structure. It is necessary to acknowledge in this instance the hidden influence of self-determination first as an irresistible "systemic value" and then as a legal principle of international law (the colonial powers did not even vote against Resolution 1514!). It is noteworthy that the transfor-

mation of self-determination into a legal norm—a crucial change in international law—preceded the loosening up of colonial ties and the unmaking of the legacy of colonial empires. The institutional catalyst and agent for this sea change was, of course, the United Nations.

2. The de facto amendments of the UN Charter on the issues in question provide another concrete example of how subsequent practice of states may change a treaty they have contracted (the Charter, though sui generis, is nonetheless a multilateral treaty).

3. The Declaration on the Granting of Independence also took care to ensure that the exercise of the right of self-determination not result in violation of general international law and the UN Charter. In no uncertain language, it called upon all states to observe the UN Charter, the Universal Declaration of Human Rights, and the Declaration on the Granting of Independence "on the basis of equality, non-interference in the internal affairs of States, and respect for the sovereign rights of all peoples and their territorial integrity" (para. 7). This requirement, in retrospect, led to the development of a law on self-determination that prohibits the right to secession. Two reasons underlie this proscription: First, secession would have entailed the violation of the territorial integrity of a sovereign entity from which a splinter group seeks secession. That eventuality would have contravened the stricture in Article 2(4) of the UN Charter, as reaffirmed by paragraph 7 of the declaration. Second, the declaration proclaims the right of self-determination to be directed against "alien subjugation," with emphasis on *alien*. The exercise of the right of self-determination to "freely determine [a people's] political status" (Article 1, Covenant on Civil and Political Rights) can therefore be directed only against a colonial, not an indigenous, rule (Nanda 1972, 326).

Right to Secession?

There is considerable consensus in scholarly opinion and state practice supporting the incompatibility of a blanket right to secession with the right of self-determination. The general agreement narrows down to interpreting self-determination as emancipation from colonial subjugation. Emerson (1971, 465) wrote that "the room left for self-determination in the sense of the attainment of independent statehood is very slight, with the great current exception of decolonization." Practice by states and the United Nations, as Nanda (1972, 326) notes, supports Emerson's conclusion. For instance, only five states recognized the Biafran claim to independence, invoking the right of secession from Nigeria.[2]

The Organization of African Unity's position is noteworthy. The charter of that organization is silent on the question of secession but specifically mentions the signatories' obligation to adhere to the principle of "respect for the sovereignty and territorial integrity of each State." Besides, the OAU charter carefully limits its concern to "total emancipation of the African territories which are still dependent" (Art. 3). On the Biafran secession, the OAU was in fact in favor of a unified Nigeria and opposed to secession (van Dyke 1970, 86).

In the 1970 UN Friendly Relations Declaration,[3] the territory of a colony or non-self-governing territory is deliberately defined as having a "status separate and distinct from the territory of the State administering it." This was lawyer's language to ensure that, from the juridical point of view, the attainment of statehood by a dependent territory (a colony or an otherwise non-self-governing territory) in exercise of self-determination would not diminish or otherwise affect the metropolitan territory of the state administering it. For example, when Nigeria or Ghana became independent, the territorial integrity of the United Kingdom was not violated by the act.

The reason for the United Nations' reluctance to acknowledge the right of self-determination in noncolonial situations is cogently stated by van Dyke (1970, 102): "The United Nations would be in an extremely difficult position if it were to invite or justify attacks on the territorial integrity of its own members." To support secession would be tantamount to endorsing interference in another state's civil conflict, which would be a breach of the international law prescription for respect for the territorial integrity of another state. For the same reason, there was little support for Biafra's secession bid in 1967. In the case of East Pakistan's secession bid in 1972, most states waited to extend diplomatic recognition until the new state, Bangladesh, had clearly shown that it had emerged from the Pakistani civil conflict in full control of its fate. The United Nations, caught in this event, was gingerly limiting its involvement to assisting in refugee repatriation in the former East Pakistan (Nanda 1972, 325). Another consideration was expressed by UN Secretary-General Boutros Boutros-Ghali that a proliferation of secessions would be at the expense of the "cohesion of states" (UN Doc. S/24111, para. 11 [1992]).

The international community, however, reacted somewhat differently to the breakup of the Soviet Union. It departed momentarily from its general reluctance to endorse self-determination in noncolonial areas. Even here, except in their prompt support for the Baltic states, most of the world reacted to the independence of the former Soviet republics very cautiously. As Müllerson (1994, 79f.) points out, no foreign state supported the self-determination right of these republics until after they had already achieved independence. There was a similar hesitancy in the international support for the secessionist claims of the component republics of the former Yugoslavia until federal authorities in Yugoslavia had unsuccessfully used military force to suppress moves toward independence in Slovenia and Croatia.

It is safe to conclude that the world's reaction to the breakups of the former Soviet Union and Yugoslavia produces no new evidence for the support of a right to secession. Nevertheless, from the experience of the Soviet dissolution we also find confirmation of something from state practices that is relevant to international law. Müllerson (1994, 79) correctly explained that international recognition of the breakaway Baltic states was more prompt than in the case of the independence of the other former Soviet republics. The reason, he said, was that the Baltic states were not incorporated into the USSR until 1940. To this late incorporation argument, I would add another possible reason: incomplete integration. The Baltic states lie on the periphery of the Eurasia landmass that was and is Russia. Although specific patterns varied, their historical ties with Russia were tenuous. Even after their 1940 annexation by force, protests and unrest continued to mar the Soviet reign (cf. Poulsen and Sharkov 1995, 152). Hence, from an outsider's point of view, whether the Baltic states were fully integrated into the Soviet Union after 1940 was an open question. Hence, their secession in 1991 met with more prompt recognition by other states.

The studied delay in the international response to the independence of the other former Soviet republics seems by contrast to offer a renewed substantiation for the concept of prescription in international law, as enunciated in the *Island of Palmas* case. To paraphrase the ruling in that 1928 case decided by the Permanent Court of Arbitration, the Soviet Union's uninterrupted, relatively peaceful administration (exercise of sovereignty) in the non-Baltic republics (e.g., Georgia and Kazakhstan) over a prolonged period of time—beyond the initial territorial acquisition—gave Moscow a firmer claim to territorial sovereignty over these lands. Their integration into the Soviet Union was more entrenched than in the case of the Baltic states. This fact may offer an additional reason the international community was initially more hesitant about recognizing these non-Baltic former Soviet republics after they had shaken off Moscow's control.

If this point can be substantiated, it adds a new dimension to the question of secession and what other states should and do consider on the question of recognition of a claim to the right of secession.

Two Ironies of History

At this point, let us take note of two ironies of history surrounding the rise of the self-determination regime. First, the land of Russia was the first to give self-determination its modern salience as a rallying point for its multiethnic nationalities. It was Lenin who used it to perfection by honing it into a tool in support of the Bolshevik revolutionary cause. After being legitimized as part of Wilson's Fourteen Points, self-determination became a systemic value, in that it was universally accepted as an axiomatic norm guiding the relations of nations. We have also noted that it was largely due to Soviet sponsorship in the United Nations that the principle of self-determination was promoted to the status of a legal right—a universal human right of all peoples. In 1960, this development served Soviet interests because it was thought that breaking up the colonial empires would strengthen Moscow's hand in dealing with the Western bloc. But who would have anticipated that in three decades, although decolonization did take place at the West's expense, no less than the Soviet empire itself died from the sword largely of its own making? The Soviet empire broke up because its disfranchised peoples and republics demanded the right to self-determination, which by the late 1980s had taken on a new significance as a claim of entitlement to democracy (Franck 1992, 59). The former Soviet Union, in the final analysis, crumbled not because of secessionist trouble, but because it had failed to satisfy its people's thirst for democracy as a fulfillment of the promise held out by self-determination, which Moscow had helped to promote internationally.

The other irony surrounds the outcome of decolonization. The anticolonial forces converged on the United Nations, making it into an authoritative medium in the deliverance of dependent peoples and nations to independence under the banner of self-determination. The one unifying belief of these forces was that only within politically independent units could the human being achieve self-respect, and that only territorially separate states could provide the framework for development. But as we witness the near-completion of the decolonization process by the mid-1990s, the gaining of statehood has brought neither development nor self-respect in many former colonial states.

With the exception of East and Southeast Asia, former colonial nations in many parts of the world have yet to show that they have achieved what the ideals of self-determination promised. The annual reports of the United Nations Development Programme showed only widening gaps and lags in the levels of wealth and health of the former colonials behind the rest of the world (*Economist,* August 19, 1995, 35). Nowhere is this more pronounced than in postcolonial Africa. The *Economist* (March 5, 1994, 21) reported not long ago: "The most dispiriting thing about [postcolonial] Africa is . . . that even if its economy (minus South Africa) were to grow at the rate confidently projected by the World Bank for the rest of the 1990s, Africans would have to wait another 40 years to clamber back to the incomes they had in the mid-1970s [when many of them were still colonies or newly independent]. Exclude Nigeria, and the wait would last a century."

Speaking of a crisis in Africa, dramatized by "failed" states such as

Somalia, Liberia, and Rwanda, Pfaff (1995, 2) pronounced that "much of Africa needs . . . what one could call a disinterested *neo-colonialism*" (emphasis added). For a people to have finally shaken off one form of colonialism to find itself in need of neocolonialism, what greater irony could there be! Almost prophetically, the UN Declaration on the Right to Development (1986) pronounced the right to development "an inalienable human right," and is the "full realization of the right of peoples to self-determination" (Art. 1). This is a right yet to be achieved.

There is another meaning to the irony inherent in the way decolonization has turned out. One of the promises of self-determination was that, within the free atmosphere of politically independent units, individuals would find fulfillment in their enjoyment of human rights, including self-respect. But the arrival of postcolonial states, following their tortuous anticolonial fight, shows that the fate of the individual in international law has not improved. All too often, instead of being a means for freeing people from unwanted political control, self-determination is being degraded into an instrument for narrow political purposes of the state. Levi (1991, 188) quite perceptively concludes that "self-determination has been thoroughly corrupted" by its being used, or abused, politically to serve the interests of the newly independent ex-colonial state (as opposed to people). One example he gave was the enactment of General Assembly Resolution 1803 (XVII) of 1962 on permanent sovereignty over natural resources. This was the work by the expanding ranks of the anticolonial and ex-colonial member states in the United Nations. But alas, out of this resolution again emerges a right of states, not individuals. Franck (1992, 58) argues that self-determination, now in its third phase of development, means the right of all peoples to democratic governance. If so, the denial of democratic rights by strong-handed governments would be a better gauge of the rise of the ex-colonial state over the individual.

Other Dimensions of Self-Determination as a Legal Right

I use *other dimensions* advisedly. Only those aspects not already covered will be addressed in this section. Here I focus on self-determination more as a legal right than as a moral principle or a political doctrine.

Self-Determination as Part of General International Law

I continue to hold that international law has to be either tested in actual cases decided in international (or domestic) adjudication or, equally important, corroborated by state practice. We have noted how in the practice of both states and the United Nations, self-determination has been accepted as a right of subjugated peoples and translated into action in the decolonization process. Now is the time to turn to the question of how the right of self-determination may have been treated in international judicial consideration.

The first opportunity for the question concerning self-determination to be reviewed by the International Court of Justice was when (in 1962) Ethiopia and Liberia, each in its own name, brought complaints against South Africa for refusing to relinquish its mandatory power over South-West Africa, a trust territory created by the defunct League of Nations. The two cases were combined by the court into the *South-West Africa* cases. The court in 1962 found that it had jurisdiction. In a final judgment in 1964, the ICJ ruled that neither complainant had *jus standi,* because neither had established any legal right or interest in the subject matter being complained of. As the court had to drop the case, the question of whether South-West Africa should be given a chance to exercise its right of self-determination and become independent became moot. The ruling followed the court's own advisory opinion given in 1950 at the General Assembly's request, which had clarified the international legal status of South-West Africa. On that occasion, the court held unanimously that the extinction of the League had not affected the administration of the territory. While suggesting that South Africa lacked the authority to change by itself the legal status of South-West Africa, the ICJ also held, by an 8-2 vote, that South Africa was not obliged to place the territory under the UN Trusteeship Council (*International Status of South-West Africa*). But that advisory opinion was rendered in 1950, or ten years before the General Assembly adopted the Resolution on the Granting of Independence.[4]

On July 29, 1970, the Security Council requested (per Res. 284) an advisory opinion by the ICJ regarding the legal consequences for states of the continued presence of South Africa in Namibia (new name for South-West Africa) after the council's Resolution 276 (1970) proclaimed South Africa's continued presence illegal. The court gave an advisory opinion known as *Legal Consequences for States of the Continued Presence of South Africa in Namibia (South-West Africa),* on June 21, 1971. It advised that, because South Africa's continued presence in Namibia was illegal, South Africa was obligated to withdraw from the territory immediately. The court also held that member states of the United Nations were obligated to recognize South Africa's illegal presence and to refrain from any dealings with South Africa that might imply recognition or support of the latter's presence and administration in Namibia; and that nonmembers should give assistance to all action by the United Nations with regard to Namibia.

Of special interest is how the court arrived at its conclusion, corroborating the absorption into general international law of the norm of self-determination created by General Assembly resolutions. The court stated:

> A further important stage in this development was the Declaration on the Granting of Independence to Colonial Countries and Peoples (GA Res. 1514 [XV] of 14 December 1960), which embraces all peoples and territories which "have not yet attained independence."
>
> . . . the Court must take into consideration the changes which have occurred in the supervening half-century, and its interpretation cannot remain unaffected by the subsequent development of law, through the Charter of the United Nations and by way of customary law.

The court then concluded:

> In the domain to which the present proceedings relate, the last fifty years, as indicated above, have brought important developments. These developments leave little doubt that the ultimate objective of the sacred trust was the *self-determination* and *independence* of the peoples concerned. In this domain, as elsewhere, the *corpus iuris gentium* has been considerably enriched, and this Court, if it is faithfully to discharge its functions, may not ignore. (*ICJ Reports* 31 [1971], emphasis added)

The above passages of the ICJ's opinion have to be read in light of the UN Charter. On the surface of it, the court's mention of Resolution 1514 (XV) may appear to suggest that the resolution was an authentic interpretation of Articles 1(2), 55, 56, and Chapter XI (on non-self-governing territories) of the Charter. It was "authentic interpretation" because it was adopted without objection (by a 40-0 vote) in the General Assembly. Yet it was more than just an interpretation, because it went beyond the more modest Charter provisions on the subject of decolonization. The Declaration on the Granting of Independence in effect tacitly amended the Charter, insofar as it transformed self-determination from a "principle" in the Charter (Art. 1[2]) into a right, and a "fundamental" human right at that; and it upgraded the goal of "self-government" in the Charter to speedy independence of all dependent territories. The court's advisory opinion of June 12, 1971, gave judicial cognizance to not only the Declaration on the Granting of Independence, but also to the fact that the norms of self-determination and decolonization have become part of general international law (*corpus iuris gentium*) that the ICJ was bound to apply.

In another case, *Western Sahara* (1975), the court had occasion to reaffirm its earlier advisory opinion and go further. In considering the decolonization of the former Spanish Sahara and the competitive claims of Morocco and Mauritania to its territorial sovereignty, the General Assembly in 1974 requested the ICJ to render an advisory opinion. The court basically decided that neither of the two named African states had legal ties that would jeopardize Western Sahara's right to self-determination.

Again, of interest to us is how the court arrived at its conclusion. In this 1975 advisory opinion, the court referred to a more recent General

Assembly resolution, Resolution 2625 (XXV), Declaration on Principles of International Law Concerning Friendly Relations and Cooperation Among States in Accordance with the Charter of the United Nations. This 1970 declaration (full text in Brownlie 1995, 36–45) reaffirms the principle of equal rights and self-determination enshrined in the UN Charter. It also states: "Every State has the duty to promote, through joint and separate action, realization of the principle of equal rights and self-determination of peoples . . . and to render assistance to the United Nations in carrying out the responsibilities entrusted to it by the Charter . . . in order . . . to bring a speedy end to colonialism." The court invoked this resolution, among others, to underscore its rejection of any claim by either Morocco or Mauritania that would obstruct Western Sahara's right to self-determination. But the very fact of the ICJ's reliance on General Assembly resolutions is indicative of something more important to international law. It provides evidence that certain norms created by General Assembly resolutions, especially those adopted by a unanimous or near-unanimous vote, may be considered to assume the character of general international law, to the extent their adoption by the General Assembly indicates the presence of an *opinio juris communis*.

In these instances, the ICJ has made it known that it considers self-determination now a requirement by general international law, quite apart from the United Nations documents cited above.

In the *Western Sahara* case, the ICJ's going beyond its 1971 advisory opinion (on South-West Africa) also clarified the meaning of "free association" and placed it in the context of alternative outcomes of a people emerging from dependency, exercising the right of self-determination. The idea of free association was later raised in General Assembly Resolution 1541 of 1960, which was meant to give effect to the essential feature of the right of self-determination as established in Resolution 1514 (the Declaration on the Granting of Independence). Principle VII of Resolution 1541 declares that "free association should be the result of a free and voluntary choice by the peoples of the territory concerned expressed through informed and democratic processes." Since the question of free association was raised in the *Western Sahara* case, the court's advisory opinion, citing Resolution 1514, pointed to the alternative modalities a non-self-governing territory emerging from its dependent status may take: emergence as a sovereign independent state; free association with an independent state; or integration with an independent state.

Nations' or Peoples' Right to Self-Determination

Is self-determination a right held by nations, or peoples? This is no trivial, linguistic question. If it is a right to be exercised by "peoples," it would open a Pandora's box as regards the definition of *peoples*. Are the Eskimos in Canada, Basques in Spain, Corsicans in France, Scots in Britain, and Indians in America entitled to the right of self-determination? If so, what would be the result? As the UN secretary-general declared in 1992, "The cohesion of States [would be] threatened by brutal ethnic, religious, social, cultural and linguistic strife."[5]

In formulating self-determination as a right, the General Assembly used the term *peoples* in almost all its relevant documents. In practice, however, it has meant the non-self-governing territories, with emphasis on territories. The United Nations practice, focusing on territories rather than ethnic identities, grew out of necessity. At the time the Declaration on the Granting of Independence and related resolutions were adopted—in the 1960s, when most African colonies gained independence from their former European masters—it was pure precolonial boundaries that were accepted for the new states. This pattern followed the precedent set in Latin America's doctrine of *uti possidetis* more than a century before.

The coincidental focus on territories was probably a blessing in disguise; if the focus had been on ethnic identity, it would not only have created enormous confusion as to how one would define the identity of the peoples entitled to self-determination, but it also would have led to a horrendous Babel. There are no ethnic-pure communities, dependent territories being no exception. If ethnic origins had to be a yardstick, purity in national identity could be achieved only by the most methodic and horrendous of ethnic cleansing.

While self-determination became a fundamental right of "all peoples" by dint of UN prescription and practice, some Western jurists still had doubts. Sir Gerald Fitzmaurice, writing in 1973 after his retirement as a judge of the ICJ, raised a challenging question: "Juridically, the notion of a legal right of self-determination is nonsense, for how can an as yet judicially non-existent entity be the possessor of a legal right?" (cited in Henkin 1993, 303).

If one traces the idea of self-determination to its Russian origins, without doubt it was *national* self-determination that was first conceived. Lenin himself indicated that the right of "nations" to self-determination not only was a stage in and condition of their final merger, but was also subordinated to the interests of socialism.[6] In Soviet literature on international law, it was said that "national self-determination" was one of the new customary norms introduced to general international law at Soviet behest (Erickson 1972, 28).

Be that as it may, the epithet of *nation* or *national* in association with self-determination may offer an answer for some, but not all, questions. For one, it confirms that self-determination should not sanction a right of secession by any subgroup from a larger group known as a nation. For another, it may give stateless nations (e.g., the Palestinians) a claim of sorts, circumstances permitting. But it offers nothing on the lingering question of whether minorities should have the same rights as the majority in which they find themselves. As Shaw and Albert (1980, 29) put it, if Quebec can opt out of Canada, then could sections in Quebec that preferred to remain part of Canada opt out of Quebec?

In any event, Sir Gerald's question defies an answer, except that in the event of decolonization, the world community as represented by the United Nations *confers* an expectant right of self-determination on an entity that does not juridically exist and whose population has been the victim of "alien subjugation," as determined by the General Assembly.

The question remains, however, as to who exactly should have the right to self-determination: nations or peoples? If peoples, then do minorities have the same right? The 1966 International Covenant on Civil and Political Rights seems to have had this question in view when it made a clear distinction between the rights of peoples to self-determination (Art. 1) and the rights of ethnic, religious, or linguistic minorities to enjoy their own culture, to profess and practice their own religion, or to use their own language (Art. 27). Although this distinction may appear to offer a right to minorities, the fact is that few successful cases of minority self-determination (including secession) are known. The Ibo people's futile quest for a Biafra state in southeastern Nigeria in 1967 is probably the most celebrated fiasco. While the Bengalis in East Pakistan succeeded in taking their land out of Pakistan to found a new state in 1971, the Chakma minority within Bangladesh have revolted in vain in their claim to self-determination (Poulsen and Sharkov 1995, 244).

It seems that what ultimately determines which minority group has the right to self-determination, and where, still depends—unlike in decolonization cases—on the "power of the gun," in the Maoist sense. This cruel reality prompted Müllerson (1994, 73) to conclude that "it would be more accurate to say that [the minorities] can exercise the right of self-determination together with the rest of the population of a given state, as part of this population." But, if that is the case, how is it different from national self-determination?

The World Community's Right to Intervene in Self-Determination

When peoples or nations are caught up in self-determination turmoil, such as that in which the former Yugoslavia is mired, does the world community have a right to intervene?

Opinions are varied. We have noted that an overwhelming body of opinion and state practice suggests that self-determination does not imply a right to secession. The world community intervenes only at the risk of violating the territorial integrity of the state from which the secessionist group seeks separation. On the other hand, the 1970 Friendly Relations Declaration (annex to GA Res. 2625 [XXV]) made it a "duty" of every state "to promote, through joint or separate action, realization of equal rights and self-determination of peoples," in order to bring about speedy decolonization (see text in Brownlie 1995, 43). As we have seen, the ICJ in the *Western Sahara* case even relied on this provision.

The West sometimes feels that if an entire population—as opposed to a targeted minority—is the object of maltreatment (say, at the hands of a dictatorial state), a revolution waged by that group as a means of redress should be considered a situation of self-determination.[7] The implied merger of revolution and self-determination prompts the question: Does the external world have an equal "duty" to intervene in the interest of promoting democracy? This question boils down to whether the "duty" of states to intervene in promoting decolonization is extended to promoting democracy. Does international law have an answer?

My view is that it does. More specifically, the answer is in the Friendly Relations Declaration, where it provides: "Nothing in the foregoing paragraphs shall be construed as authorizing or encouraging any action which would dismember or impair, totally or in part, the territorial integrity or political unity of sovereign and independent States conducting themselves in compliance with the principle of equal rights and self-determination of peoples as described above and thus possessed of a government representing the whole people belonging to the territory without distinction to race, creed, or color" (Brownlie 1995, 44).

Current international law, which sanctifies external intervention in behalf of decolonization, does not accept intervention in the name of promoting democracy. Self-determination thus implies neither a right to secession nor a right to revolution in the name of democratization, strictly speaking. The cases of the Soviet implosion and the Balkan split-up are sui generis and in no way create a precedent. The reason is that we still live in a multistate system in which all states have a reciprocal vested interest in the protection, at all costs, of state sovereignty and hence territorial integrity and political independence.

The United States in 1992 passed the Cuban Democracy Act in an attempt to push Castroite Cuba to move toward democracy and greater respect for human rights. Washington began to interfere in the trade of other countries with Cuba, even trying to dictate trading practices to them. The Helms-Burton Act, passed in 1996, would have the United States go even further. It requires that the president approach the UN Security Council in an effort to have other countries join America's embargo against Cuba (Smith 1996, 52f.). Are efforts like these, aimed at promoting democracy in another country, presumably in furtherance of the self-determination right of the local population, legal under international law?

To answer this question, we have to posit one assumption and suggest one test required by international law on the question of self-determination. The assumption is that the development of self-determination has by now, as Franck (1992, 58) writes, entered into the "third phase," whereby it now denotes access to democratic governance, or entitlement of peoples to democratic participation (the two preceding phases being independence of specific territories detached from defeated enemy states from both world wars, and liberation of the trust territories and colonies from Western colonial rule). The assumption that self-determination has advanced beyond the stage of decolonization into an "entitlement" to democratic government was endorsed by Halperin and Scheffer (1992, 60–65).

The test alluded to is a reference to an obligation to ascertain the will of the people involved (Principle VII, GA Res. 1541 [XV]), that is, the intended beneficiaries of self-determination. The Cuban Democracy Act is one such example of action that can possibly be undertaken by the world community. If a claim of self-determination is made by or on behalf of a population against a state (such as Cuba), international law requires that the will of the intended beneficiaries must be ascertained. Under international practice, plebiscites have been a favored means for determining the free choice of peoples. The United Nations has conducted plebiscites in several cases involving ex-colonial territories, though not with regard to claims of groups in sovereign states (Johnson 1967, 71–98). A unique case is the UNTAC-supervised elections in Cambodia in May 1993. Presumably, these can be analogies to draw on during the alleged third phase of self-determination at work. Means of ascertaining the will of the people other than voting may also be appropriate (Gordon 1971, 563f.). Hence, the legitimacy of the Cuban Democracy Act turns on whether the U.S. government, acting as a presumptive benefactor on behalf of the world community, has taken the required steps to ascertain the free choice of the intended Cuban beneficiaries. The test is a prerequisite lest self-determination become "external" determination, which would violate the territorial integrity of another state.[8]

Conclusion

The post–World War II period has witnessed a proliferation of states, thanks to three sources: (1) divisions or diminution of ex-enemy states by agreement reached by victor powers (such as the emancipation of Korea from Japanese control, the division of Germany until 1990, and the placing under trusteeship of certain territories detached from defeated powers); (2) decolonization under the aegis of self-determination; and (3) split-offs following unfinished insurgencies (such as in Indochina). Of the three categories, there is no leftover business from category (1), as all the eleven trust territories have gained independence. For category (2), however, Halperin and Scheffer (1992, app.) have established an exhaustive list of more than sixty real or potential self-determination cases pending final outcome in all regions. Some cases are more trying than others, such as East Timor and Chechnya.

On the other hand, there are few cases left over in category (3). Possibly the most noteworthy instance, dating from the pre-1945 era, is the square-off across the Taiwan Strait. The conflict stems from the unfinished civil war that divided China into a mainland known as the People's Republic of China (PRC) and an island ruled by the Republic of China (ROC) regime that retreated to Taiwan in 1949 after losing out to the communist insurrection.

This case could conceivably be one of the most disturbing and destabilizing ones as the world sails into the twenty-first century. Of late the PRC hinted a timetable to take control of Taiwan by force if necessary, following the scheduled return to Chinese sovereignty of Hong Kong (in 1997) and Macao (in 1999) (*New York Times,* January 31, 1996, 2). The news attracted unusual worldwide attention, since mainland China had resorted to nuclear bluster across the Taiwan Strait and suspended many contacts in retaliation for an "unofficial" visit to the United States by Taiwan's president Lee Teng-hui in June 1995. The PRC insisted that the Lee visit was one more indication of a Taiwanese attempt to secede from the "one China" ideal held sacred by Chinese the world over. The latest rupture followed a third missile testing by Beijing across the Taiwan Strait in March 1996. It simply reversed the steady trend of cautious normalization between the two sides begun in late 1986 after thirty-seven years of incessant armed confrontation.

The question raised for international law in the PRC-Taiwan division is that both sides are hung up on a false dichotomy, between unification and Taiwan separatism. Purely from the international law perspective, the physical detachedness (avoiding the word *separation*) of Taiwan from the mainland is simply the result of the unfinished Chinese civil war. It is neither a question of division of sovereignty, which Beijing insists is unacceptable, nor Taiwan's secession, since the island has never been under PRC jurisdiction—hence, there is nothing to secede from. Nor is it a case even of self-determination, because in repeated public opinion polls, the percentage who supported separatism was rarely over 12 percent. If these pollings represented the required ascertainment of the free will of the people, there is no legitimate basis for self-determination, notwithstanding occasional idiosyncratic and nonrepresentative writings by foreign-based Taiwan scholars to the contrary.[9] If the three-way choice suggested by the International Court of Justice in the cognate *Western Sahara* case is any guide, the unification versus separatism for the Chinese situation is a false dichotomy. In a three-way outcome, Taiwan separatism would be only one option, the other two being a free association between the two sides across the Taiwan Strait (presumably a Greater China association in the economic sense), and a Taiwan-mainland integration (i.e., unification) scenario. Once this three-way choice replaces the false dichotomy, chances are that the present Chinese division problem may lend itself to a non-zero-sum solution. If so, it illustrates that, no less than with political issues, familiarity with international law and imaginative application of it may hold the key to many seemingly intractable problems, international or domestic.

On the subject of self-determination, we may draw the following conclusions based on the preceding discussions:

1. The world community may confer a right on a "judicially as yet non-existing entity" (Sir Gerald Fitzmaurice's words), whose population is the victim of alien subjugation. A prior condition for any vicarious exercise of the right of self-determination, however, as confirmed in United Nations practice, is that the world community has to discharge an obligation to ascertain the free will of the people. Only after the free will of the people has been ascertained can it be certified as "self" determination. Otherwise, it would be "external" determination, which is not supported by international law.

2. A derivative conclusion is that, as demonstrated in the practice of the United Nations, especially in the area of decolonization, the very fact that the world community may "confer" a right on a dependent people under alien subjugation is the best indication of the rise of a modern community that takes at least part of the rough edge off the systemic anarchy inherent in the Westphalian world we live in.

3. As in other areas (e.g., human rights, see Chapter 6), self-determination is also liable to political use and maneuver by external forces. As we have seen, the first prime mover of the self-determination campaign was the Soviet Union. In introducing in the General Assembly the resolution that became the Declaration on the Granting of Independence, the Soviet intention was to undercut the West. But the irony is that the Soviet empire was to break up three decades later when its disfranchised peoples and republics demanded their share of self-determination, or their right to democratic participation, which Moscow could not deliver.

4. There is no permanent conflict between self-determination and respect for territorial integrity nor between international law and municipal law. We have seen that in the practice of states and the United Nations, self-determination has been mainly limited to colonial cases and does not imply the right to secession. And, as in other areas, international law often limits

itself to flaunting certain generic principles (in the present case, the right of self-determination) as broad guidance for the conduct of international relations. But the rest is pretty much left to municipal law, as in the definition of what constitutes the private acts (*acta gestionis*) of a foreign sovereign, which modern international law says should receive no immunity from other states (see Chapter 5). In the case of self-determination, which is upheld by international law, much of the detail is likewise left to domestic jurisdiction, as in the disposition of all matters relating to state succession.

5. To Neorealism, self-determination is not a concern, because this is an area involving "nations," "peoples," and nationalism, all of which fall outside the Neorealist state-centric bailiwick. But this anomaly merely illustrates the insufficiency of a paradigm of international relations based purely on state centricity. As an increasing number of scholars have suggested, we need not only a state-centric but also a nation-centric approach to the study of international relations.[10]

A nation-centric approach is all the more necessary if we are to adequately cope with the expanding structural fluidity in the post–Cold War world (Lapid 1991, 11, n.10). The following are some of the phenomena indicative of increasing structural fluidity that demand greater attention on our part: the rise of stateless nations (e.g., Palestinians, Kurds, Gypsies, and Inuits) and nationless states (e.g., Lebanon); the delegitimation and "implosion" of empires (e.g., the Soviet Union); and the near breakup of multinational states (e.g., Yugoslavia and Canada).

Notes

1. The General Assembly, on November 25, 1992, set the goal of complete decolonization by the year 2000. It reaffirmed its declaration of the decade beginning in 1990 as the International Decade for the Eradication of Colonialism. See *U.N. Chronicle,* March 1993, 88.

2. For the text of Biafra's declaration of secession of May 30, 1967, see *ILM* 6 (1967):679.

3. The full title is United Nations Declaration on Principles of International Law Concerning Friendly Relations Among States in Accordance with the Charter of the United Nations, GA Res. 2625 (XXV), 1970. Text in GAOR, 25th sess., Supp. 28, 121.

4. *ICJ Reports* (1950):128; digested in *AJIL* 44 (1950):757.

5. Boutros Boutros-Ghali, *Agenda for Peace,* UN Doc. 3/24111, para. 11; text also in *ILM* 31 (1992):953.

6. V. Lenin, "Theses on the Social Revolution and the Right of Nations to Self-Determination (March 1916)," in V. Lenin, *Selected Works* (London: Lawrence & Wishart, 1969), 37.

7. Cf. Franck 1990, 168. His view apparently is not widely shared, especially in the Third World.

8. In the case of the Helms-Burton Act, there are more than U.S-Cuban relations involved. The law permits U.S. companies whose properties were seized by President Fidel Castro's government to file suits in U.S. courts against foreign companies that are using them in Cuba. Since it would punish all countries doing business with Cuba, it created a hornet's nest among the world's trading nations, including Canada and European and Latin American states (*New York Times,* July 16, 1996, 9; November 12, 1996, 5). The European Union was reportedly agreed on possible countermeasures in retaliation, including blacklisting U.S. companies, requiring visas for business travelers, and taking the matter to the World Trade Organization (*New York Times,* July 16, 1996, 9).

9. For example, Lung-chu Chen, *Formosa, China, and the United Nations* (New York: St. Martin's Press, 1967).

10. See W. Connor, "Nation-Building or Nation-Destroying," *World Politics* 24, 3 (April 1972); A. D. Smith, *The Ethnic Revival* (New York: Cambridge University Press, 1981); Joseph Rothschild, *Ethnopolitics* (New York: Columbia University Press, 1981); Daniel P. Moynihan, *Ethnicity* (Cambridge: Harvard University Press, 1975); and Benjamin Akzin, *States and Nations* (New York: Anchor Books, 1966).

8

Control over the Environment: Common Legacy of Humankind

The subject of this chapter is international control over two areas beyond national jurisdiction: global commons and the environment. These areas are often lumped together in discourses on an emergent international environmental law and the role it plays in the preservation of community interests therein. For this book, there is special significance in the emergence of an international environmental law: It offers tangible evidence of the rise of community interests over those of sovereign states.

Traditionally, the first premise of international relations was an international society composed of sovereign states that held supreme power over their respective territories and that created legal norms to apply in their relations only if those norms supported their national interests. Traditional international law as well as realist theory was based on this vision. Cumulative global change since the end of World War II, however, has modified the state-centric reality and calls for a new perspective. The belief that the human community has interests that are superior to those of individual states, and that may be larger than the sum of the latter, is becoming more wide-spread. As Kiss (1992, 331f.) argues, the peaceful uses of outer space and the oceans and the conservation of the biosphere—no less than issues like the protection of human rights, decolonization, and the development of poor countries—cannot be properly understood apart from the concept of a common interest for humankind. Some of these vital community concerns are addressed in Part 3 (Chapters 5 and 6) dealing with "sovereignty in check." In this chapter, our focus is on the community's interest in maintaining order in, and preserving the quality of, the global commons and the environment, often over the particular (even contrary) interests of the individual states. As we go along, we will see how the ascendancy of the community's environmental order represents a further advance beyond the phenomena discussed in Part 3. Certainly there is no similar dissension on the imperative and meaning of environmental control as there is, for instance, on the specific meaning of human rights.

Coping with the Tragedy of the Commons

The global commons, sometimes known as common-pool resources, is a catchall phrase for vast reservoirs of natural resources that exist on planet earth, such as the deep seabed and the high seas and their fisheries; outer space; the Antarctic; the atmosphere, including the ozone layer; the carbon dioxide balance; and the electromagnetic frequency spectrum for broadcasting. The concept may even include clean air and water, arable land, and energy sources such as petroleum, coal, natural gas, and wood. All the world's resources are finite and can be used up. Yet the property rights of these resources cannot be defined and enforced by economic means (Russett and Starr 1992, 457). Save for community action out of an enlightened human interest, there is no hope for the protection of these common-pool resources. Motivated by competitive egoistic interests, individual states can destroy an existing commons—such as the ozone layer in the atmosphere, animal and fish species, forests, and topsoil—through over-exploitation, ecological pollution, or just negligence.

Another disaster that could befall a global commons—for instance, Antarctica or outer space—is the declaration by any single state or group of states, especially if backed by brute power, that the area is its exclusive domain and off limits to all other states. A worse disaster would be if overlapping and conflicting claims to parts of a commons should lead to eruptions of international violence. In any event, the ultimate solution lies with the world community, which can act through the medium of international law.

In this discussion, I treat the solution to the last mentioned scenario (conflicting territorial claims) as the control of the global commons, and control of the environment as the remedy to the other hazards. While both could fall under the rubric "international environmental law," I shall for clarity's sake limit the discussion in the present section to the control of the global commons. The rest will be reserved for a separate section, on the question of the environment and the making of an international environmental law.

Tragedy of the Global Commons and Remedies

The metaphor "tragedy of the commons" was first developed by Garret Hardin (1968, 142): Just picture an open pasture, the commons, that belongs to all members of a group. As a rational being, each herdsman seeks to maximize his gain, measured by the increment of the number of animals in his herd. Adding together the component partial utilities, the rational herdsman concludes that the only sensible course for him to pursue is to add another animal to his herd—and another, and another. This is the conclusion reached by each and every rational herdsman sharing a commons. "Therein is the tragedy," writes Hardin, adding: "Each man is locked into a system that compels him to increase his herd without limit (i.e., egoism)—in a world that is limited. Ruin is the destination toward which all men rush, each pursuing his own best interest in a society that believes in the freedom of the commons. Freedom in a commons brings ruin to all." This last sentence catches the essence of the "tragedy of the commons." Substituting *states* for the *herdsmen,* we find the same phenomenon duplicated in the international community. Freedom bred by systemic anarchy could spell ruin to all in the global commons, unless the world community acting counterintuitively can find a way to regulate the behavior of states in relation to the commons.

I use the word *counterintuitively* because Neorealists, intuitively viewing the world system purely from the anarchic paradigm (lack of a higher authority than the states), would believe that egoism and relative-gains calculations prevent states from being able to work together (cooperate) in meting out the necessary regimes for eliciting mutually acceptable behavior in the commons. Yet the record of state practice is that workable solutions were found to obviate disputes and avert possible ruin to the global commons—from Antarctica to outer space to deep seabed. These developments were therefore counterintuitive.

While each of these commons is a vast topic, my purpose here is to show how unexpected solutions were found, through community effort, to remove competitive claims and preserve the integrity and environmental soundness of the global commons.

The Antarctic. The first situation that called for a collective solution concerned the Antarctic. The existence of a landmass in this polar region—with no community-defined rules of conduct—prompted competitive territorial claims by a variety of states (the rational herdsmen in Hardin's open pasture). Numerous and conflicting claims were put forth over the decades by the United Kingdom, Argentina, Norway, Australia, New Zealand, France, and Chile. While most claims were founded on discovery, the claims by Great Britain, Argentina, and Chile were based on a degree of permanent settlement (i.e., display and exercise of sovereignty), as in the Palmer Peninsula region, achieved through bases these nations maintained over a number of years (von Glahn 1992, 385; Bishop 1962, 356, n. 18).

The United States did not assert any official claims to territory in the Antarctic, although Congress, in the 1950s, wrestled unfruitfully with proposed declarations of U.S. sovereignty over portions of the region. The official U.S. policy, first enunciated by Secretary of State Hughes in 1924, was based on the theory that no claims in Antarctica could be recognized until discovery had been followed by effective occupation or control, including settlement and development.

By contrast, other countries not only laid claims, but also in several cases recognized one another's claims as valid. In other instances, overlapping claims caused considerable friction, such as between Britain and Argentina/Chile. The British suggestion that the disputes be taken to the International Court of Justice was rejected by the other two countries. Attempts were made, without success, to have the matter of the Antarctic taken up by the UN General Assembly (Bishop 1962, 357).

Had the situation continued without a solution, it would have brought disaster and war to the region, not to mention the possible competitive plundering of resources to the detriment of the environmental quality of the region. The solution was the Antarctica Treaty of 1959, creating the so-called Antarctic Treaty System (ATS). The twelve countries that produced the treaty, at a conference, in Washington from October 15 to December 1, 1959, became the original "consultative members" (voting members): Argentina, Australia, Belgium, Chile, France, Japan, New Zealand, Norway, South Africa, USSR, UK, and the United States. After the instrument came into force on June 23, 1961, Poland, West Germany, Brazil, China, Uruguay, and India also became consultative members. Adhering to the instrument but lacking voting privileges are the "acceding" members: Austria, Papua New Guinea (as successor state), Bulgaria, Czechoslovakia, Denmark, East Germany, Finland, Hungary, Italy, the Netherlands, Romania, Spain, Sweden, Cuba, Peru, Finland, Ecuador, Greece, South Korea, and North Korea (von Glahn 1992, 384).

The treaty suspends, without prejudice, all territorial claims previously asserted by the contracting parties (Arts. IV, VIII). No new claim or enlargement of any existing claim to territorial sovereignty in Antarctica shall be made while the treaty is in force (Art. IV[2]). The treaty reserves the Antarctic region for peaceful use only, committing the parties to cooperate in scientific investigation, freedom of which is also specifically guaranteed (Arts. II, III). Freedom of access is guaranteed to all the contracting parties "at any time to any or all areas of Antarctica" (Art. VII[2]). But nuclear explosion is prohibited in the region (Art. V). Disputes of any kind between contracting parties, either with regard to the exercise of jurisdiction in Antarctica or to the interpretation or application of the provisions of the treaty, shall be settled by peaceful means (Art. XI).

The so-called ATS is founded on the bedrock of the 1959 treaty, which by virtue of its required suspension of territorial claims preserves the integrity of Antarctica as a commons. Its other component mechanisms aimed at the protection of the region's environment are:

- Agreed Measures for the Conservation of Antarctic Fauna and Flora (1964)
- Convention for the Conservation of Antarctic Seals (1972)

- Convention for the Conservation of Antarctic Marine Living Resources (1980)
- Convention for the Regulation of Antarctic Mineral Resource Activities (1988)
- Protocol on Environmental Protection to the Antarctic Treaty, known as the Madrid Protocol (1991)

Blay (1992, 377–399) offers a detailed account of the regimes for the protection of the Antarctic environment. Our interest here is in how the Antarctic was saved from the proverbial "tragedy of the commons" by the device of a multilateral convention dispensing with egoistic sovereign claims, made possible by a combination of factors: the inconclusiveness of the rivaling claims to the region; the explosive danger of serious international conflicts stemming from the inconclusive overlapping claims; and the undesirability of possible ruin to the integrity of the Antarctic from the prospect of resource plundering by rational states scrambling to maximize their egoistic gains. Despite the anarchic condition (i.e., lack of a supranational authority) of the world, enough nations saw the need for a solution that would require constraint on their own sovereign claims. They responded to the imprimatur of the United States, which hosted the 1959 conference, to fashion the Antarctic Treaty, laying the foundation of the ATS (Hayton 1960, 348ff.). The significance of the instance is twofold: First, it shows that under conditions of anarchy, it is possible for states, contrary to Neorealist expectations, to cooperate and agree to sacrifice some of their own sovereignty to preserve some perceived higher community good. They did so not under coercion (the United States simply served as the host country), but out of enlightened concern for community interests over and above their own. Second, the precedent set for Antarctica was to serve as a guide for saving other global commons from ruin, i.e., outer space and deep seabed in tandem.

Outer space. The increasingly common penetration of the upper layers of the earth's atmosphere, made possible by the advent of modern aviation technology, marked outer space as one of the next targets for voyages of discovery. This development posed wide-ranging legal questions for space travel and exploration. Not the least of these were how far a country's territorial sovereignty should extend into air and outer space; and how liabilities should be determined in the event of mishaps from space exploration (cf. Whiteman 1970, vol. 2, 1285–1321). The competition between the two superpowers in their race to outer space, following the Soviet launching of Sputnik in 1957, lent urgency to the search for a permanent solution that would demilitarize outer space and maintain both terrestrial and environmental integrity.

In 1961, the General Assembly tried to offer an answer by making the UN Charter, and general international law, applicable to outer space; it adopted the Declaration on Peaceful Uses of Outer Space (text reprinted in *AJIL* 56 [1962 Supp.]:946). The declaration regarded outer space as well as other celestial bodies as free for exploration and peaceful use by all states. These concepts were expanded in a later General Assembly document, the 1963 Declaration of Legal Principles Governing Activities in Outer Space. An important advance in the development of a nascent outer space regime was the notion that space exploration and the use of space were to be for the benefit of all humankind (von Glahn 1992, 415).

The idea of a common heritage of humankind gradually crystallized and inspired subsequent agreements that defined the regime of outer space, including:

- Treaty on Principles Concerning the Activities of States in the Exploration and Use of Outer Space, Including the Moon and Other Celestial Bodies (1967)
- Treaty Banning Nuclear Weapon Tests in the Atmosphere, in Outer Space, and Under Water (1963)
- Treaty on the Rescue of Astronauts, the Return of Astronauts, and the Return of Objects Launched into Outer Space (1968)
- Convention on International Liability for Damage Caused by Space Objects (1971)
- Agreement Concerning the Activities of States on the Moon and Other Celestial Bodies, commonly known as the "Moon Treaty" (1979)

Article I of the 1967 Treaty on Principles sets the tone for the nascent regime of outer space, now juridically cordoned off and preserved as a global commons. It declares that "the exploration and use of outer space, including the moon and other celestial bodies, shall be carried out for the benefit and in the interests of *all countries,* irrespective of their degree of economic or scientific development, and shall be the province of *all mankind*" (emphasis added). On the other hand, states pledge not to subject outer space to "national appropriation by claim of sovereignty, by means of use or occupation, or by any other means" (Art. II). By 1993, ninety-five countries had ratified the treaty. As in the Antarctic case, the willingness of states to accept an obligation to forgo all claims of territorial sovereignty, in favor of preserving the integrity of a commons (outer space) and regulating all activities within its confines, is an amazing development in that states literally pledge to forsake egoistic pursuit, because of their preference for order in an anarchic system.

Deep seabed. If the idea of the "common heritage of mankind" had thus far been implicit as well as novel, it was made explicit in the 1982 Convention on the Law of the Sea (CLOS III). In no uncertain terms, Article 136 states: "The Area and its resources are the *common heritage of mankind*" (emphasis added). "The Area" is defined in Article 1(1) as "the sea-bed and ocean floor and subsoil thereof, beyond the limits of national jurisdiction."

Under Article 137, which defines the "legal status of the Area and its resources," claims of sovereignty by any state party are prohibited. No part of the area is subject to national appropriation; all rights in the resources of the area are "vested in mankind as a whole." On behalf of all humankind, an International Seabed Authority (ISA) shall be established, consisting of all states parties to the convention (Art. 156), with the power to "organize and control activities in the Area, particularly with a view to administering the resources of the Area" (Art. 157). Under rules and procedures enunciated in a separate annex (III) to the convention, the ISA has the authority to approve "plans of work for activities in the Area," including exploration and exploitation. The Enterprise, which is an arm of the ISA, states that parties, and certain other entities (e.g., state enterprises or private miners possessing the nationality of a state party, when sponsored by the latter), may apply for approval of their plans to the ISA. According to Article 3 of Annex III, all approved plans of work, except those presented by the Enterprise, shall be in the form of a contract between the ISA and the applicant or applicants.

The International Seabed Authority in a way personifies the human community in enforcing control of all activities in the deep seabed. Its functional arm, the Enterprise (established pursuant to Art. 158), shall carry out activities in the area directly (pursuant to Art. 153, para. 2[a]), as well as transport, process, and market minerals recovered from the area (Art. 170). All states and private miners wishing to engage in activities of prospecting, exploration, or exploitation can do so only under licensing by the ISA.

This development is remarkable if one keeps in mind that under the traditional concept of sovereignty, states should be free to exploit the resources in any place like the seabed, to the extent it is a place analogous to a *res nullius*. It is a well-established principle that a no-man's territory and its resources are subject to national appropriation. But this is drastically changed by the 1982 convention and, for that matter, by the emergent international environmental law.

Following U.S. objection, first raised in 1982 by the Reagan administration in its refusal to sign the convention, informed consultations later led to agreements that removed the obstacles to wider adherence to CLOS III.

The "Agreement Relating to the Implementation of Part XI of the U.N. Convention on the Law of the Sea of 10 December 1982" was adopted by the General Assembly on July 28, 1994. Now made into a single instrument with CLOS III, this 1994 agreement is in effect an amendment to Part XI of the treaty (Oxman 1994, 687). Part XI contains the provisions regarding the establishment and functions of the ISA and the Enterprise, as described above. The United States voted for the adoption by the General Assembly of the agreement and signed it in late 1994. This cleared the way for the submission of the 1982 convention to the U.S. Senate for ratification (Charney 1994, 705).

In rejecting CLOS III, the Reagan administration took issue with the deep seabed mining regime, but embraced the rest of the convention (Reagan's statement of March 10, 1983, reprinted in *ILM* 22 [1983]:464). In the 1994 agreement that the United States signed, the purported changes to Part XI of the convention concerned technical issues such as decision-making in the council of the ISA (the United States is given a guaranteed seat as the world's largest economy); production limit; technology transfer to the Enterprise; access to the deep seabed; the Enterprise itself, including its financial and regulatory burdens; and the distribution of revenues (Oxman 1994). Other than Reagan's lip-service deprecation of the idea of a "common heritage of mankind" as advancing socialism by treaty, the initial U.S. objection was based on more practical grounds. Removal of these specific obstacles made it possible for the United States to endorse the 1982 convention.

It appears that the concept of a "common heritage of mankind" is now generally accepted. By deduction, it means that the idea of a community with interests superior to those of its component units (states) is also established as a (new) premise of contemporary international relations.

An Emergent International Environmental Law

A good illustration of the linkage between the preservation of the commons and the control of the environment is in the extensive component mechanisms aimed at the protection of the Antarctic environment in the Antarctic Treaty System. The 1959 treaty marked Antarctica off as a commons not subject to national appropriation. But the other ATS-supporting agreements, including the Convention for the Regulation of Antarctic Mineral Resource Activities and the Madrid Protocol, provided for the environmental protection of the region. Likewise, in the outer space regime, the 1967 Treaty on Principles establishes outer space, including the moon and other celestial bodies, as a new frontier commons belonging to all humankind, not subject to national appropriation. Other agreements provide for the demilitarization of outer space and set the criteria for ascertaining international liabilities for damage by space objects. These are ultimately concerned with maintaining the environmental integrity and security of outer space as a global commons, or common legacy of humankind.

We have seen that the deep seabed is preserved and protected under the law of the sea regime, culminating in CLOS III, as a global commons. CLOS III would also appear to have supporting agreements for the protection of the marine environment, which bespeaks the linkage between environmental control and the preservation of the commons.

For the control of marine pollution alone, there exist the following multilateral environmental treaties:

- International Convention for the Prevention of Pollution of the Sea by Oil (1954; TIAS No. 4900; amended, No. 8505)
- International Convention Relating to Intervention of the High Seas in Cases of Oil Pollution Casualties (1969; TIAS, No. 8068)
- Convention on the Prevention of Marine Pollution by Dumping of Wastes and Other Matter (1972; TIAS, No. 8165)
- International Convention for the Prevention of Pollution from Ships (1973; *ILM* 12 [1973]:1319)
- International Convention on Oil Pollution Preparedness, Response and Cooperation (1990; *ILM* 30 [1991]:733)

For the protection and conservation of marine living resources, the following should be mentioned: the International Convention for the Regulation of Whaling (1946; TIAS, No. 1849); and the Convention on Fishing and Conservation of Living Resources on the High Seas (1958; TIAS, No. 5969).

The Environment and International Law

Let us play the skeptic for a moment and raise some fundamental questions. First, what is meant by *environment*? There is almost no way to define the term. Birnie and Boyle (1992, 2) lament that none of the major treaties, declarations, codes of conduct, or guidelines on the development of an international environmental law has ever offered a definition. Dictionary definitions range from "something that environs" to "the whole complex of climactic, edaphic, and biotic factors that act upon an organism or an ecological community and ultimately determine its form and survival; the aggregate of social or cultural conditions that influence the life of an individual or community."[1]

The first community-wide deliberations on the implications of the deteriorating environment of the human habitat took place in 1972, at the

United Nations Conference on the Human Environment (UNCHE) in Stockholm. However, the historic UNCHE declaration simply refers to man's environment "which gives him physical sustenance and affords him the opportunity for intellectual, spiritual, moral, and social growth" (UN Doc. A/CONF.48/14/Rev.1; reprinted in *ILM* 11 [1972]:1416).

The next document of comparable importance, the Rio Declaration on Environment and Development (A/CONF.151/5/Rev.1, reprinted in *ILM* 31 [1992]:874), was adopted by the UN Conference on Environment and Development (1992), which was reputed to be a sequel to the 1972 Stockholm meeting. It highlights the linkage between "environmental protection" and "sustainable development" (Principle 4). Despite its copious references to "environmental issues," "environmental standards," "environmental impact assessment," "environmental management," etc., the Rio declaration does not try to one-up the Stockholm document by offering a definition of the term *environment.*

A survey of the various environmental treaties reveals that, although each instrument makes specific references—to the "Antarctic environment," the "marine environment," etc.—none offers a definition of *environment.* Article 194(5) of CLOS III, which specifies "measures to prevent, reduce, and control pollution of the marine environment," refers to "rare or fragile ecosystems" and "habitat of depleted, threatened, or endangered species or other forms of marine life," to which the specified measures are to be applied. This phraseology comes closest to a definition of what are to be found *within* a "marine environment." But what actually constitutes "marine environment" remains elusive.

As Caldwell (1980, 170) explains, most conventions avoid defining environment because "it is a term that everyone knows and no one is able to define."

The second fundamental question is whether there is an international environmental law after all. On the con side, one may question whether there is any distinct "environmental" body of law with its own sources and methods of lawmaking deriving from principles peculiar or exclusive to environmental concerns. On the pro side, a clearly identifiable body of norms, both customary and conventional, now exists for the protection of the environment, including norms created by the various conventions. *International environmental law* is often used as a shorthand label very much after the fashion of the terms *law of the sea, human rights law,* and *international economic law.* Put another way, it is the aggregate of all the norms and principles aimed at protecting the global environment, including the commons, and controlling activities within national jurisdiction that may affect another state's environment or areas beyond national jurisdiction (Birnie and Boyle 1992, 9). Environmental protection is now extended to other jurisdictions, such as the commons mentioned earlier. As such, environmental law involves questions of sovereignty, jurisdiction, regulation, and state responsibility.

Making of the International Environmental Law

How is international environmental law made? Or, an international lawyer might ask, what are the "sources" of this body of international law?

Because international environmental law is such a vast subject, the discussion in this chapter focuses on one aspect: the "making" of the body of norms regulating the environment, or the intersecting of international law and politics. Of interest is how, despite their egoistic proclivity, states accept binding norms in the protection of the environment, and how the world community has shown a certain ingenuity in developing a relatively coherent body of environmental norms over a short period of time. Considering the absence of a world legislature, the emergence of this body of law cannot but be amazing. The "legislative" process is piecemeal and fragmented, but the body of norms created somehow seem to cohere into an integral whole.

At the risk of overgeneralization, three overall propositions might be made: (1) a common purpose, representing the will of the community of nations, seems to have inspired and steered the development of the international environmental law (IEL) beyond its initial haphazard beginnings; (2) there is in IEL a unique fusion of science, economics, and law; and (3) the evolution of IEL seems to have followed a dual track of treaty making and—though less perceptible to the uninitiated—of analogizing from municipal law (comprising both judicial decisions and juridical doctrines) and other parts of general international law.

Common purpose. Concededly, occasional international agreements—mostly bilateral—occurred as far back as the late nineteenth century on questions relating to the protection of such resources as fisheries, fur seals, birds useful to agriculture, and boundary waters.[2] But in the paradigm of traditional international law, the legal status of states is characterized by three principles: sovereignty, independence, and equality. The awareness of and willingness to accept an obligation by states to protect the environment beyond national jurisdiction is a more recent development. The earliest modern indication of this awareness is found in the 1968 African Convention on the Conservation of Nature and Natural Resources. According to this convention, where an animal or plant species threatened with extinction is represented only in the territory of one state, that state has a particular responsibility (toward the human community) for its protection (Art. 8) (Weiss 1992, 13).

I say *modern* for three reasons. First, unlike most other similar international agreements before, this 1968 convention was multilateral, in fact continent-wide. Second, this one covered the whole range of "nature and natural resources" in its call for protection, not just one animal or plant species as in most previous agreements. Third, and most important, parties to the convention demonstrated a commitment to the world community—not just to another contracting party or parties as in past agreements—in taking on conservational responsibility. With the demonstration of such a common purpose of community, the world entered into a new era. Typically, the UNCHE declaration (1972) names the defense and improvement of the human environment, for the present and future generations, "an imperative goal for mankind" (para. 6). To achieve this environmental goal, it requires "the acceptance of responsibility by citizens and communities and by enterprises and institutions at every level" as well as states, "all sharing equitably in common efforts" (para. 7). Thus, the modern international environmental law is a spinoff from this common endeavor of a world community, inspired by a common purpose.

Fusion of science, economics, and law. The IEL is influenced by a range of nonlegal factors, not the least of which are science and economics. There is no doubt that the likelihood of achieving an agreement increases with great *scientific* consensus about the cause and seriousness of a problem (Hahn and Richards 1989, 433). In an agreement to regulate marine pollution, for example, specification of the criteria for pollution assessment and the quality standards depends on scientific knowledge (Barros and Johnston 1974, xv–xvi, part I). IEL also bears a close relationship to economics in two ways. First, although rarely expressed in quantitative terms, faithfully implemented environmental protection measures may result in the preservation of countless resources from waste and destruction. Second, short-term rules adopted to protect the environment can impose enormous costs on the parties complying with the protective measures. Most environmental treaties do not provide for financial resources to be made available to compensate for the additional costs of protective measures, partly because at the time of their negotiation their economic consequences were not fully known. The 1973 Convention on International Trade in Extinct Species (CITES), for instance, does not compensate African nations for loss of revenue due to the 1989 ban on trade in ivory (Sands 1995, 12). It is hardly surprising that in recent years environmental concerns have become economic concerns. One indication of this was the combination of development and the environment as the theme for the 1992 UN Conference on Environment and Development in Rio de Janeiro.

Dual track. What we have called the "dual track" in the genesis of the international law of the environment has two meanings. First, it derives equally from treaty making and borrowings from municipal law. Second, it means there is both a "hard-law" component and a "soft-law" component.

Dual Track in the Origins of International Environmental Law

Treaty Law. The use of treaties, along with custom, is said to dominate the process by which the international environmental law is made (Palmer 1992, 264ff.). In the jurisprudential sense, the sources of IEL go beyond treaties and custom to include UN General Assembly resolutions and declarations; general principles of law; judicial decisions; the writings of publicists, such as reports and drafted articles by the International Law Commission (ILC); and other UN reports and drafts, including those by specialized agencies (Birnie and Boyle 1992, 10–26). A confusion for the uninitiated is whether the resolutions and reports are additional "sources" of international law. The answer is no. The question of the sources of international law was addressed in Chapter 1, and the question of the so-called soft law will come up later. However, I hasten to add the following two points: To the extent certain General Assembly resolutions represent a consensus of nations, so much so that they embody an *opinio juris communis,* they may arguably represent a body of norms *de lege ferenda* or at a minimum may be considered to have a "legal effect" or constitute a "subsidiary means for the determination of rules of law" (Parry 1965, 21); and writings by publicists and drafted articles by ILC and other UN agencies may provide either evidence of extant rules of law or a subsidiary means for the determination of customary norms, which exist independently of treaties.

Over a long period, numerous treaties have created binding obligations to regulate the environment. In the list compiled by Sands (1995, xix–xl) one can count 155 signed during the period 1972–1993 alone. The total number increases to 261 if the time period is pushed back to 1867, when the Anglo-French Convention on Fisheries was concluded. The year 1972, when the Stockholm conference not only yielded a harbinger Declaration on the Human Environment, but also mandated the creation of the United Nations Environment Programme (UNEP), is sometimes considered the beginning of modern international environmental law. The average annual yield of more than seven environmental treaties since 1972 is impressive.

The subject matter regulated by these agreements include prevention of marine and air pollution and waste dumping; preservation of water quality and river flow; protection of endangered species, wildlife and natural habitats, and other living resources; prohibition of military or other hostile use of environmental modification techniques; cooperation in combating oil spills on the high seas; protection of the ozone layer and of fauna and flora; safety in the use of asbestos; assistance in the case of a nuclear accident;

control of the transboundary movement of hazardous waste; protection and use of transboundary watercourses and international lakes; civil liability for damage resulting from activities dangerous to the environment; and protection of specified regional environment.

It is common practice to use a three-tiered approach to the making of environmental treaties. The first tier, a framework treaty, sets out general obligations, creates the basic institutional arrangements, and provides procedures for the adoption of detailed obligations in a subsequent protocol, at the second tier. At the third tier, framework treaty or protocol will frequently have one or more annexes or appendixes, which include scientific, technical, or administrative provisions (such as dispute settlement and information exchange). An example is the 1985 Vienna Convention for the Protection of the Ozone Layer, with a 1987 Montreal Protocol, plus the 1990 and 1992 adjustments and amendments. The third-tier instrument (annexes or appendixes) may also list the species, substances, or activities that are regulated, as in the CITES (1973). The use of this three-tiered approach is to allow flexibility in making possible legal amendments or other changes in accordance with political, scientific, or economic developments (Sands 1995, 106).

Customary law. In the international law of the environment, customary norms play a necessary role. Like in other areas of international law, the significance of custom lies in the fact that it creates obligations for all states, including those that are not parties to a particular environmental treaty that codifies certain norms in custom that exist in generic form. Customary law usually manifests itself in state practice and is often tested by adjudication. A problem is that state practice is notoriously difficult to prove, and little empirical research has been carried out on state practice relating to international environmental obligations (Sands 1995, 118).

However, this problem in no serious way vitiates the usefulness of customary law in regulating environmental behavior. Suppose a nation—say, state X—allowed unlimited manufacture and use of chlorofluorocarbons, to the detriment of the ozone layer. And suppose state X was not a party to either the 1985 Vienna Convention or the 1987 Montreal Protocol, which regulates liability for damage to the ozone layer. It would still be possible to hold state X responsible under the customary norms on state responsibility, if the case is submitted to a competent international tribunal. The *Trail Smelter* case (U.S. v. Canada, 1941) comes to mind as a precedent. The case was decided by a Special Arbitral Tribunal under an existing U.S.-Canadian convention. It grew out of a complaint about air pollution from sulphur dioxide fumes emitted by a smelter plant at Trail, British Columbia, owned by a Canadian corporation. In holding Canada responsible for its negligence in preventing the damage caused to the state of Washington by fumes emitted from Canadian territory, the tribunal, citing Professor Clyde Eagleton (1928, 80) of New York University, declared: "A State owes at all times a duty to protect other States against injurious acts by individuals from within its jurisdiction" (UN *Rep. Int'l Arb. Awards* 3 [1941]:1963f.). The principle that grave omissions engage the international responsibility of a state was upheld by the International Court of Justice in the *Corfu Channel* case (1949). Under the doctrine of "objective responsibility" in customary international law, there is a breach of duty by result alone, provided that agency and causal connection are established. There is no need to establish the existence of malice in an act or omission causing damage (Brownlie 1973, 423–428). Hence, there is enough in customary international law to find state X guilty of having breached its state responsibility by negligence (omission) resulting in damages to the ozone layer caused by the overproduction and use of chlorofluorocarbons by citizens within its borders.

Earlier we saw that the international law of the environment is made in part by analogizing from municipal law. In fact, the borrowings from municipal law are mainly in the customary part of the international environmental law. A couple of examples will serve to illustrate this point. In assessing when and where marine pollution exists, two criteria often used are "unassisted senses" and the amount of dissolved oxygen (DO). These criteria were first affirmed in domestic cases, *Missouri v. Illinois* (1906) and *New York v. New Jersey* (1921) (Barros and Johnston 1974, 13). Besides, some of the doctrines in municipal law borrowed into the international law of pollution were negligence (or fault), strict (or absolute) liability, nuisance, riparian rights, and trespass (p. 22).

In the *Trail Smelter* case, the tribunal also discussed some of the domestic cases—*Missouri v. Illinois* (1906), *New York v. New Jersey* (1921), and *New Jersey v. New York* (1931)—dealing with water pollution. Then it cited *Georgia v. Tennessee Copper Company* (1907 and 1915) dealing with air pollution.

These borrowings from municipal law revealed something significant about one aspect in the "sources" of international law. It concerns "general principles of law" (Cheng 1993, 1–26), which are usually considered a third source, following custom and treaty, as is shown in the enumeration in Article 38 (1-c) of the ICJ Statute. It means that when neither treaty nor custom offer anything relevant for a legal situation so novel that there is simply no precedent in existing international law, a logical solution is to reach down to municipal laws in search of principles that might offer a guide (Lauterpacht 1970). In the past, the Soviet view, in disagreement with the West, always insisted that "general principles of law" meant general principles of international law (not domestic law).[3] In light of the development of the international environmental law, when borrowings from municipal law were made necessary precisely because of lacunae in existing international law, the Soviet view would make no sense.

One of the general principles of law originating in municipal law is that of good faith in the exercise of rights. Another relates to prohibitions on the abuse by a state of a right it enjoys under international law (cf. Cheng 1993, 121–136). Both these were invoked by international arbitral tribunals when they were considering environmental issues, including those in the classic *Fur Seals* arbitration (1893; for discussion see Sands 1995, 415–419). The abuse of rights doctrine provides a basis for the rule that a state must not interfere with river flow to the detriment of other riparian states. The doctrine is related to the rule requiring respect for the environment of other states or areas beyond national jurisdiction, as reflected in Principle 21 of the Stockholm Declaration and Principle 2 of the Rio Declaration.

Hard law and soft law. In the province of international environmental law, a consensus among scholars and international lawyers is that while certain norms form a body of "hard law," which establishes legally binding obligations, there is also a body of "soft law" (Birnie and Boyle 1992, 26; Palmer 1992, 269; Sands 1995, 103; Szasz 1992, 70). Soft law, though not binding, often plays an important role by pointing to the likely future direction of formally binding obligations, by informally establishing acceptable norms of behavior, and by "codifying" or possibly reflecting rules of customary law.

In international trade law, where soft-law norms are used extensively, there is a sizable literature on what soft law is and whether it is really law.[4] A similar situation obtains in international environmental law. Palmer (1992, 269) made an interesting observation about one particular way in which soft law can be useful: it allows politicians to change their minds. "Soft law," he commented, "is where international law and international politics combine to build new norms." The Helsinki Declaration on the Protection of the Ozone Layer (1989) provides an example of how a soft-law instrument helped pave the way for hard amendments to be adopted at the 1990 London meeting, affecting the 1987 Montreal Protocol. Not all "soft" instruments necessarily become "hard" law, nor is that an inherent aim of each one. But several have. For example, the UNEP's Cairo Guidelines and Principles for the Environmentally Sound Management of Hazardous Waste (1987) anticipated a partial "hardening" into the 1989 Basel Convention on the Control of Transboundary Movements of Hazardous Wastes (Birnie and Boyle 1992, 27f.).

The soft-law approach allows states more flexibility in dealing with problems on which they wish to retain freedom of action because the needed scientific evidence is either incomplete or inconclusive or because the economic costs are uncertain or too burdensome. Yet soft-law solutions allow commitments to be made pending further developments. In a new, largely uncertain, and surely unsettled field like the environment, the soft-law approach has proven to be highly useful and has in fact made important contributions in establishing a legal order. Partly as a result of the soft-law approach, the world has seen, in the two decades since the 1972 Stockholm conference, a remarkable growth not only in the vast array of environmental treaties as discussed above, but also in new legal concepts and principles that, as Birnie and Boyle (1992, 31) suggest, increasingly call into question traditional boundaries between "public" and "private" international law, and between international and municipal law. In the political sense, this development bespeaks the lowering of barriers between sovereign states and their fuller integration into a world community in the true sense of the phrase.

Conclusion

We have seen the unmistakable growth of a body of norms regulating the environment outside national (states') jurisdiction, despite the world's lack of a central legislature. Its growth is a spin-off of a combination of two prior conditions: a prevailing common purpose of the community, and a widespread willingness on the part of states to accept the premise that certain community interests, e.g., the integrity and security of the environment, including the global commons, should reign over the individual interests of states. The making of the international environmental law has progressed by stage. As we have seen, the development of a regime of the global commons began with the Antarctic, shifted to outer space, and finally moved to deep seabed. With the progression, the concept of a "common legacy of mankind" became further crystallized, until it was thoroughly established and enshrined in hard-law instruments.

Cynics may try to fault the law by raising the habitual question about its enforceability. My answer on this, as on other aspects of international law, is that it is the wrong question to ask. Since there is no central enforcement agency in our anarchic system, compliance, not enforcement, should be the question for us to ponder. Once the gaze is shifted to compliance, one would be amazed at how often, in the absence of an enforcement agency, states comply with the obligations created under environmental as well as general international law. Just as the absence of a central legislature did not prevent the rise of an environmental law, the lack of an enforcement agency has not changed the fact that most of the obligations are more often than not met in state practices. Over the years, a range of techniques, drawing on other developments in international law, have been adopted and used to improve compliance with environmental obligations. One such mode of settlement in the event of a dispute over compliance is arbitration, following the tradition created by the classic *Fur Seals* arbitration of 1893. We already have a body of jurisprudence growing out of various environmental disputes submitted to international dispute resolution arrangements. These include disputes in transboundary air pollution (e.g., *Trail Smelter*); the diversion of the flow of international rivers (*Lac Lanoux* arbitration; *Diversion of Water from the River Meuse*); conservation of fishery resource (*Fisheries Jurisdiction* cases); and responsibility for rehabilitation of mined lands (*Yellow-Fin Tuna* case).

A more recent dispute between Hungary and Slovakia is instructive on the wide range of mechanisms available in disputes over environmental obligations. In a 1991 application, Hungary unilaterally referred to the International Court of Justice its dispute with Slovakia over the Gabcikovo-Nagymaros dam and the diversion of the Danube. Then the two countries explored other forums, including arbitration, conciliation by the EC Commission, and the emergency procedures of the Conference of Security and Cooperation in Europe (CSCE). Finally, they agreed to return to the ICJ in a new but joint application in 1993, which superseded the one filed by Hungary two years before (Sands 1995, 142).

Clearly the question of dispute settlement is closely related to, and reveals a lot about, the question of compliance with environmental guidelines. Another way to assess the compliance is to examine the practical "impact" of the environmental treaties on environmental quality. Although some qualitative measures may be used to gauge the effectiveness of these treaties (Haas 1995, 409), my own view is that the task of ascertaining whether the environmental treaties have resulted in a tangible improvement in environmental quality is still an elusive undertaking. We know of no successful effort at measuring the effectiveness of environmental treaties in bringing about environmental improvement. Even to come up with a workable methodology would not be easy. One way would be to look at the number of subsequently enacted domestic legislations aimed at, for example, the preservation of certain resources or the reduction in hazardous waste dumping, using the standards set by an environmental treaty a state has signed as a guide. But, although quantitative, this method can only measure a treaty's impact on domestic environmental policy, which is not exactly the same as impact on international environmental quality.

More important than compliance and treaty effectiveness is still what the rise of the international environmental law signifies for the global structure and tenor of international relations. A number of observations may be derived from the above discussion.

First, there seems to be a tendency for a decline in the role of the state, as in matters concerning environmental damages calling for payment of compensation or other reliefs. As Kiss (1992, 329) notes, international practice concerning liability in the environmental field shows a distinct change in the global system. Liability in traditional international law is generally understood as resulting from damage done by one state to another, creating an obligation for the first state to repair the damage, usually by paying an adequate compensation. International practice in the area of environmental protection, however, shows a departure from this traditional standard. States now prefer to transfer the problem of compensation for environmental damages from the interstate to the interindividual level. In certain instances, procedures are now available that allow the victim of environmental damage to seek compensation by suing the source (offender) directly, who is generally a private person.[5] Article 235 of the 1982 Convention on the Law of the Sea reflects this trend: "States shall ensure that recourse is available in accordance with their legal systems for prompt and adequate compensation or other relief in respect of damage caused by pollution of the marine environment by natural or juridical *persons* under their jurisdiction" (emphasis added).

Second, there seems to be a diminution of the place of state interests and of the state's role in espousing them relative to the interests of the human community. As manifested in the international environmental law, the recognition of common interests of humankind is an ongoing process. More and more legal instruments (e.g., treaties) embrace this idea of a body of common interests of the community over the states. Rather than just proclamations in the abstract, the environmental regime established by treaty suggests that the common interests of humankind are identifiable and are to be materialized in specific fields, such as the deep seabed's mineral resources, the moon and other celestial bodies, and the world's cultural and natural heritage (Kiss 1992, 335).

Third, the main thrust of the legal instruments underlying the environmental regime seems to be focused not on the sharing of benefits but on the conservation and, as a consequence, obligations of the present holders of such goods; they should be considered trustees acting on behalf of all humankind (Kiss 1992, 335). In this sense, the concept of the common heritage of humankind implies the conservation of the ozone layer, tropical forests, the global climate, and genetic diversity, among others.

Fourth, as is shown in the report of the Brundtland Commission (1987), the notion of the common legacy of humankind has an intertemporal and intergenerational implication. One of the principles proposed in the commission report is that of "intergenerational equity," to the effect that "states shall conserve and use the environment and natural resources for the benefit of present and *future generations*" (p. 348) (emphasis added). Thus, like never before, international relations today are concerned with intergenerational equity (Choucri 1995, 487).[6] Our international system, perhaps because of the political awareness that has come with our sharpened environmental keenness, has become what Choucri and North call a "distributive mechanism" (p. 480).

Telescoping all this, it is not hard to see a simultaneous ascendancy of community interests and the status of the individual on the one hand, and the decline of the state on the other—in terms of the latter's role in asserting its own interests and espousing a cause on behalf of its subjects (such as in seeking compensation for environmental damage). Even more than any other reason, this change calls into doubt the adequacy of the Neorealist paradigm, if it still adheres to a state-centric world characterized by unmitigated systemic anarchy.

Notes

1. Webster's *New World Dictionary,* 3d College ed. (Cleveland: Merriam-Webster, 1988), 454.
2. Many of these treaties are listed in Sands (1995, xix–xl).
3. The most authoritative exposition of this position was given by G. I. Tunkin; see Ramundo (1967, 65).
4. See, for example, "A Hard Look at Soft Law," *ASIL Proceedings* 82 (1988):371; John King Gamble, "The 1982 United Nations Convention of the Law of the Sea as Soft Law," *Houston Journal of International Law* 8 (1985):37.
5. World Commission on Environment and Development, Experts' Group on Environmental Law, *Environmental Protection and Sustainable Development, Legal Principles and Recommendations* (The Hague: Martinus Nijhoff, 1987), 118.
6. Edith Brown Weiss has written extensively on this question. See her "Intergenerational Equity: A Legal Framework for Global Environmental Change," in Weiss (1992, 385–412). See also her *In Fairness to Future Generations: International Law, Patrimony, and Intergenerational Equity* (Irvington, NJ: Transactional Press, 1989); and her "Our Rights and Obligations to Future Generations for the Environment," *AJIL* 84 (1990):198ff.

Part 5

Summary and Conclusions

9

Three Perspectives in International Relations: Hobbesian, Kantian, and Grotian

It should be clear by now that this book is concerned not only with the interplay of international law and politics, but also with the question of whether contemporary International Relations scholars acknowledge this crucial interplay in their interpretation of the Westphalian system. As we have noted, especially in Chapters 3, 6, and 7, the politics/law interplay also extends to the realm of international organization (as typified by the United Nations). Since the IR field is currently dominated by the Neorealist school, I have singled out the Neorealist paradigm as an object of my criticisms of the IR field's neglect of the role and reach of international law in the domain of international politics.

Inquiring into the question of order in world politics, a Realist (Bull[1] 1977, 24–27) observed that, throughout the history of the modern multistate system, there have been three competing traditions of thought:

- The Hobbesian or realist tradition, which views international politics as a state of war
- The Kantian or universalist tradition, which sees at work in international politics a potential community of mankind
- The Grotian or internationalist tradition, which views international politics as taking place within an "international society," or a community within which order is possible because its members crave order in conditions of anarchy

These three perspectives (or traditions) anticipated the subfields of international politics, international organization, and international law, which constitute most of the IR field.[2]

In this chapter, I address these three perspectives and link them to the three named IR subfields they anticipated or inspired. I do so not for their own merits, but to ascertain whether the three domains can be viewed together to provide a more comprehensive understanding of IR as an integral field.

The Hobbesian Perspective: Realist International Politics

The Hobbesian tradition sees international relations as a state of war of all against all, as in the state of nature described in *Leviathan* (Hobbes 1909, 94–98). International relations is an arena in which each state is pitted against every other in a zero-sum game. Peace, in this view, is a period of recuperation from the last war and preparation for the next.

From the methodological standpoint, what led Hobbes to his pessimistic conclusion was his point of departure, i.e., human nature and, more specifically, the "equality of ability" that Mother Nature bestows on individual human beings. In Hobbes's logic, this equality of ability begets diffidence, which breeds war. The Hobbesian prescription for international conduct is that the state is free to pursue its goals in relation to other states without moral or legal restrictions of any kind. Preoccupied with conflict, the Hobbesian view rules out any possibility of a harmony of interests among peoples and nations.

Hobbesian thought is linked to modern realism by its pessimistic premise of human nature. Morgenthau (1985, 4–7), the best-known spokesman for modern realism, began his discourse on the "Six Principles of Political Realism" in these words: "Political realism believes that politics, like society in general, is governed by objective laws that have their roots in *human nature*" (p. 4; emphasis added). From this premise, Morgenthau derived the rest of his principles, including his famous thesis regarding national interest defined in terms of power. In light of human egoism, Morgenthau echoed Weber's observation that "interests (material and ideal), not ideas, dominate directly the actions of men" (p. 11). Recalling the Hobbesian postulate about humanity's equality of ability, Morgenthau then proceeded to pontificate about the necessity, and virtue, of the balance of power as a statecraft for coping with nations' competitive drive for power.

Political realism, according to Morgenthau (p. 13), counsels the disaggregation of the moral aspirations of a particular nation from the "moral laws that govern the universe," setting the stage for Realist and Neorealist[3] belief in the inherent conflict of a nation's interests and those of the community.

Citing the Hobbesian state of nature, where "life is . . . nasty, brutish, and short," Waltz (1979, 103) obliterates incidence of violence as a valid criterion distinguishing the international system from domestic systems.

Nevertheless, he holds out self-help (i.e., use of force) as a constant or inherent attribute in our anarchic system. Conflict is the rule, rather than the exception. Recalling the Hobbesian denial of harmony of interests among men and nations, Waltz (1959, 160) asserts:

> In anarchy, there is no automatic harmony. . . . Because each state is the final judge of its own cause, any state may at any time use force to implement its policies. Because any state may at any time use force, all states must constantly be ready either to counter force with force or to pay the cost of weakness.

The dictum "every state is the final judge of its own cause" is ominous—just as it is crucial to Neorealism—in that it rules out acceptance by states of any community-centered interests and any body of norms, moral or legal, held out by the community as obligatory on all states in their mutual relations.

Not all realists, however, are agreed on the exclusion of normative principles. Carr (1939) believed that "politics are made up of two elements—utopia and reality" (p. 93). He called the theory separating the spheres of politics and morality superficial, because it evades the "insoluble problem of finding a moral justification for the use of force" (p. 100). In contrast to Hobbes, who proceeded from the premise of human nature, Carr arrived at his conclusion from the perspective of how the individual acts in groups, not in isolation. "Man," Carr began his chapter on politics, power, and morality, "has always lived in groups" (p. 95). Man in society, he counseled, reacts to his fellow men in two opposite ways. "Sometimes he displays *egoism,* or the will to assert himself at the expense of others. At other times, he displays *sociability,* or the desire to cooperate with others, to enter into reciprocal relations of goodwill and friendship with them" (p. 95; emphasis added). Obviously, Waltz and Waltzian Neorealists looked only at the egoism of nations, not their sociability.

Realist Bull (1977, 51f.), agreeing with fellow realist Carr, considered order both possible and desirable in the anarchic system, which actually reflects the coexistence of all three elements: war and struggle for power, transnational solidarity and conflict, and cooperation.

In an eloquent critique of the "poverty of Neorealism," Ashley (1986, 290) noted that "Neorealism's totalitarian implications are only partly to be discovered in its celebration of *power before order*" (emphasis added). Placing power over order is precisely the reason international law is factored out of the Neorealist paradigm of international politics. More specifically, it is why Neorealism defines the international system purely in terms of power and its distribution, to the exclusion of law, morality, and ideas. Throughout this book, I have tried to demonstrate the inadequacy of the

Neorealist single-factor (power alone) analysis, by showing the indispensable role and reach of international law in international politics. Power, as we have seen, does not at all times prevail over the community's urge for order.

I would like to add a footnote that even in Hobbes there is allowance for the mitigation of the war of everyone against everyone else. In his *Leviathan* he speaks of "the passions that incline men to peace." These passions are "fear of death, desire of such things as are necessary to commodious living; and a Hope by their Industry to obtain them" (Hobbes 1909, 98). Waltz and the Waltzians speak of no such passions that would incline nations to peace. The Waltzian pessimism about the jungle in the Westphalian system even exceeds that of Hobbes in the proverbial state of nature. Writing about the international state of nature, Waltz (1988, 39–52) had this to say: "In the anarchic domain, a state of war exists if all parties lust for power. But so too will a state of war exist if all states seek only to ensure their own safety. . . . In an anarchic realm, peace is fragile . . . the price of inattention or miscalculation is often paid in blood.

I do not dispute the fact that, combining power and structuralism, Waltz has constructed a parsimonious theory that is neat and logically self-enclosed, nay, hermetically sealed. But, with due respect, I have doubts about its empirical application or actual explanatory power. Where, in the real world, would one actually find *empirical* referents for the kind of system Waltz has painted in blood and tears? The only possible place might be the Middle East, as Waltz (1979, 66) himself inadvertently reveals the locality on his mind: "Whether in the second century before Christ or in the twentieth century after, Arabs and Jews fought among themselves and over the residues of northern empire, while states outside of the arena warily watched or actively intervened." Is it possible that the Waltzian Neorealist model of the Westphalian system is a caricature (analogue) of the Middle Eastern subsystem writ large? If true, it may explain why Waltzian Neorealism allows no place for international law or, for that matter, morality or what we have called "systemic values," because these, if one could generalize, would seem irrelevant in contemporary Middle Eastern international politics. But it may also explain why the Waltzian theory does not hold up to the real world at large—unless, of course, it could be assumed that the world at large is but a macrocosm of the Middle East in terms of relations between nations.

Keeping in view the Hobbesian allowance for some "passions" inclining nations to peace, it seems to me that the kind of egoist behavior ascribed to nations in the Waltzian Neorealist rendition of the Westphalian "state of nature" is more Hobbesian than Hobbes's view as expressed in *Leviathan*.

The Kantian Perspective: Liberalism and International Organization

At the other extreme from the Hobbesian view, the Kantian or universalist tradition sees the essential nature of international politics to lie, not in conflict among states, but in the transnational social bonds that link the individual human beings who are the subjects of states. In the Kantian view, international relations ultimately boil down to the relationship among all men and women in the human community. The Preamble of the UN Charter, which begins with the words "We the *peoples* of the United Nations . . ." is indisputably Kantian in spirit (cf. Claude 1964, 46).

Within the human community, according to the universalist view, the interests of all nations are one and the same. Hence, peace is indivisible, just as the global commons are the shared legacy of humankind. International politics from this perspective is not purely distributive, but is a cooperative, not zero-sum, game.

Kant (Frederich 1948, 20, 51, 239) distinguishes between "noumenal" awareness (things in themselves) and "phenomenal" experience (things as perceived and constructed in our mind). This suggests the duality of two realms or, in Kant's words, "the starred heaven above me and the moral law within me." Noumenal awareness reveals the basic equality of all humans and the priority of human freedom, especially the freedom to be moral (Cassirer 1947, 40–42).

While "the natural state is one of war" (Kant 1957, 10), the central problem for Kant is to create conditions in the phenomenal world that make it possible to provide the *freedom to act morally*. Reduced to the simplest terms, the Kantian model called for the creation of a federation of liberal republics as the foundation for "perpetual peace" (Huntley 1996, 48). The idea of a league of democracies was revived in Wilsonianism, which inspired the building of a modern collective security system institutionally anchored in universal peace organizations such as the League of Nations and its successor, the United Nations (Claude 1964, 46). While this conviction about democracies' disposition toward peace distantly anticipated the current interest in "liberal peace" (Huntley 1996), it also inspired the UN Charter provision (Art. 4[1]) that membership in the United Nations is open only to "peace-loving states."

The Kantian-Wilsonian idealist paradigm proceeded from two *institutionalist and globalist* assumptions: the development of formal intergovernmental organizations was at least as relevant to concerns about international order (and justice) as the development of less formal or demanding modes of interstate cooperation; and any efforts at international institution building had to focus on the global level (Rochester 1995, 201f.). The development of formal machinery and rules is, quite appropriately, the concern of international organization (IO).

For the uninitiated, let me suggest that three general principles have guided and pervaded modern human efforts at international organization, as concertized in the United Nations system: universality (globalism), regionalism, and functionalism. Since peace is indivisible, the response to threats to peace (a fortiori aggression) must therefore be "all against one," i.e., action by all the community against that one aggressor (cf. Chapter 3). Like the League of Nations before, the United Nations is based on such a globalist conviction.

Regionalism is an alternative to (but not substitute for) globalism. Because the world is diverse and unwieldy, the universality of any world organization almost inevitably tends to weaken its appeal to particular loyalties and particular interests (Carr 1945, 45). However, within a region, adaptation of international solutions to real problems can be intelligently carried out, because commitments by the area states to each other can be confined to manageable proportions and sanctioned by clearly evident bonds of mutuality (Claude 1964, 95). A good example is found in Europe and, to a lesser extent, Latin America. Not only does the UN Charter (Arts. 52–53) provide for a role by "regional arrangements" for peace (such as the OAS and NATO), it also mandates a role for functional agencies such as the regional commissions under the Economic and Social Council. Other organizations such as the ASEAN, EEC, OAU, OECD, and OECS are examples of international governmental organizations (IGOs) outside the United Nations framework, but conceived in the spirit of regionalism.

Functionalism is a principle of international organization that postulates that development of international economic and social cooperation is a major prerequisite for the ultimate solution of political conflicts and the elimination of war (Claude 1964, 345). The functionalist theory, as first developed by Mitrany (1946), is predicated on the assumption that the cooperative habit once developed in the economic and social (hence, functional) spheres will spill over into the political relations among states. Mitrany hypothesizes the development of successive layers of functional collaboration, in a process that would "suffuse the world with a fertile mingling of common endeavor and achievement" (p. 63). Mitrany calls this process "federation by installments," which in Frederick L. Schuman's felicitous phrase was called "peace by pieces" (Claude 1964, 347). A combination of the functionalist and regionalist principles underscore the efforts at regional integration (cf. Haas 1968), as typified by the evolution of the European Union.

As academic fads and fashions come and go, international organization as a focus of study has fallen out of favor in the aftermath of the behavioral revolution in the political science discipline and, especially, after the rise of

Waltzian Neorealism. As Kratochwil and Ruggie (1986, 753) graphically put it, "The leading doctors have become biochemists and have stopped treating and in most cases even seeing patients." Reflecting the rising influence of Neorealism, most IR scholars now tend to either avoid mention or treat sparingly the subject of IO in their writings and analyses of important questions in International Relations. So finds Rochester (1995, 202f.) from a survey of the literature. This contrasts, ironically, with a clear contrary trend in the irreversible proliferation of IGOs, numbering over a thousand in the contemporary global system (Jacobson, Reisinger, and Mathers 1986, 141).

The United Nations may be primitive, flawed, and fragile, but as an exemplification of the international organization approach and process, it is a very real part of the life of relations among nations. The United Nations is an important stage on which much of the drama of international politics unfolds in our time and an important forum where important new rules of conduct are written—for example, in the issue areas of decolonization, human rights, and environmental law. In short, the United Nations is the only global organization charged with and capable of effecting peaceful change (Art. 14, UN Charter; Hanrieder 1968, 281f.).

The Neorealist neglect of IO is unfortunate. It offers its fervent critics yet another ground for attacking its irrelevance ("poverty"?), owing to its inability to explain the totality of politics unfolding on the world stage at large, except in the narrow sphere of instinctive conflict and struggle.

The Grotian Perspective: International Law and World Order

The Grotian internationalist tradition stands between the realist and universalist traditions (Wright 1955, 222; Bull 1977, 51f.). Contrary to the Hobbesian tradition, the Grotians contend that the states are not engaged in simple struggle, like gladiators in an arena, but are limited in their conflicts by common rules and institutions. This characterization of the behavior of states emanates from the Grotian premise that international politics does not take place in a vacuum or wilderness, but in an international society, however primitive a community it is (Masters 1964, 607). In contrast to the Kantian or universalist perspective, the Grotians accept the Hobbesian premise that sovereign states (rather than individuals) are the principal actors in international politics (Bull 1977, 51f.).

As explained in Chapter 1, this discussion accepts the Neorealist paradigm based on systemic anarchy, but believes that there is a place for law in such a system. In fact, the need for order is made all the more acute precisely because of the anarchy of the system. Throughout the book, the goal has been to show that international law is not incompatible with systemic anarchy; and its role in ensuring a modicum of stability and facilitating international exchange—i.e., the transfer of goods, people, capital, and technology across national boundaries—is an indispensable one. International law is in fact a creation of the society of states to meet their mutual need for order, for the sake of which they are willing to set confines on their freedom of action relative to each other and to the community at large. In a feedback loop, the law in turn becomes part of the context within which the society of states must act, constraining them through a set of rules that alter the incentives, costs, and benefits of various possible choices and behaviors (Starr 1995, 301).

Despite the Neorealist neglect of law, it is possible to reconcile international law with the anarchic system as described in the Neorealist paradigm. If we can pick anarchy, self-help, and freedom of states as the three key concepts summing up the Neorealist paradigm, their counterpart key words in international law are sovereignty, independence, and equality. There is a close correspondence between these two parallel sets of epithets: Because the system is *anarchic,* each state is *sovereign* (having no higher authority over them). Each state in an anarchic system has to fend for itself through *self-help,* which is as much an indicator as a result of its *independence.* And the fact that each state enjoys as much *freedom* as any other in the anarchic system connotes *coequality* among states. Thus, the three conceptual pillars of international law—sovereignty, independence (which also means noninterference by other states), and equality—are all derivatives of the anarchic system of states, Neorealist nonrecognition of this fact notwithstanding.

In fact, in the positivist sense, the bulk of international politics can be said to consist in the alternate assertion and limitation of state sovereignty, employing an international law concept. Certain phenomena in international relations may be described variably in terms of what happens to state sovereignty, for example: the transcending of state sovereignty—as in the emergence of a transcendental entity such as the European Union; the circumvention of sovereignty—as in the boundaryless prevalence and evasiveness of the multinational corporations (MNCs); the harnessing of sovereignty—as in the rise of human rights protection; the splintering or undercutting of state sovereignty—as found in the breakup of the Soviet Union and Yugoslavia and the separatist challenges in Chechnya; and the enlightened constraint of sovereignty—as required in environmental protection. In each of these genres, there is an inevitable role of international law in the playing out of international politics.

The sanctity of international law, or the law's obligatory basis, is intractably linked to the sovereignty of states. In the positivist theory, the basis for obligation derives from self-interest, utility, and consent (Starr 1955, 300). Treaties are binding because the contracting parties have given their consent to be bound by the mere act of signing and ratifying the treaties, under the principle of *pacta sunt servanda*. The obligatory character of customary norms comes from repeated practice, which conveys a sense of obligation (known as *opinio juris*) to follow the same norm with regularity and consistency. Ultimately, positivist international law[4] is based on the consent of states, whose sovereignty is upheld and restricted by a body of norms by which they have generally consented to be bound.[5]

This situation is consistent with the concept of an anarchic system made up of sovereign states. The consent by states to observe a body of norms, even if those norms circumscribe states' conduct internationally, is an option equivalent to an act of self-help that sovereigns voluntarily take in an anarchic system.

Thus viewed, there is nothing in the Neorealist model of the Westphalian system that should deny a place, and role, to international law. Its exclusion from the model, therefore, is not compelled by the Neorealist logic. Nor is it justified by the reality of international politics, as the preceding chapters have illustrated.

International Law in the Hobbesian System of International Politics

In a timeless piece written long before the rise of Neorealist dominance, Hoffmann (1961) identified the intricate relationship between international law and international systems. Without duplicating his lengthy arguments, I would single out a few of his observations for amplification and update: international law reflects the *structure* of the world system; international law reflects the pattern of power and the political culture of the main actors; extraneous factors such as technological change also affect the shape of international law; and the law reflects the relations among the units of the international system (in Falk and Handreider 1968, 95).

These observations have found empirical corroboration in this book. For example, we have discussed how international law has evolved over time, mirroring the transformation in the structure of the international system from the nineteenth century balance of power to the postwar bipolar world (Chapter 1); how during the Cold War era the law underwent new rule-making endeavors that enshrined self-determination as an overriding "human right," responding to the demands of a growing Third World—in league with the Soviet bloc—for speedy decolonization (Chapter 7); and how advance in technology has complicated the application of international law in the control of armaments (Chapter 4) and how it has called for an environmental law (Chapter 8).

As regards the last link on Hoffmann's list—that international law reflects the normal conduct of relations among sovereign states—we have also seen how international law, in addition to the above functions, supports and guides international political relations in the following ways: by mitigating the security dilemma (Chapter 2); by controlling the self-help reflex (Chapter 3); by enhancing the chances of war avoidance and facilitating dispute settlement (Chapter 4); and by constraining the effects of anarchy by delineating the jurisdictional boundaries of sovereign states, guiding the grant or denial of immunities to foreign sovereigns and their diplomatic and consular agents, and defining the extent of state responsibility (Chapter 5). In all four functions, international law plays the role of a "facilitator," not just a "reflector." This finding confirms Burley's (1993, 220) point about the "facilitative properties" of international law.

Considering that there is no central legislature in the anarchic system, the growth and development of international law in the conduct of normal international relations, stretching across all these and other areas, is truly amazing. International law not only regulates the status quo, but also displays an enormous self-renewing ability in response to changes in the international system, including changes in the tenor of relations among the system's units (states) and new demands posed by the changing political, socioeconomic, and ideological contexts in which those relations take place.[6]

In Hoffmann's (1961, 96f.) formulation, it is possible to distinguish three kinds of international law in stable systems: (1) the law of political framework—i.e., the network of agreements that define the major conditions, and certain of the cardinal rules, of the political game among the states; (2) the law of reciprocity, which defines the conditions and rules of international relations in the practical issue areas, as circumscribed by the prevailing law of the political framework; and (3) the law of community, which deals with problems that can best be handled not on the basis of a reciprocity of interests of states understood as separate and competing units, but on the basis of a community of action transcending narrowly conceived national interests, e.g., problems of a technical or scientific nature for which borders are irrelevant.[7]

I shall discuss these three kinds of international law separately to illustrate how each interfaces with international politics.

Law of Political Framework

In the nineteenth century, the world was Eurocentric in that international politics was either dominated by European powers or played out mostly among European actors, both on the continent and in their overseas empire-building competition. The law of the political framework was the law of the

Concert. It was the instrument of the society of the major powers for the supervision of the small states and the control of the individual ambitions of each member. But the law was a balancing technique, not a way of overcoming the balance. Many rules merely expressed the independence of states in such a system (Hoffmann 1961, 103) or upheld the powers' overseas interests in Africa, Asia, and Latin America, much of which was "outside" the system. For instance, Turkey ("the Porte") was not admitted to the "public law of Europe" until after the Crimean War in 1856. An Anglo-Franco-Austrian treaty, of April 15, 1856, agreed to consider any infringement of Turkish integrity or independence a *causa belli* and a cause for consultation among the three European powers (Albrecht-Carrie 1958, 93). The agreement, in other words, formally accepted Turkey, the former "outsider," into the then Eurocentric international system.

In our time, however, the law of political framework is the UN Charter, the ideology and reality of which is superimposed on the state system, to some extent as both its complement and supplement (Falk 1975, 69). Most important, the Charter ushered in a new era—and UN practice has confirmed it—in which sovereign equality of all states gains distinct ascendancy, while a limited Big Power condominium is reserved mainly in the security domain. Such peculiar symbiosis is reflected in the respective roles played within the UN by the General Assembly and the Security Council. Unlike in the League of Nations, the unanimity rule is dispensed with, except in the Security Council, where each of the five permanent members wields a veto on substantive issues (Art. 27[3]). Characteristically, the council is given the "primary responsibility for the maintenance of international peace and security" under the Charter (Art. 24). The substitution of majority rule for unanimity rule in the United Nations (except on matters involving the veto in the council) bespeaks, both figuratively and realistically, the advent of quasi-parliamentary diplomacy beyond the traditional mode of bilateral and conference diplomacy. This new modality is duplicated in other international organizations, including NATO. And in the 1990s, parliamentary diplomacy became a permanent fixture in the institutions of the European Union (Sbragia 1992, 77–105). Furthermore, the idea of universality inherent in the Charter also signifies an acknowledgment that there is no longer any state that is "outside" the world system.

Instead of a concert of the major powers supervising the small states as during the nineteenth century, the political framework after the advent of the UN Charter supports the diffusion of sovereignty and respect for sovereign equality. The former has come about following the disintegration of larger units into an ever growing number of smaller political entities (Friedmann 1964, 31). This trend continued into the 1990s, although in the more recent cases it was due to the breakups in Eastern Europe, including the implosion of the Soviet empire. The trend was only partially offset by the conglomeration of sovereign states into a larger superentity, the European Union.

Respect for sovereign equality, which is highlighted perhaps to a higher degree than ever before in the political framework supported by the law of the Charter, means the leveling of the relative hierarchy among states found in the nineteenth-century system. The de facto pecking order of states gradually gave way to an increasing crescendo of sovereign equality. Juridically, the Charter makes sovereign equality the central premise of the United Nations organization (Art. 2[1]) and, by extension, an obligation for all states. Both the Charter (Art. 1[2]) and the Declaration of Principles of International Law Concerning Friendly Relations (annex to GA Res. 2625 [XXV]) upheld the "principle of equal rights and self-determination." Politically, the resultant decolonization was largely a tribute to this emphasis on self-determination and sovereign equality in the international law of the post-1945 era.

The decolonization process and its outcomes were dealt with in Chapter 7. The point to be made in the present context is that the breakup of colonial empires and the resultant rise of a multitude of Third World states is in itself an indicator of the leveling process among the system's units in the second half of the twentieth century. This political change was, in retrospect, partly due to the bisuperpower conflict, in which each side was conscientiously seeking wider support from the rest of the world. The arrival of a massive number of postcolonial countries, in turn, contributed to the further loosening up of the traditional grip of the major powers over the course of events in international politics. In sum, the underpinnings of the political framework of international relations in our time, which we have called the law of the Charter, can be appropriately characterized as an international law of sovereign equality, with these connotations.

In Chapter 1, we noted that landlocked nations, which would otherwise be denied transit rights under the pre-1960 international law, now enjoy the freedom of transit to and from the sea through the territory of neighboring transit states by all means of transport, as codified in CLOS III (Art. 125). This change is one concrete example of the distinct ascendancy of weak and disadvantaged states and the concomitant leveling of the relative hierarchy of states that existed in the Westphalian system.

Ironically, the trend toward greater respect of sovereign equality may face the fate of being interrupted, if not significantly modified, by the crucial transformation in the system following the disappearance of Soviet power that ushered in a monopolar system. The removal of restraint on superpower behavior and the end of the erstwhile bisuperpower competition for Third World support may weaken the rationale for greater respect on the part of the remaining superpower for the sovereign equality of the lesser states, although the results are hard to predict.

Considering the proliferation of nonstate actors, from multinational companies to IGOs, the law circumscribing the political framework of our time also has a transnational component cutting across public and private international law (Friedmann 1964, 65–67). Although the subject is too technical for us to go into, its mention is necessary, if only to acknowledge one more dimension to the interplay between law and politics in the changing structure of international relations.

Law of Reciprocity

In the era of the UN Charter, which coincided for four and a half decades with the Cold War, the law of reciprocity manifested a rare combination of what Friedmann (1964, 60–63) called the International Law of Coexistence and International Law of Cooperation. The former was so called because international law during the Cold War period concerned matters of life and death for everyone in the world. At a minimum, it provided a modus vivendi for the communist and anticommunist camps whereby routine relations could be maintained, including diplomatic and consular exchanges. Reflecting the complex intertwining of international politics and law, the ideological division of the two opposing camps—complicated further by the proliferation of sovereignties and consequent multiplication of clashing national interests—prevented the world from seeing its way through in its search for answers in international law on many practical issues. For instance, for the resolution of maritime issues, two Geneva conferences on the law of the sea were held, in 1958 and 1960. But the major agreement reached was on the continental shelf, i.e., an extension of exclusive national claims to resources hitherto included in the freedom of the seas. Neither in 1958 nor in 1960 was agreement achieved, or achievable, on the extent of territorial waters and other issues.

Conflicting claims on the question of the length of a coastal state's territorial sea—ranging from the communist bloc states' 12 miles, the Western states' 3 miles, and Japan's 1 mile to the 200 miles claimed by Chile and Peru—may have been due to geographical, economic-technological, and military factors (cf. Friedmann 1964, 61). But the ideological division, and the radiating tension because of it, certainly did not help in the world's quest for definitive answers in international law pertaining to these and other issues affecting the national interests of states in different camps. Typically, those answers did not come until late 1982, but only after nine years had been spent in a third law of the sea conference. By then, the Cold War protagonists had learned the dire need for negotiated settlement in lieu of confrontation. It was nineteen years after the first partial nuclear test ban treaty, fourteen years after the nuclear nonproliferation treaty (NPT), ten years after the anti–ballistic missile (ABM) treaty, and three years after SALT II had come into being.

Both superpowers, under the crushing burden of their escalating nuclear arms race, were deep "in crisis" (Krickus 1987). By then, both Washington and Moscow were finally convinced that despite their ideological disagreements, they had to mend their ways and learn how to look to a future of peaceful coexistence in the world. Even without a Gorbachev coming to power in Moscow three years thence, it was obvious that the way was paved toward "peaceful coexistence." The conclusion in 1982 of CLOS III, despite Reagan's last-minute demurrer, was a clear indication—and one more piece of convincing evidence—of the unmistakable culmination of what Friedmann (1964, 61) had called an International Law of Coexistence.

Law of cooperation. Friedmann (1964, 104) observed that in the nineteenth-century system, the law of cooperation progressed considerably in two areas: free trade and pacific settlement of disputes. We dealt with the latter question in Chapter 4; let us here examine how the post–World War II international law supports progress in the area of free trade.

In the post–World War II era, the foundation of a liberal structure of peace was laid with the inauguration of the Bretton Woods system and the GATT regimes. International lawyers may speak in isolation of the "regulation of international economic relations through law" (Kohona 1985). International political economy (IPE) scholars, on their part, speak only of the "politics of global economic relations" (Walters and Blake 1992). Rarely are the political and legal and economic strands of IPE discussed in the same breath. Here I provide evidence that there is always an interlinking of the legal and political strands (plus an economic strand in this case) in international relations, and demonstrate that we, as IR scholars, ought to recognize this simple yet important fact. It is not my intention to duplicate what Morgenstern (1986) has done in explicating the "legal problems of international organizations." If anything, the ensuing discussion is to elucidate the larger environment in which politics and law interact in the realm of post–World War II international relations.

The liberal international economic system (IES) established at the end of World War II reflected lessons from mistakes made in the settlements following the previous world war (Ray 1987, 15f.). The exorbitant reparations imposed on defeated Germany after World War I led to its economic ruin, catapulting Hitler to power in 1933 and, equally important, indirectly exacerbating the world's drift toward the Great Depression of the 1930s

(Shirer 1960, 57f.). The most decisive factor leading to the Great Depression was the competitive protectionist walls erected by the world's major trading nations, following the example of the United States' Smoot-Hawley Act of 1930 (Kindleberger 1986, 151). Therefore, the victors of World War II decided not only that there should be no reparations paid by the defeated enemy states, but also—and more important—that the postwar IES must be pro–free trade, antiprotectionist, and antimercantilist. The inauguration of the new IES coincided with the advent of the United Nations, whose mandate was broader than that of its predecessor, the League of Nations. The broader mandate made the United Nations a promoter of economic prosperity and social justice as well as a universal security organization and center for harmonizing international relations (Claude 1964, 58ff.). Inherent in the postwar liberal IES, which included the Bretton Woods system and the GATT, is a liberal "economic theory of peace" predicated on two assumptions: that free trade substantially reduces the number of targets to which force might be applied in the pursuit of state interests (Knorr 1975, 196); and that free trade increases the mutual vulnerability of actors (because of their increased interdependence), making them disinclined to use force (Keohane and Nye 1977, 28).[8]

As a result of the early onset of the Cold War, the Soviet bloc states either chose not to join or were kept out of the IES by the Western trading nations. Access to the World Bank and the International Monetary Fund (IMF) was not open to the Soviet bloc nations until after the end of the Cold War (Haus 1992). On the other hand, the post-1945 liberal IES has served well the economic interests of the industrial West and Japan. In fact, the free world's extraordinary economic progress owes a great deal to the flame of international trade, thanks to the GATT. Between 1950 and 1975 alone, the volume of trade expanded by as much as 500 percent, against an increase in global output of 220 percent (*Economist,* September 22, 1990, 7).

Much has been written about the GATT and the Bretton Woods system or, for that matter, the postwar IES as a whole. Yet very little has been said about what holds them together in the formal or legal, as opposed to organizational or procedural, sense: Both institutions were created and are held together by international agreements—the Bretton Woods system since 1944 and the GATT since 1947. A brief discussion here on the origins of these vital institutions can serve a number of purposes: it can provide a glimpse into the international law of cooperation; it can provide an example of the process by which the so-called international economic law is made in connection with the postwar IES; and, above all, it can illustrate that law is an indispensable part of institution building, just as the latter is an integral part of the political process in international relations.

• The Bretton Woods system comprises the IMF and the World Bank. The articles of agreement of the International Monetary Fund were drawn up in 1944 at the Bretton Woods conference. Membership is open to all countries. The articles have since been amended twice, in 1969 and 1978. The first amendment provided for the creation and allocation of Special Drawing Rights (SDR) to improve the liquidity of the international monetary system. The second amendment implemented a review of the fund's responsibilities and operations conducted from 1972 to 1976, following the collapse of the fixed exchange rate system. The collapse in turn had resulted from President Nixon's decision to discontinue the use of the dollar as the measure on which all other currencies, and gold value, were pegged at a fixed conversion rate. (Here is an example of further interlinkage of international and domestic politics.) The articles of the International Bank for Reconstruction and Development (IBRD, known as the World Bank) were drawn up at the same 1944 Bretton Woods conference. Membership in the World Bank, which began operation in 1946, is restricted to those members of the IMF that ratify the articles of the agreement creating the Bank and accept the terms laid down by it. The structure of both the IMF and the Bank is laid down in the respective agreements under which they were each created (Henkin et al. 1993, 1181–1195; UN, *Handbook 1991,* 143–145, 169ff.).

• The instrument that created the GATT is credited with being the first *global* commercial agreement in history (Henkin et al. 1993, 1165). By Resolution 13 (I) of 1946, ECOSOC decided to call an International Conference on Trade and Employment to promote the expansion of production, exchange, and consumption of goods. When the conference was held in Havana, it was presented with the proposal of an international trade charter, which contained sections dealing broadly with trade, investment, and economic matters, and, above all, the functions and administration of an International Trade Organization (ITO). As governments proved unwilling to approve the Havana charter, the ITO was stillborn. The results of the initial negotiations, conducted at meetings of the preparatory committee preceding the Havana conference, were incorporated into the General Agreement on Tariffs and Trade, or GATT, of October 30, 1947 (UN, *Handbook 1991,* 125). What had been intended as an interim arrangement came down as the principal instrument for regulating the international trade of the world's trading nations, at least until the projected inauguration of the WTO in January 1997.

Strictly speaking, the GATT itself has never entered into force. Instead, it has been applied in truncated form pursuant to the Protocol of Provisional Application, of October 30, 1947 (TIAS, No. 1700). In effect, what is now loosely called the GATT descended from a web of bilateral agreements, first made by the states that participated in the Havana conference. By 1992, some 105 countries had become members of the GATT (Henkin et al. 1993, 1398).

Technically, the GATT is defined in the text of the General Articles, not counting the tariff schedules that constitute the basic trade policy commitments of the contracting parties. These articles, thirty-eight of them covering about eighty pages, contain a number of detailed rules and obligations designed generally to prevent protectionism, or to prevent "beggar thy neighbor" trade policies that would be self-defeating if duplicated by other nations.

These articles in general purport to achieve a number of goals: to limit tariffs on particular items by the amount negotiated and specified in each party's tariff schedule; to prevent nontariff barriers (NTBs), such as quotas and stringent product inspection requirements, that would inhibit exports; to make "national treatment" an obligation by all GATT members; and to promote free competition by preventing and penalizing state subsidies and state trading (cf. UN, *Handbook 1991,* 125f.).

Unlike the IMF and the World Bank, the GATT lacks a permanent administrative structure. It has only a secretariat, located in Geneva. The GATT refers only to action by the contracting parties in case of complaints filed against a member for violating the articles. The action has generally been restricted to fact finding and mediation (Henkin et al. 1993, 1398). However, despite its institutional deficiency, the GATT has been more effective than it would seem in controlling tariff and nontariff violations, thanks to three principles at work: reciprocity, nondiscrimination, and transparency (*Economist,* September 22, 1990, 7).

In fulfilling its general objectives, the GATT uses a continuing program of consultations and negotiations designed to expand international trade and reduce or remove both tariff and nontariff barriers. To date, eight rounds of general negotiations have been held, including the last one, the Uruguay Round (Winham 1992, 43–106). The Uruguay Round, completed in April 1994 after eight years, was convened to revamp and revise the GATT. Instead, an agreement was reached at the end of the marathon conference to replace the GATT with a new World Trade Organization (WTO). The successor organization, though officially inaugurated on January 1, 1995, was to become fully operative in January 1997. During the interval the GATT continued to guide global trade, gradually winding down until the WTO took over. In many ways, the WTO is the realization of the 1940s vision of a strong international trade organization, with what promises to be a more effective dispute settlement mechanism (Crowley and Jackson 1996; Feinerman 1995, 17).

From this brief review of the Bretton Woods and GATT systems, what might be nonobvious to a casual IR observer is that while international commerce and finance are regulated by interstate agreements, the latter were established by political units (states) to create joint rules and thereby create stability and certainty in trading and related relations (Winham 1992, 23). Stability and certainty are especially important in international trade and financial transactions because the system itself is anarchic. In the absence of a world government, sovereign nations within the Westphalian system are relatively unconstrained in the pursuit of their own interests. International agreements create the necessary conditions and rules, including a structure of expectations—i.e., an international law of cooperation—whereby normal cooperative relations among sovereign states are possible within certain preset confines. In international trade, for instance, agreements such as GATT promote cooperation because they forestall *policy* competition by states and generate *private* competition. Thus, rules of order perform a necessary function by controlling anarchy and keeping egoistic behavior in check. From the operation of the GATT system, one thing remarkable, though nonobvious, is that agreements do not have to be formal; what counts is explicitly stated commitments. This, in fact, is nothing new in customary international law: in the *Eastern Greenland* case, the PCIJ actually held the Norwegian foreign minister to his oral commitment to his Danish counterpart. But to the layperson, this point should be emphasized as a reminder that international law does not just consist of formal tangible documents. Commitment (*opinio juris*) creates binding obligations in international relations.

The international law of cooperation is made up of more than multilateral agreements. It also comprises bilateral agreements—for example, the so-called friendship, commerce, and navigation (FCN) treaties; the principles of international commercial law developed from the ancient *lex mercatoria* (law merchant); and a whole body of decisions from international commercial arbitration (cf. Janis 1993, 273–282).

From a rational-choice point of view, the serial-conference modus operandi such as used by the GATT in its periodic negotiating rounds converts international trade relations into an iterated game, thus enhancing the chances of cooperation. Revisions of the rules, which may have occasioned the negotiating rounds, further contribute to making the game continue on less bumpy terrain.

The Law of Community

The last component of international law in Hoffmann's formulation is the law of community (1961, 97). This body of law also was expanded through agreements reached at countless conferences, conventions, and institutions, as well as through custom. We have seen this in our discussions on the emergence of an international environmental law (Chapter 8), and of a body of norms promoting the community's concerns in self-determination (Chapter 7) and human rights (Chapter 6). A compelling conclusion from these developments is that, in support of the ascendancy of community interests over those of individual states, there is an expanding body of norms that constitutes what can be truly called the *law of community* in the sense Hoffmann used the term.

One inevitable question is: Considering the disappearance of the Soviet bloc regimes, and with it a rudimentary source of the world's ideological dissension, what are the prospects of an accelerated expansion in the law of community? The answer is not so clear-cut. The main reason is that the ideological divide that existed during the Cold War was not the only factor that caused dissension and heterogeneity in the world. Our system today continues to display a structural disparity between different kinds of states: those that meet the traditional criteria of statehood—a population, a territory, a government, etc.—and those that are still governments in search of a country (e.g., the Palestine Liberation Organization Authority) or a nation (e.g., Lebanon). Then there is heterogeneity in the domestic regimes and levels of economic and technological development. What this means is that these domestic differences may affect the different things they value in an international law of community. Issues like environmental protection and decolonization are atypical; the wide consensus in these areas is not likely to be duplicated in other issue areas.

One encouraging development is the universal acceptance of the concept of *jus cogens,* or a body of peremptory norms that transcend, and override, the wills of national sovereignties. The concept, a legal emanation that grew out of the natural law school, was known to exist as *ordre public international* (Schwarzenberger 1965, 100–103) in Europe,[9] where the concept of and conviction about an international community has existed the longest in modern history. It was first broached as a guiding principle for global adoption during the course of negotiations for a convention on the law of treaties, or a codified body of norms governing the making and breaking as well as interpretation of international agreements. It was written into the 1969 Vienna Convention (1969) on the Law of Treaties as Article 53. *Jus cogens* is nonderogable and invalidates subsequent norms generated by treaty or by custom that militate against some larger community interests. An example is a hypothetical agreement contracted by two or more sovereign states to engage in, say, slave trade or narcotics trafficking. Under traditional, positivist international law, any two or more consenting sovereign states would have been perfectly within their right to enter into an agreement committing them to any such endeavor as they chose. But the *jus cogens* rule means that any such endeavor detrimental to larger community interests is null and void (cf. Charney 1993, 534). The International Court of Justice, in a case decided in 1969 (*North Sea Continental Shelf* cases), gave judicial cognizance to this principle: It explicitly put itself on record as not "attempting to enter into, still less pronounce upon any questions of *jus cogens*."

This is remarkable in the development of international law, with far-reaching effects. It signifies that states, at least the contracting parties of the 1969 Vienna Convention,[10] other states that accept the convention, and the International Court of Justice, now endorse and observe the dictate, as upheld by *jus cogens,* that the world community has interests and stakes that prevail over the sovereign wills of individual states.[11] It also gives hope that a "universal international law" (Charney 1993) is perhaps on the horizon.

Conclusion

For IR students, the preceding discussion confirms the following truisms, as expounded by Starr (1995, 310): that international law facilitates international communication, including diplomacy; that diplomacy (political relations and state practice) generates treaties and customary norms, which become more international law; and that both law and diplomacy create international organizations, which facilitate more diplomacy as well as more international law. In sum, international law is fundamentally important in the creation, maintenance, and operation of regimes, which generate and promote more international law. One truism not articulated in the Starr formulation is that international organizations, which in turn are creations of the political will of sovereign states, are solidified by treaties and may serve as a medium in the promotion of diplomacy and the creation of new legal norms. Thus, in a crosstemporal way, the Hobbesian, the Kantian, and the Grotian traditions are blended into one coherent whole. This is because "international relations" comprises all the relations of sovereign states and other actors, circumscribed as they are by a code of conduct called international law, oftentimes with the participation and assistance of international organizations, all of it taking place within the Hobbesian international system.

In view of the development of the international law of community, I would like to add that as the world community is politically disposed to accept some higher, overriding community interests (such as protection of environmental soundness and human rights), international law converts political consensus into legal commitment. Once corresponding norms are incorporated into international law, they enter into the vocabulary of international politics and, more important, provide the parameters within which sovereign states have to calibrate their behavior in order not to deviate from the expectations created by the preestablished code of conduct, as in the environmental area. Here is one more good reason, outside the reciprocity of bilateral relations, that law and politics solidify into an integral whole. Neorealism, with its eyes ever trained on the power structure of the Hobbesian system, overlooks the fact that international law, as described and explained in this book, is a product of the anarchic system, and that it functions despite the condition of anarchy. (Similarly, more or less the same can be said of international organization in relation to international politics.) We have seen that states under anarchy can and do create international laws and institutions, accord legitimacy to those laws, and comply with them (Nardin 1992; D'Amato 1985; Franck 1990; Kratochwil 1989; Milner 1991; Kocks 1994). Once this plain reality is understood and acknowledged, all the dispute between neorealism and neoliberalism is superfluous. The question is not whether the two traditions can be synthesized (Kegley 1995), but whether one is to recognize that the two traditions actually belong to a coherent whole. The answer would depend on whether one examines the reality of international relations as a whole organic forest or as individual clusters of trees.

Notes

1. In case of skepticism about my characterization of Hedley Bull as a realist, one who is familiar with the literature should know that Bull is consistently identified as a realist. Kegley (1995, 36), for example, lists Bull among the stalwarts of modern realists, along with Carr, Spykman, Herz, Aaron, Morgenthau, Kennen, Niebuhr, etc. Dougherty and Pfaltzgraff (1990, 256) explicitly place Bull in the same company as Neorealist Kenneth Waltz.

2. The field of International Relations has many components; this discussion, however, will be mainly confined to international law, politics, and organization—three of IR's older subfields. For a masterful treatise on IR as a field in analytical and pedagogical perspective, see Wright's classic (1955).

3. As throughout this book, Realism (capitalized) refers to the particular realist school associated with Hans Morgenthau, while Neorealism (capitalized) denotes the paradigm developed by Kenneth Waltz and his supporters and followers. The rationale is that there can be, and are, other strands of realist and neorealist thought.

4. "Positivist international law" conveys three alternative meanings: "as opposed to natural law," "state-centric" law, and treaty law.

5. The question may arise as to whether a state is nonetheless bound by a particular norm or body of norms that either existed before the state came into being or did not receive the state's specific consent. The answer is provided under the doctrine of generality, which means that general international law, which is binding on all states regardless of specific consent, does not depend on universal acceptance. As to how many states are needed to establish a threshold of "generality," or general acceptance, international law, being not an exact science, provides no definitive answer. Cf. Charney (1993); also see Friedmann (1964, 297ff.); and Lissitzyn (1965, 6).

6. For a good discussion of the linkage between changing contexts and inter-

national politics, and how changing contexts influence the way states act, see Gary Goetz, *Contexts of International Politics* (Cambridge: Cambridge University Press, 1994).

7. Hoffmann's tripartite classification of international law recalls a similar formulation by Schwarzenberger (1967, 11): (1) law of power (dealing with conflicting interests); (2) law of reciprocity (compatible interests); and (3) law of coordination (identical interests).

8. Realists disagree with this liberal theory of peace and reject generally the linkage between a liberal IES and international security. See Barry Buzan, "Economic Structure and International Security: The Limits of the Liberal Case," *IO* 38, 4 (fall 1984):597–624.

9. This should not be confused with the concept of "order public" in domestic law, such as Swedish law, as discussed in H. Eek, "Peremptory Norms and Private International Law," *Recueil des Cours* 139 (1973-II), Hague Academy of International Law; Christopher R. Rossi, *Equity and International Law* (Irvington, NJ: Transactional Publishers, 1993), 177.

10. By 1992, some ninety states had become parties to the 1969 Vienna Convention of the Law of Treaties, which entered into force in 1981. Text appears in *AJIL* 63 (1969):875. Other states not a party to the convention are bound by customary international law, into which *jus cogens* arguably is integrated, as implied in the ICJ's decision in the *North Sea Continental Shelf* cases.

11. For the benefit of the uninitiated, I must hasten to point out that *jus cogens* should not be confused with a "source" of international law. It is a precept that certain peremptory norms of general international law are not derogable by the sovereign will of states. The prohibition of such criminal acts as slave trade, narcotics trafficking, and unprovoked use of force is one such peremptory norm. For another, states are called on to cooperate in the observance of human rights, respect for sovereign equality, and respect for self-determination. See definition of *jus cogens* in Article 53 of the 1969 Vienna Convention on the Law of Treaties; *ILM* 8 (1969):679. Article 53 also provides that a peremptory norm can be modified *only* by a subsequent norm of general international law "having the same character." For a commentary on *jus cogens,* cf. *Oppenheim's International Law,* 9th ed. (1992), 7–8.

10

ORDER AMIDST ANARCHY: THE WESTPHALIAN SYSTEM INTO THE TWENTY-FIRST CENTURY

In this concluding chapter, we shall take a final look at the question of the interplay of international law and politics, and do some prospective thinking about the paths the Westphalian system and international law will take into the twenty-first century. The chapter begins with a brief review of the essential lessons that can be drawn from the discourses in preceding chapters.

A Retrospective Look

International Law and Order in Anarchy

Throughout this book, I have used international law and systemic order in close association. I have suggested that the urge for order by nation-states in the anarchic system invariably leads to the discovery of international law. Hence, international law is that body of norms created by nation-states to regulate the conduct of their mutual relations, in the interest of ensuring a modicum of stability and predictability (cf. Falk 1970, xii), or order in our language. While international law may not provide a fail-safe guarantee of order, states' craving for order in the anarchic system invariably leads to the creation of international law. In summing up, we need to spell out what specific needs international law is created to serve.

The answer lies in the law's intended functions. The usual enumeration in the literature includes the conflict-related functions of international law; its facilitative, management, and coordinative functions; and its communication function (Starr 1995, 308). In his seminal work, Coplin (1966, 169–176) sees international law as a quasi-authoritative communication system, a primary device for *socializing* policymakers to the prevailing consensus in the international system and its changing expectations as to the rights and duties of international actors. Starr (1995, 308) considers the communication function to be a prerequisite for the facilitative function. In Chapter 7, we saw how international law and UN practice *facilitated* the realization of self-determination and decolonization, precipitating a transformation of the international system. At the same time, the collapse of colonial empires and the consequential rise of massive numbers of postcolonial states effected crucial shifts in the system's power balance.

The lessons from the preceding chapters suggest that international law performs two additional functions: the mitigative function, and that of sanctifying the global community's interests over those of individual states, as in the area of environmental protection (Chapter 8). As to the mitigative function, we have seen that international law has the potential to:

- Mitigate the effects of the security dilemma (Chapter 2)
- Narrow the perimeter of self-help options open to states (Chapters 3 and 4)
- Restrict the discretion of states in going to war (*jus ad bellum*), and in the conduct of war (*jus in bello*); and impose an obligation, and prescribe the modes, for the pacific settlement of disputes (Chapter 4)
- Curb the arbitrariness of national human rights policies by holding up a set of international standards for emulation (Chapter 6)

Although not fully explored in this book, another mitigative function of international law is to constrain the mercantilist impulses of states by substituting an externally imposed market-centered regime (GATT/WTO) for the egoistic policies of individual states (Chapter 9).

The cumulative impact of this array of functions performed by international law is that, by containing the egoistic bent of states' policies, it *mitigates* the anarchic character of the Westphalian state system. Mitigation of anarchy is the beginning of order. The loop from the states' urge for order to international law and from there to a modicum of order in an otherwise anarchic system is thus complete. This much can be explained by Neorealist logic. Neorealism is correct in deducing systemic anarchy from the lack of a world government. But it errs in that it ceases to look beyond anarchy to the role and reach of international law in mitigating the extent of anarchy and in thereby changing its sweep and character.

International Law Versus Waltzian Neorealism

Neorealism (lower case), or structural realism that views international politics from a systemic (as opposed to a purely statist) perspective, has no reason to reject international law. The latter's place is inherently, though imperceptibly (to the undiscerning), compatible with the neorealist paradigm built on systemic anarchy, as I have demonstrated in this book. States' urge for order, in fact, owes itself to systemic anarchy. The neorealist logic can, indeed, explain the symbiotic existence and close interlinking of international law and politics under conditions of anarchy (Chapter 2).

But the Waltzian brand of neorealism (i.e., Neorealism)[1] rejects international law probably because, as was suggested in Chapter 9, of the empirical referent (Middle East) from which it derived much of its theoretical formulation. Onuf and Klink (1989) cogently point out that Waltzian Neorealism artificially dichotomizes anarchy on the one hand, and authority and rule on the other. The reason for the unnatural opposition, however, lies in Waltzian Neorealism's central premise, which is also the way it defines anarchy. According to its central premise, each state is the final judge of its own cause (Waltz 1959, 160); therefore, no state will accept constraints on its sovereignty (Waltz 1979, 91). This Waltzian premise is irreconcilable with—in fact, falsified by—findings on the behavior of nations under the influence of international law. For instance, we have seen that, with only rare exceptions, sovereign states have voluntarily accepted mutuality over unilateralism, and constraint on their self-help discretion (Chapter 3). They have created international organizations endowed with certain juridical competence to act, sometimes even in constraint of state sovereignty—for example, in the human rights and self-determination movements. Even the Soviet bloc and Third World countries accepted international law (Chapters 5 and 6) during the height of the Cold War.

Neorealism contends that anarchy inhibits cooperation between nations because of the relative gains inhibition (who gains more?). In reality, as in the area of adjudicated settlement of disputes, states accept international law because it mitigates the relative gains problem. As was shown in Chapter 4, states accept a third-party settlement mechanism for disputes because it changes the choice from either A's or B's terms (relative gains) to the choice between having a solution—even a perfunctory one—and having a stalemated nonsolution, which may be worse than an unsatisfactory one. Furthermore, international law regimes accentuate iteration, such as in the prolonged arms control process and the GATT's serial consultation rounds, converting single-act games into iterated games, in which the shadow of the future mitigates the uneven gains problem and engenders cooperation. When the iteration is long enough, such as in the history of customary norms, international law may transform norm-driven behavior into habit-driven behavior (Chapter 2).

We have also seen that infraction of international law by one state can be a sure imprimatur to copycat violations or counterviolations that may make the first violator worse off. An example was Nasserite Egypt's nationalization of the Suez Canal in 1956 in violation of the 1888 Constantinople

Convention. It triggered the Anglo-French expedition and Israeli occupation of the Sinai, both of which were, strictly speaking, violations of Article 2(4) of the UN Charter prohibiting the use of force other than in self-defense. If Nasser had hoped to use the push to boost his own sagging prestige, he found that he had lost more than he had imagined (Chapter 2). In this light, it is ultimately to the self-interest of states to act within the boundaries set by international law. Thus, when one speaks of system-induced behavior, international law desiderata are part of the system (along with its power distribution) that shapes the behavior of nations.

Waltzian Neorealism, with its exclusive concern with pure power, cannot explain many important developments in the international system. One example is Gorbachev's rapprochement with the West, not the least of which was his acceptance of the 1987 Intermediate Nuclear Force (INF) Treaty. Clearly it was not motivated by a concern for relative gains: the Soviet Union agreed to remove more missiles from the European theater than did the United States. As Koskowski and Kratochwil (1994) point out, the INF Treaty was widely interpreted as advantageous to the West. But the uneven gains did not stop Gorbachev from cooperating by signing the treaty. To anticipate a Waltzian riposte, I hasten to add that Gorbachev's downfall and the eventual Soviet demise was not due to his acceptance of a single treaty disadvantageous to his country.

Equally, Neorealism cannot explain the rise of an international environmental law, which graphically places community concerns over and above those of sovereign states. Much less can Neorealism account for the leveling of the relative hierarchy of states (Chapter 9), each allegedly positioned according to its power in the system's structure. Its explanatory power is especially inadequate when one considers that the leveling is disproportionate to the diffusion of power in the real world. Woefully for Neorealism, it failed to anticipate the collapse of Soviet power and, much worse, it cannot even provide a convincing explanation for its sudden collapse. This episode prompted Gaddis (1992–1993, 18) to pronounce the Neorealist-dominated IR field bankrupt.

This book is not intended to be a general critique of Neorealism. Nor do I want to join the fracas in the running debates between Neorealism and Neoliberalism.[2] As I said in Chapter 9, the two schools are mutually complementary, just as international politics, international law, and international organization are inseparable components of the universe we study as IR students. Our basic concern is rather that Neorealism of the Waltzian tradition painted itself into a corner by insisting that only power shapes the international behavior of states. In Chapter 9 we noted that Neorealism, though admittedly Hobbesian in its inspiration, evinces a pessimism that goes even beyond that in Hobbes's own view of the state of nature.

Whereas Hobbes still allowed for a few "passions" inclining men and nations to peace, Waltzian Neorealism sees only war and no letup whatsoever. My problem with Neorealism is not its "false promise" (Ruggie 1995), not even its undue pessimism, but its self-laceration. By that I mean that while it has all it takes to be a well-rounded theory, capable of accommodating both tangible power and intangible values as the motivating force for the behavior of states, Neorealism chose to shortchange itself by opting for monofactor (power) analysis. The presence of anarchy does not by and of itself permit inferences about the structure of the international realm, much less a system driven solely by power. To do so would be like the proverbial blind man determining that the elephant is the trunk he "sees" with his hand. An easy remedy, as we see it, would be for Waltzian Neorealism to live out its unrealized potential by giving to values the same weight it gives to power as a force shaping the system-induced behavior of states.

Kocks (1994, 535) argues that "since international law does exist, a theory of international politics should instead equate international structure with the legal principles regarded by states as imposing binding constraints on their strategic actions." This statement, Kocks admits, may strike some as fanciful, as it directly contradicts Neorealist arguments that have acquired the status of conventional wisdom. Nevertheless, he adds, "the assumption that international structure consists of legal norms is more firmly grounded in logic than contrary Neorealist assertions" (p. 539).

As we have seen in this book, Neorealism cannot explain why nations voluntarily choose restraint of their sovereignty (as in accepting the law of state responsibility); why they choose constraints of their sovereign interests in favor of some higher community interests (as in environmental control); and even why they choose restrictions on their self-help discretion (as in the proscription of all uses of force except in self-defense). Neorealist counterarguments may be that, despite the international law prescriptions, there is no central agency to guarantee enforcement; hence, states are in the final analysis motivated by power. We have seen, however, that despite the absence of enforcement (a typical consequence of anarchy), states observe international law norms more often than not; more states do so than do not; and these norms do matter in strategic decisionmaking.

In Chapter 4, we noted that while not all states accept the compulsory jurisdiction of the International Court of Justice, the revealing question to ask is: Why would *any* state voluntarily accept the court's compulsory jurisdiction after all? To do so would mean surrendering the immunity that a state is entitled to by dint of its sovereignty. In Neorealist parlance, it would mean surrendering the state's capacity to resort to self-help. It follows that no state would be expected to do so. Nonetheless, the fact is that as many as fifty-eight states (by 1994) have filed declarations under the "optional clause" (Art. 36.2 of the ICJ Statute) accepting the court's compulsory jurisdiction. Where does that leave us in terms of IR theory?

The truth is that power alone cannot adequately account for these types of nation-state behavior. It is patently necessary to supplement the power assumption with a concomitant assumption about normative desiderata (including norms of international law) as part of the invisible force motivating and guiding the behavior of nations in their mutual relations. To do so would not require a revamping of the Neorealist logic about anarchy and its consequence. The Waltzian reasoning, however, simply leaps from the anarchic premise to the conclusion about the power determinant, to the exclusion of all other factors that may equally mold the behavior of nations.

A Prospective View

To forecast the future of the Westphalian system is risky enough, but to venture a prevision of the likely directions of the global system and international law is a hazardous and thankless endeavor. What follows is only a sketch offered largely for heuristic purposes, to illustrate the importance of two cardinal premises that the juxtaposition of the two elements implies: (a) that there is a close relationship between the structure of the global system and international law—one subsuming the other in determining, along with power (i.e., power distribution across the system), how the units (nation states) are to behave; and (b) that changes in the system's structure will set the condition for corresponding changes in the norms governing relations within the system, according to which states in turn will recalibrate their strategic actions.

Structural Change in the New World Order: A Neorealist View

Elsewhere (Hsiung 1993, 3–5) I have defined the post–Cold War world order by referring to three key characteristics: multipolarity, decline in the salience of nuclear deterrence in favor of conventional deterrence, and rise of geoeconomics, or the mounting paramountcy of economic security over military security. This analysis is neorealist (lower case) in spirit, as it focuses on changes at the global level (instead of the unit level) and on the new power distribution across the system. The implications for international law are that the new multipolar system will provide an environment approximating a loose balance of power system, which will be conducive to international law (as explained in Chapter 2); attention of states in the security and arms control areas will be redirected to missile defense and the control of conventional, biological, chemical, and other weapons of mass destruction; and greater emphasis will be placed on a far more important international economic law.

We noted in Chapter 9 that the WTO, with a more effective dispute settlement mechanism, was replacing the relatively more lax GATT system. This trend is a good beginning for a greater role of international law in the age of geoeconomics. While the term *geoeconomics* has been bandied about by many, to my knowledge nobody has to date offered a precise definition of what it means, much less what the "age of geoeconomics" entails. Because of its importance, let us venture to suggest what should go into a definition of the concept. On the macrolevel, in the age of geoeconomics, all matters pertaining to manufacturing, marketing, financing, and research and design (R&D) are globalized. On the microlevel, national power is no longer measured exclusively, even mainly, by a state's military might. In fact, economic security has eclipsed or overtaken military security in importance. National power in the geoeconomic context is the aggregate of a number of components, such as human and technological resources, exportable capital, efficient production of modern goods, influence over global economic decisionmaking, and the will to mobilize economic capacity for national ends (cf. Hunter 1992, 9).[3]

Nations will find an increasing role for international law in the control and facilitation of the globalized processes of manufacturing, marketing, financing, and R&D. The law will figure heavily in protecting the security of human and technological resources and the export of capital and modern products. And it will play an enhanced role in regulating global economic and financial decisionmaking in and through institutions such as the IMF, the World Bank, and the WTO.

The New World Order and International Law: A Neoliberal View

Nonstate actors. In the new world order, while states remain essential actors, nonstate actors are expected to assume important roles in developing transnational practices and norms and in influencing governmental actions. The emergence and ascendancy of an ever expanding list of nonstate actors both calls into question the neorealist state-centric premise and poses new challenges to international law. Weiss (1994, 1) expresses this phenomenon most eloquently: "The new model is a network of states, intergovernmental organizations, transnational corporations and industry associations, national and subnational nongovernmental organizations, transnational expert communities, and *ad hoc* associations that are intricately connected through binding and nonbinding international legal instruments and associated institutions." All this, she notes, can be seen in different areas of international law: environment, economics, human rights, telecommunications, even peacekeeping. She sees in all this change important implications for the transformation of sovereignty.

In retrospect, we come to the realization, as never before, that in the post-1945 global system, certain nonsovereign units have behaved independently and have greatly influenced outcomes, such as Al Fatah, the Viet Cong, the European Common Market, and even the Mafia, which plays a larger role in global transactions than is customarily recognized (Mansbach, Ferguson, and Lambert 1976, 27). Organizations like the United Nations and its agencies, NATO, and even the International Red Cross, while possessing neither legal nor territorial attributes, are significant actors on the world stage. UN organs and agencies have been allowed to seek advisory opinions from the International Court of Justice, which otherwise is restricted to disputes among sovereign states (Barton and Carter 1992, 281).

But in the new era, nonstate actors might include private firms—for example, the miners licensed by the International Seabed Authority (ISA) to prospect and exploit seabed resources in competition with the Enterprise, an arm of the ISA. They might include private individuals (investors) who seek relief in investment disputes with a sovereign state under the Convention on the Settlement of Investment Disputes Between States and Nationals of Other States (1965; TIAS, No. 6090). Or they might be individuals seeking compensation from insurance companies for damages caused by states or other individuals in violation of the international environmental law, as discussed in Chapter 8.

Since the Nuremberg Trials, natural or juridical persons have increasingly been accepted as independent actors, subject to and benefiting from international law. Individuals now enjoy even procedural rights in certain areas, such as the competence to file complaints before a competent tribunal against alleged human rights violations by their own government at home (Chapter 6). This has changed traditional international law, according to which only states have *locus standi* to bring a case before an international tribunal or espouse a cause internationally (*Mavromatis* case). If the trend continues, the distinctions may blur between public international law regulating interstate relations, and private international law dealing with activities of individuals.

A simple example of the difference between public and private international laws is provided by Barton and Carter (1992, 282): The Iraqi invasion of Kuwait in 1990 and the resulting UN economic sanctions involved traditional issues of public international law. Yet the implementation of the sanctions very much affected a U.S. or European bank with Iraqi or Kuwati deposits. Courts, national governments, and international organizations struggle with the vexing mixtures of public and private issues cutting across the two international laws. Thus, when the European Community developed its judicial system, it realized that individuals would have to be able to appeal to or against community action, just as much as governments do. What has happened in the European Union, knocking down the artificial barriers separating public and private international law, may well be a harbinger for the global community in the future.

International institutions and collectivism. The years since 1919 have seen the development of more numerous, larger, more expensive, more complex, and more varied international organizations. These institutions have become increasingly involved in the conduct of a growing list of functions and are making more demands on the attention and resources of governments (Claude 1988, 114). A casual look into the latest editions of the *Yearbook of International Organizations* would turn up a list of hundreds, even thousands, of IGOs and NGOs. The phenomenal growth stems largely from the policies of governments. Ultimately, it suggests that decisionmakers are now more willing to emphasize collective, rather than merely unilateral, approaches to a wide range of issues for the management of international relations.

The collectivist (multilateralist) bent can be seen in the imperfect institutions of collective security and peacekeeping. It is increasingly evident in the propositions of collective responsibility in the promotion of sustained economic development, and in the endeavors of integrative community building, of which the EU is the first concrete example on a grand scale.

The EU, which is founded on both treaty law and a long tradition (since 1957) of state and community practice (customary law), has its own lawmaking institutions and procedures (Folsom 1992, 25). The European Community Law today not only regulates relations and policies within the community—including taxation, trade, monetary, equal-pay, and worker and consumer protection matters—but it also provides for litigation (of the European Community Law) in national courts and tribunals and in the European Court of Justice (67ff.).

While the details of the European Community Law and how it works need not detain us here, what is relevant is that this body of regional law may herald the future of international law at large. At its present stage of development, the European Parliament does not yet have the power to propose legislation or to enact it, although it has the potential to be endowed with such power. The decisions of the European Commission and the resolutions and declarations from the Council of Ministers, like the guidelines from the European Council, together constitute the equivalent of what is known in the cognate development of an international environmental law as the soft law (Chapter 8). The hard law of the European Community is founded on treaties, the cornerstone being the Treaty of Rome (1957), but is augmented by the regulations and directives from the Council of Ministers.

If the European experience is any guide, a possible development in general international law is that soft-law instruments will play a wider role. This development may soon foreshadow the acceptance of soft-law instruments as an auxiliary source of general international law.

One overwhelming reminder that collectivism is the trend of the future is the first summit of members of the EU and its Asian counterpart, the Asian Pacific Economic Cooperation (APEC) forum, which met in Bangkok in March 1996. Fifteen European and ten Asian countries met to pledge a "strong partnership" in trade and investment (*New York Times,* March 3, 1996, 3). In what was billed as a "wake-up call" for Asia Pacific, the fastest-growing region destined to lead the world in trade and investment well into the next century, the summit was only the first step to more ambitious joint undertakings. These include the establishment of more institutions, such as the Asian-Europe Environmental Technology Center in Thailand and the Asia-Europe Foundation in Singapore. Other measures include an Asia-Europe university program and links integrating a trans-Asian railway network with the trans-European railway network (*AWSJW,* March 11, 1996, 5).

The cooperation between the two supertrading blocs is significant for theory in a number of ways. First, it confirms the collectivist proclivity, including a reliance on institutions—at least those of the most successful economies. Second, it was an obvious snub to the United States, as the meeting's "mutual respect" motto turned out to mean noninterference in the internal affairs of other countries, a veiled criticism of the U.S. policy of making trade with Asian countries dependent on progress in combating child labor, improving worker-safety conditions, and allowing the formation of independent labor unions (*New York Times,* March 3, 1996, 3). Third, the alliance making between the world's largest (EU) and smallest (APEC) of the three supertrading blocs goes against the balance of power rules adhered to by nations ever since 1648. The rules of the balancing game, deducible from past practice, would call for APEC teaming up with the North American Free Trade Association (NAFTA), the second largest among the three groups, in order to balance EU, the largest, hence most threatening, bloc.

In my 1993 study (Hsiung 1993a, 254f.), extrapolating from an earlier study (1985) of triadic games, I calculated that there was a 67 percent chance that North America and Asia Pacific would align on the same side, against Europe, which is the largest bloc in terms of total combined GDP and a number of other measures (p. 251). This finding, based on realist power-ratio calculations, corroborates both the alliance-making records of nations and Waltzian theory. Consistent with his theory that in anarchy, power calculations determine states' alliance behavior, Waltz (1979, 127) counsels: "Secondary states, if they are to choose, flock to the weaker side; for it is the stronger side that threatens them."

The fact that the Asian group chose instead to ally with the stronger side testifies that either geoeconomic alliance making calls for different strategies or that some extraneous factor(s) tipped the balance, making pure power calculations an inadequate guide for action. As it turned out, the United States was shunned by the Asian countries because Washington's human rights foreign policy was a great turnoff (*New York Times,* March 3, 1996, 3). If there is any doubt, Bangkok, where the recent Asian-European summit was held, had hosted an earlier conference, on March 29, 1993, that produced the joint Bangkok Declaration of the forty-nine Asian nations in attendance. The declaration (UN Doc. A/CONF.157/ASRM/8 [1993]) disputed the West's (mainly U.S.) right to impose its human rights definition on Asia (see discussion in Chapter 6, text at reference for n. 1). Hence, normative, not power, considerations were the rationale behind Asia's choice to team up with Europe, to the exclusion of the United States and NAFTA.

As interregional integration initiatives gain momentum, it is obvious that international law will be tapped to play an ever increasing role in regulating relations between economic blocs—between the blocs and in relations across trading blocs as well as within each bloc. The Asia-Europe alignment provides evidence that the traditional balancing pattern no longer holds, and Neorealist theory has yet to explain why the pattern ceases to hold. It may also intimate a formidable challenge to international law, if indeed its new role called for by possible expanded interregional integration should materialize. As international law becomes increasingly indistinguishable from inter-regional law (law among regions), as is likely, its ability to retain a coherent body of norms known as general inter-national law (law among nations regardless of regions) may be severely strained.

Sovereignty and International Order

The advances in regional integration (culminating in the EU thus far) together with the rise of the individual in international law seem to convey a steady challenge to the traditional sovereignty of states. However, the erosion of sovereignty is obvious only if viewed internationally. Looking from domestic contexts, even though peripherally comparing Northern and Southern states, Thompson (1995, 230) analytically takes exception to the suggestion that sovereignty has eroded. Although professing to examine "state sovereignty in international relations," she defines sovereignty as "authority," or the state's (domestic) ability to make authoritative decisions—in the final analysis, the decision to make war.

So far, except for the few "failed states" (such as Somalia and Rwanda) and the even fewer countries caught in the abyss of internal breakup and internecine fighting (such as the former Yugoslavia), one finds almost no state facing serious problems in its (domestic) ability to make authoritative decisions (Thompson's definition of sovereignty, p. 216). Theory aside, the merit of the Thompson demurrer, nevertheless, is that it reminds one that the question of the alleged transformation of sovereignty is not a universally accepted conclusion. Many of the non-Western nations—including the forty-nine Asian nations that signed the 1993 Bangkok Declaration, defending their sovereign rights in the face of the challenge posed by the U.S. human rights foreign policy—would reject any insinuation that traditional sovereignty has gone over the hill.

Empirically, the erosion of sovereignty is discernible only from an external (international) perspective in four contexts: (1) when protection of a state's interests internationally pales in competition with the seeming preeminence of some overriding community interests (as in environmental issues); (2) when a state's "eligibility"[4] to represent the country internationally is impaired by its loss of legitimacy in the eyes of the world, due to internal strife or simply to the rise of "nation over state" (Gotlieb 1993, 20); (3) when world sentiments, backed by a changing international law, support conferring procedural rights on individuals such as in their newfound competence to bring human rights violations charges against their own government to an international forum or otherwise seek relief in their own right against foreign states in investment disputes; and (4) when a state finds its ability to act on the international scene hampered by the activities of multilateral institutions such as IGOs and NGOs in and outside the United Nations family, and by those of the ubiquitous transnational corporations (TNCs).

To elaborate on the last point, how is sovereignty eroded by the existence and activities of these nonsovereign institutions? Mingst and Karns (1995, 3) provide an answer: Global telecommunications and economic interdependence diminish the control governments can exercise over the information their citizens receive, the value of their money, and the health of the country's economy. In Chapter 5, we noted the jurisdiction-without-sovereignty phenomenon, wherein actions by IOs, including the United Nations and its affiliated agencies such as ICAO and IMO, have far-reaching effects on sovereign states.

Multilateral institutions, in theory, take actions that constitute intervention in states' domestic affairs only with consent. There is, nevertheless, a growing number of precedents in humanitarian intervention, which has emerged as a legitimate undertaking in the community's name, without the consent of the "host" country (Mingst and Karns 1995, 3). Viewed from outside looking in, it is indisputable that state sovereignty is now more porous. The question is: What might be the consequences?

In a nutshell, it is bound to affect the nature of world order and the modality by which it is maintained. Traditional world order is built on the state-centric premise; and positivist international law reinforces state centricity by its unequivocal support of sovereign equality and inviolability of states. If decline in state sovereignty by contrast shifts the limelight from state to community, one consequence would be a corresponding rise in the legal capacity of international multilateral institutions. In a time-honored advisory opinion (*Reparation,* 1949), the International Court of Justice concludes that the United Nations, although not a superstate, does possess "a large measure of international personality" and the "capacity" to operate on the international plane. In the circumstances, three developments among many are conceivable: (a) the rise of an integrated community such as the EU, having not only a legal capacity within its territorial and functional confines vis-à-vis its members, but also a comparable measure of "international personality" such as that of the United Nations, to act on the international plane; (b) an increasing call for international accountability of states and individuals, including their leaders, for violations of the law, even in noninternational conflict (e.g., Bosnia), as concretized in the institution of an "international criminal court"; and (c) greater reliance on collectivism, in lieu of unilateralist self-help, as manifested in a return to collective security.

In the preceding discussion, we touched on the gravity of a European community law marking the successful community-building efforts on that continent. The meaning of the rise of this continent-wide integrated community in Europe and what it entails is self-apparent. The following discussions therefore address only (b) and (c) among the three suggested developments and their implications for the unfolding links between international politics and law.

International Accountability: An International Criminal Court?

In Chapter 4, we noted that although resort to adjudicative settlement of disputes has a long history, declines in the use of arbitration after 1945 and the relatively sparse acceptances of the ICJ's compulsory jurisdiction can be traced to two sources: state sovereignty and the Cold War ideological conflict, which inadvertently gave a fillip to the jealous safeguarding of state sovereignty. The reported decline in sovereignty following the lifting of the Cold War impediment should augur well for a wider use of arbitration and judicial settlement of disputes between states. As discussed in Chapter 4, one untapped resource for enhancing the enforceability of ICJ decisions is the measures (including sanctions) the Security Council can take, under Article 94(2) of the UN Charter, to give effect to ICJ awards. In the post–Cold War era, as the Security Council is not ideologically deadlocked as before, fuller use of this resource would appear to be feasible.

The solution holds the potential of encouraging wider use of the ICJ for the judicial settlement of international disputes.

The idea of an international criminal court (ICC) predated the Nuremberg Trials, but the main hindrance has always been the barrier of state sovereignty. States cannot be counted on to turn over their citizens, a fortiori national leaders, who have committed delicts or even crimes against humanity according to standards of international law. The Bosnia tragedy provided a rare occasion for the realization of the ICC ideal in peacetime. By a 1993 resolution of the UN Security Council (Res. 48/827), the legal foundation was laid for the establishment of a UN International Tribunal for the Prosecution of Serious Violations of International Humanitarian Law Committed in the Territory of the Former Yugoslavia (Slomanson 1995, 387).

Concededly, many problems, substantive and procedural, surrounded the founding of the International Tribunal. The most challenging one was whether the Security Council, which premised the tribunal's jurisdiction on its "Chapter VII" powers in the UN Charter, has the power to create an international criminal court of this sort. Article 39, which contains the central theme of the Charter-vested powers for the council in Chapter VII, reads: "The Security Council shall determine the existence of any threat to the peace, breach of the peace, and act of aggression and shall make recommendations, or decide what measures shall be taken . . . to maintain or restore international peace and security."

Slomanson (1995, 388) correctly notes that no UN entity has the power to create a subsidiary organ to carry out functions not conferred on the endowing UN entity by the Charter. This point was in fact enunciated in a 1973 opinion by the ICJ in a similar case, albeit involving the General Assembly. In its advisory opinion on the case, known as *Review of Judgment No. 158 of the UN Administrative Tribunal,* the court states: "But a subsidiary organ could not have a competence falling outside the competence of the principal." It is noteworthy that neither the General Assembly nor individual states are known to have challenged the legality of the International Tribunal thus created by the Security Council. If the implication of the quiescence is that the world community is disposed to accept an international criminal tribunal, using the Bosnia case as a good start, it merits our close attention, for several reasons.

First, the tacit universal acceptance of the International Tribunal and, more important, the idea it represents, may hold the hope of humanity. It seems to convey a coherent sense of community held by nations as never before. All previous antecedents of an ICC were constituted at the end of a major war by the victor powers to try the culprits from among the vanquished (Slomanson 1995, 382). The International Tribunal for the former Yugoslavia is probably the first exception in that it was not a tribunal set up by the victors; besides, the end of the civil war in that country was not yet in sight. Rather it was established by the world community as represented by the UN Security Council. This development is a giant step toward a community-wide consensus regarding collective action on behalf of international peace and justice. Ultimately, if this trend continues, it means that states are not just "units of the system," as in Neorealist parlance, but members of a world community bound together by a heightened sense of a common destiny. It speaks loudly for an emergent collective will of the community, as a *corpus iuris communis*. It is a wake-up call for those who are still singularly harnessed to the unilateralist self-help reflex of the sovereign state.

Second, according to its statute (text in *ILM* 32:1159ff.; also in Brownlie 1995, 456–468), the tribunal is empowered to prosecute grave violations of the international humanitarian law (Art. 1). By usage, the term *international humanitarian law* is usually considered to encompass the 1949 Geneva Conventions, the laws or customs of war, the Genocide Convention (1948), and norms on "crimes against humanity," as last reformulated and applied at the Nuremberg and Tokyo trials. In its provisions (Arts. 2–5) on the laws the tribunal shall apply, the statute reconfirms this formulation of international humanitarian law.

Third, the establishment of the tribunal raises several variations on the theme of "accountability" (O'Brien 1993, 639). The most pertinent for us in this context is the issue of *international accountability* of individuals, who may be prosecuted for violating international humanitarian norms. Mandating the tribunal to prosecute "persons" who have violated international criminal law, the statute contains a "personal jurisdiction" clause (Art. 6): "The International Tribunal shall have jurisdiction over *natural persons* pursuant to the provisions of the present Statute" (emphasis added). In addition, *individual criminal responsibility* is defined in Article 7(1), in the following terms: "A person who planned, instigated, ordered, committed or otherwise aided and abetted in the planning, preparation or execution of a crime referred to in Arts. 2 through 5 of the present Statute, shall be individually responsible for the crime."

That the tribunal was created to take on not small cogs but big wheels—in fact no less than key decisionmakers ultimately responsible for the crimes committed—is clearly indicated in the sweep of its mandate to reach to even the level of heads of state and government (Art. 7).

Edith Brown Weiss, former president of the American Society of International Law, may have a point when she commented that the tribunal "must be given every opportunity to carry out its task successfully," lest cynicism mount at the international community's response to the crisis in the former Yugoslavia; and "it would be a blow to the rule of law."[5] I would add, however, that even if the tribunal should in the end fail because of circumstances beyond its control, its very establishment would have contributed something important to theory on law and politics. It would have shown to the world that the world community, by this example, is now receptive to the idea that the international humanitarian law is higher than any domestic jurisdiction; that crimes against humanity must be tackled at the highest decisionmaking levels; and that internal strife and noninternational crimes against humanity are just as offensive as international wars and the crimes committed therein. The ultimate contribution of even a failed ICC would be that it would have served notice that the world has become so interdependent (in security as in economic matters) and close-knit that peace in any domestic jurisdiction is invariably tied to peace and stability in the world community at large. Besides, as the world grows more psychologically geared to these truths and becomes more experienced, the next time around, any culprits in domestic or international conflict may not find themselves so lucky as to escape international accountability.

Already, the International Tribunal, while awaiting the arrest and delivery of all the culprits, is making a contribution in the further clarification of international law on war crimes. One example is the tribunal's formulation that sexual assault on Muslim women during the Balkan conflict constituted a "war crime" (*New York Times,* June 28, 1996, 1). This is the first time ever that rape has been pronounced by a competent international tribunal as a war crime. Even if the elusive culprits should never be brought to justice, reformulations of the law as such by the tribunal will serve as a powerful deterrent to potential rapists among future combatants in both noninternational and international conflicts.

The single most important lesson from the establishment of the International Tribunal on the former Yugoslavia is that the world community now calls for international accountability of both states and individual decisionmakers (as well as policy-executing persons).

The resurgent salience of *international accountability* is probably the most important development in the realm of international politics of the new world order beyond the end of the Cold War. It stems from the three phenomena we spoke of above, namely: the ascendancy of the community over states, the rise of individuals in their status under international law, and the concomitant (though controverted) decline in state sovereignty.

Collective Security: New Meaning and New Context

The return to collective security is also associated with the erosion of sovereignty but may be attributable to other systemic factors as well. One of the reasons for the erosion of state sovereignty is the ascendancy of the community—as seen in the arrival of an integrated European Union. If the EU fully develops its potential, it may assume community-wide (collective) security responsibilities for its members. Its security system now rests on three pillars: the Western European Union (WEU), the Organization for Security and Cooperation in Europe (OSCE), and NATO.[6] Within the EU community, member states will find it less likely to fight wars with a fellow member and therefore less necessary to prepare for one. There is reason to expect that collective security will take care of member states' defenses within the community. A failure to understand this modern trend of collectivism would lure one into believing in and forecasting the demise of NATO, as Waltz (1993, 76) did.

A careful reader will find that I used the words *return to* collective security, not *return of*. The implied message is that, as an idea and institution, collective security has been in place since 1919, even in the hardest of times. Although the collective security system, as envisaged in the UN Charter design, has never been allowed to fully play out its potential because of the Cold War divisions in the Security Council, the idea of collective security has remained alive and has inspired regional institutions such as NATO, OAS, CSCE, and even the Warsaw Treaty Organization.[7] It is not a question of the return *of* collective security, since it has never departed from the scene. The idea of a return *to* collective security has another connotation: The likely shift from the unilateralist reliance on self-help to a collective approach to peace maintenance does not necessarily suggest a wider use of the latent collective security mechanism inherent in the UN system, now that it is finally freed from the erstwhile bondage imposed by the Cold War.

Admittedly, since 1987, when the Soviet Union changed its policy toward the world organization, the United Nations has been able to play an ever expanding role in peacekeeping. A comparison of the number of peacekeeping missions sent by the UN before and after 1987 would be instructive. In the thirty-one years from 1956 to 1987, the United Nations dispatched a total of thirteen peacekeeping missions. But in the following seven years (1988–1995) alone, another sixteen missions were commissioned. Whereas the pre-1987 peacekeeping operations were more geographically limited—eight of the thirteen to the Middle East alone—the post-1988 peacekeeping operations were more scattered, including six in Africa, one in Asia, one in the Middle East, and one in Latin America.[8]

By return *to* collective security, however, I am both mindful of the potential of the United Nations in the post–Cold War era (cf. Weiss, Forsythe, and Coate 1994; Mingst and Karns 1995) and wary of possible competition from other institutions, some yet unborn. I say this for two reasons. One, given the trend of collectivism, the number of institutions capable of assuming collective security responsibilities, such as the WEU, OSCE, and NATO in Europe alone, is likely to increase. Second, according to the theory of collective action (Olson 1971), the "free-rider" problem makes it especially difficult for large groups to act collectively. Between the United Nations and a much smaller and regionally focused security organization like NATO, the former is too unwieldy and cumbersome and intractably burdened by the free-rider problem (cf. Oneal 1990). Besides, unlike during the initial years of the Cold War, when the United Nations was an automatic legitimizer of U.S. foreign policy, the United States is no longer willing to play the role of both banker and hegemon (as required by the theory of collective action) to crack the free-rider problem in an organization that produces "collective goods," such as peacekeeping and peaceful change. Hence, other peace and security institutions may have a chance (even better one) of fulfilling the need of collective security in the new world order. While the UN is not out, the bottom line is that collective security cannot be automatically equated with the United Nations.

Agreeing that collective security is the trend for the twenty-first century, Kegley and Raymond (1994, 212ff.) suggest a "concert-based" collective security system, which in fact may take "alternative frameworks" (pp. 220–229), the UN being only one of them.

Still another reason for a wider endorsement of collective security, in contrast to reliance on unilateral self-help, is that the meaning of security has changed; so have the requirements for meeting nations' security needs. Security used to mean the protection of a country's territorial integrity and political independence, essentially by military means. Today, in the geoeconomic age, sources of security threats have grown to include environmental hazards, resource depletion, external population explosion, and mass migration. Any or a combination of these could lead to international conflict or serious deprivation, hence become a security problem. For instance, environmental hazards could mean ozone depletion, global climate warming, or loss of biological diversity, which could result in health hazards or the destruction (even extinction) of species and crops and of natural substances that might hold the cure for diseases. Population explosion elsewhere, especially if accompanied by poverty, might trigger mass exodus, posing threats to the target country or countries of immigration. Disputes between states over control of shared resources (e.g., shared water resources of international rivers) may lead to international conflicts. Conversely, renewable resources (e.g., fish stocks) may be depleted as a result of international conflicts (Porter and Brown 1996).

These, plus increasing instances of international terrorism, are going to plague the world's nations as modern threats to their security, more than military threats in the traditional sense. A cursory scanning of the agendas of UN General Assembly meetings shows the centrality of the world's concern with terrorism, narcotics trafficking, and environmental issues, among others. These are the kinds of new security issues that cannot be tackled by individual countries through unilateral (self-help) means. They have to be responded to and contained by collective action. Hence, collective security, which will increasingly become "other help," has a new meaning and new manifestations in the changed systemic context.

There is always a legal dimension not only to international politics, but also to international organization and, in particular, collective security. For instance, collective security carries with it the necessity to create a set of legal provisions spelling out obligations for members and the limits on the system itself (Weiss 1993, 9). Without a legal structure, the system will not have the certainty when the chips are down that each member is committed to repressing peace disturbers. Not having centralized decisionmaking, it will leave the determination of a breach of the peace to the haphazard perception of individual governments.

Conclusion

In this book we have been concerned with the interplay of international politics and law, which is also found duplicated in the area of international organization. The relationship between politics and law, as has been shown, is one of mutual reinforcement and mutual pervasion. If all that has been said could be reduced to a few words, they probably would be that both power and normative desiderata, including international law, have an equal effect on the strategies and behavior of nations. This is something the pure-power Neorealist theory fails to convey and account for.

In this concluding chapter, I have both taken a retrospective view, summing up from preceding chapters, and ventured a cavalier look into the future. In periscoping into the twenty-first century, we see in the unfolding interactions between politics and law a number of major developments surrounding the apparently increasing (though controvertible) erosion of state sovereignty. Other findings include a distinct trend toward the use of collectivism, which augurs well for adopting a new version of collective security (other help?), as opposed to the traditional reliance on unilateral self-help.

All these transformations pose a serious challenge to IR theory as we know it. In its present shape, Neorealism (that is, of the Waltzian school) does not seem to be up to the new challenge. Nonetheless, its structural emphasis and logic based on the anarchic premise is sound, and its theory does seem to have the potential of self-renewal. At its present stage of development, though, Waltzian Neorealism is stunted by its beeline rush from the anarchic premise to the summary conclusion that power (i.e., power distribution in the system) determines all things—from unilateral state behavior to alliance formation and performance—in international relations, to the exclusion of all other equally decisive guiding forces, international law being foremost among them.

Lest the assertions made earlier about changes in sovereignty be misunderstood or taken out of context, let me add a few caveats. First, despite the rise of the community and the status of the individual in international law, and despite the suggested collectivist trend pointing unmistakably to a growing role for multilateral institutions and collective security, the sovereign state is here to stay—that is, unless the Westphalian system we live in ceases overnight to be an anarchic system (i.e., lacking a "common power" over the states). Second, although state sovereignty may be more porous internationally, its domestic face has not likewise changed. The state's other attributes, such as territoriality and nationality, will remain as strong as ever. In Chapter 5, we noted that nationality appears to have emerged as the most important principle by which jurisdiction is determined, eclipsing all other competing bases of jurisdiction with the possible exception of territoriality.

As Ruggie (1993, 174) perceptively reminds us, the subject of territoriality is little studied and hence not fully understood. Its empirical significance can be seen from the fact that so many of the contentious cases brought before the ICJ in the years immediately following the Cold War have been concerned with territorial claims, the use of land along international boundaries, or riparian issues concerning international rivers. Recall the attitude of the Southern nations in their disputes with the West (read: United States) regarding its alleged invasions of their sovereignty under the guise of human rights. The admittedly increasing porous quality of state sovereignty, therefore, is by no means a reliable clue to the alleged disappearance of sovereignty as a factor in international law and politics. Any gratuitous report of the demise of sovereignty is premature.

In view of the systemic transformations discussed, I think it appropriate to conclude this book by offering a few suggestions, bold but studied, on how international law is likely to be upgraded in line with the sea changes in the world system's political underpinnings.

- One of the first items up for review might be: Who are the "subjects" of international law? Traditionally, only states are subjects. In view of the rise and future importance of integrated communities (united Europe is the first example), and the enhanced status of IOs and other multilateral institutions—and individuals—the concept of subjects of international law may need to be enlarged to include at least some of the nonsovereign entities (including some of the ones I have characterized in Chapter 5 as having jurisdiction without sovereignty).
- The body of norms currently pertaining to the "responsibility of

states" may also have to be expanded to accommodate the responsibility of nonstate actors, such as multilateral institutions, as they become more like equal participants with states on the international scene in their capacity to incur delinquency.

- With regard to the "sources" of international law, it is likely that what is now known as *soft law,* a term often used in the development of international environmental law—consisting of declarations, resolutions, memoranda, and other instruments during the negotiating stage before a treaty is concluded—may be admitted as an auxiliary source.
- The law of treaties, likewise, may have to be expanded to accommodate the legal capacity and consequence of nonstate actors concluding international agreements both among themselves and with sovereign actors.
- In the human rights area, the "right to sustained development" of nations, which belongs to what we have called the third genre of human rights (Chapter 6), will likely receive further attention. This will be the Southern nations' response to the West's call for respect for an earlier generation of human rights, which are individual oriented.
- International economic law will become even more important with the removal of the Cold War barriers that prevented former communist bloc countries from participating in the global economic system for so long.
- The international environmental law too is likely to play a bigger role, as a result of both the universal acceptance of the superiority of certain community interests and, equally, states' concerns for environment as a security problem.

Finally, conditions prevailing in the new world order will most likely conduce to the "enforceability" of international law, as a number of avenues previously closed by the Cold War are now open. Some examples are the solution available through Article 94(2) of the UN Charter, which gives the Security Council the equivalent of a "collection agency's" role to play, in behalf of unenforced awards handed down by the ICJ; the 1958 New York Convention on the Recognition and Enforcement of Foreign Arbitral Awards (TIAS, No. 6997; 330 UNTS 38); and the 1965 Convention on the Settlement of Investment Disputes (575 UNTS 159; TIAS No. 6090). Other avenues include the role of domestic courts in enforcing international law, including international arbitral and judicial awards. Although municipal courts, as other domestic authorities, have always had the competence to enforce international law at their discretion, without the Cold War hindrance, the chances of their actually taking the initiative to do so are reasonably improved.

Considering the far-reaching systemic changes, the term *inter-national law* may even prove to be inadequate, as the scope of the emergent law will no doubt expand in accordance as the role of the nonstate actors expands on the world scene. Nevertheless, regardless of what it is called, there will always be a normative side to international politics. Anarchy and order will remain the dual central fixtures of international relations and IR studies, unperturbed by the tumultuous turns of events punctuating the march from the close of the bipolar era into the twenty-first century.

Notes

1. As throughout this book, *Neorealism* (capitalized) is reserved for neorealism of the Waltzian brand, as expounded in Waltz 1979. The word *neorealism* (lower case) refers to any structural update of traditional realism, viewing international relations from the standpoint of the structure, however defined, of the international system (as opposed to the state-centric view). To Neorealists, the structure is defined exclusively by its power distribution.

2. For the running debates, see generally Keohane 1986; Baldwin 1993; Kegley 1995; Mearsheimer 1994; Keohane and Martin 1995; Ruggie 1995; Wendt 1995.

3. Of the two parts in my definition here, the first part (macrolevel) may find echoes in the globalization literature (e.g., Mittelman 1996); but the latter has nothing to say on the microlevel. My formulation, which combines both a change in macrolevel economic power management and the new era's microlevel implications for individual states caught in the shifting global power game, captures, I think, the essence of the age of geoeconomics.

4. Alan James defines jurisdiction as "what makes a territorial entity *eligible* to participate in international relations" (emphasis added). See his "Comment on J. D. B. Miller," *Review of International Studies* 12, 1:91–93.

5. See Edith Brown Weiss, "Message from the President," *ASIL Newsletter,* June-August 1994.

6. Cf. Janier Solana, "The European Security Agenda," *NATO Overview,* no. 6 (November 1995): 11–14. CSCE is now OSCE.

7. For an interesting analysis of the respective roles played by the UN and regional organizations in the management of conflict, see Haas 1986.

8. For the pre-1987 period, data are based on *The Blue Helmets: A Review of U.N. Peacekeeping* (New York: United Nations, 1990). Data for the post-1988 period are from my own tabulations.

INTERNATIONAL LAW CASES CITED

Alabama Claims (U.S.–Great Britain Arbitration). Digested in Bishop 1962, 864–869.
Alcoa (U.S. v. Aluminum Company of America). Court of Appeals, U.S.; 2d Cir., 1945. 148 Fed. 2d 416.
Alvarez-Machain (U.S. v. Humberto Alvarez-Machain). Sup. Ct. of U.S., 1992. 504 U.S. 114.
Anglo-Iranian Oil Company. 1951 ICJ Rep. 89.
Asylum (Colombia v. Peru). ICJ, 1950. 1950 ICJ Rep. 266.
Barcelona Traction, Light and Power Company (Belgium v. Spain). ICJ, 1970. 1970 ICJ Rep. 43.
B. E. Chattin Claim (U.S. v. Mexico). United States and Mexico General Claims Commission, 1927. 4 UN Rep. Int'l Arb. Awards 282.
Bering Sea Fur Seals Fisheries Arbitration (Great Britain v. U.S.). Moore's *International Arbitrations* 755 (1893):28:415–419.
Berrizi Brothers Company v. S.S. Pesaro. Sup. Ct. of U.S., 1926. 271 U.S. 562; 46 Sup. Ct. 611.
Blackmer v. U.S. Sup. Ct. of U.S., 1932. 284 U.S. 421.
Caroline, The (U.S. v. Great Britain, 1837). Digested in John Moore, *A Digest of International Law* (Washington, DC: Government Printing Office, 1906), 2:412.
Certain Expenses of the UN. ICJ Advisory Opinion, 1962. 1962 ICJ Rep. 151.
Competence of the General Assembly for the Admission of a State to the UN. ICJ Advisory Opinion, 1950. 1950 ICJ Rep. 4.
Corfu Channel (Merits; UK v. Albania). ICJ, 1949. 1949 ICJ Rep. 4–224; Judgment (Merits), April 9, 1949.
Cutting (U.S. v. Mexico). Moore, *International Law* 2:231–232; Dickinson 404.
Diversion of Water from the River Meuse (Netherlands v. Belgium). PCIJ, 1937. PCIJ Ser. A/B, No. 70, 76–78.
Eastern Greenland, Legal Status of (Denmark v. Norway, 1933), PCIJ, Ser. A/B, No. 53.
Factor v. Laubenheimer. Sup. Ct. of U.S., 1933. 290 U.S. 276.
Factory at Chorzow. PCIJ, 1927. PCIJ Ser. A, No. 9, 5–34; PCIJ Ser. A., No. 17 (1928, Merits).
Fawas Yunis (U.S. v. Fawas Yunis). U.S. Ct. of Appeals, Dist. of Columbia Cir., 1991. 288 U.S. App. D.C. 129.
Fisheries Jurisdiction (UK v. Iceland, 1972, 1973, 1974). ICJ Rep. 1972:12; 1973:3; and 1974:3. Also *Fishery Jurisdiction* (Fed. Rep. of Germany v. Iceland, 1983) (Jurisdiction). ICJ Rep. 1983:96.
Flores (U.S. v. Flores). Sup. Ct. of U.S., 1933. 289 U.S. 137.
Fur Seals Arbitration. See Bering Sea Fur Seals Fisheries.
Hilton v. Guyot. Sup. Ct. of U.S., 1895. 159 U.S. 113.
Interhandel (Switzerland v. U.S.). ICJ, 1959. 1959 ICJ Rep. 6.
Island of Palmas (U.S. v. the Netherlands). PCA, 1928. 2 UN Rep. Int'l Arb. Awards 829.

Jesse Lewis (David J. Adams Claim, U.S. v. Great Britain). Claims Arbitration under the Special Agreement of August 18, 1910, 1921. Nielsen Report, 526; 6 UN Rep. Int'l Arb. Awards 85.

Lac Lanoux Arbitration (France v. Spain). 24 International Law Reports 101 (1957).

Laura M. B. Janes Claim (U.S. v. Mexico). United States and Mexico General Claims Commission, 1926. 4 UN Rep. Int'l Arb. Awards 82.

Legal Consequences for States of the Continued Presence of South Africa in Namibia (South-West Africa). ICJ Advisory Opinion, 1971. 1971 ICJ Rep. 16.

Lotus, S.S. (France v. Turkey). PCIJ, 1927. PCIJ Ser. A, No. 10.

Matta-Ballesteros (U.S. v. Matta-Ballesteros). F. Supp. 700:528 (N.D. Fla. 1988).

Mavromatis Palestine Concessions (Jurisdiction; Greece v. Great Britain). PCIJ, Ser. A, No. 2, 11ff.

Naulilaa Incident Arbitration (Portugal v. Germany). Portugal-Germany Arbitral Decision of July 31, 1928. UN Rep. Int'l Arb. Awards, 2[1949]:1011.

Nicaragua v. the U.S. (Military and Paramilitary Activities in and Against Nicaragua). ICJ Judgment of June 27, 1986. 1986 ICJ Rep.

North Sea Continental Shelf (Fed. Rep. of Germany v. Denmark; Fed. Rep. of Germany v. Netherlands). ICJ, 1969. 1969 ICJ Rep. 3.

Nottebohm (Liechtenstein v. Guatemala). ICJ, 1955. 1955 ICJ Rep. 4.

Paquette Habana, The; The Lola. Sup. Ct. of U.S., 1900. 175 U.S. 677.

Pink (U.S. v. Pink). Sup. Ct. of U.S., 1942. 315 U.S. 203.

René Martin Verdugo-Urquidex (1985). As discussed in Andreas Lowenfeld. 1990. "U.S. Law Enforcement Abroad: The Constitution and International Law, Continued." *AJIL* 84, 2:448.

Reparation for Injuries Suffered in the Service of the UN. ICJ Advisory Opinion, 1949. 1949 ICJ Rep. 174.

Schooner Exchange v. MacFaddon. Sup. Ct. of U.S., 1812. 7 Branch 116.

South-West Africa (Ethiopia v. South Africa; Liberia v. South Africa). 1966 ICJ Rep. 34.

Texaco Overseas Petroleum et al. v. Libyan Arab Republic. International Arbitral Award, January 19, 1977. 17 *ILM* 1 (1978).

Trail Smelter (U.S. v. Canada), 1941. 3 UN Rep. Int'l Arb. Awards 1911.

U.S. Diplomatic and Consular Staff at Tehran (U.S. v. Iran). 1979 ICJ Rep. 7 (Order of Provisional Measures, December 15, 1979); 1980 ICJ Rep. 3 (Judgment of May 24, 1980).

Western Sahara. ICJ Advisory Opinion. 1975 ICJ Rep. 12.

Wildenhus. Sup. Ct. of U.S., 1887. 120 U.S. 1.7.

William Way Claim (U.S. v. Mexico). United States and Mexico General Claims Commission, 1928. 4 UN Rep. Int'l Arb. Awards 391.

Abbreviations and Acronyms

ABM	antiballistic missile
AJIL	*American Journal of International Law*
APEC	Asian Pacific Economic Cooperation
ASEAN	Association of Southeast Asian Nations
ASIL	*American Society of International Law*
ATS	Antarctic Treaty System
AWSJW	*Asian Wall Street Journal Weekly*
CFE	conventional forces in Europe
CITES	Convention on International Trade in Extinct Species
CLOS III	(UN) Convention on the Law of the Sea
CSCE	Conference on Security and Cooperation in Europe; now OSCE
ECOSOC	Economic and Social Council
EEC	European Economic Community
EU	European Union
GATT	General Agreement on Tariffs and Trade
IAEA	International Atomic Energy Agency
ICAO	International Civil Aviation Organization
ICBM	intercontinental ballistic missile
ICC	international criminal court
ICJ	International Court of Justice
IEL	international environmental law
IES	international economic system
IGO	international governmental organization
ILC	International Law Commission
ILM	*International Legal Materials*
ILO	International Labour Organisation
IMO	International Maritime Organization
INF	Intermediate Nuclear Force (Treaty)
IO	*International Organization*
IPE	international political economy
IR	International Relations
IS	*International Security*
ISA	International Seabed Authority
ISQ	*International Studies Quarterly*

LNTS	League of Nations Treaty Series
MASA	mutually agreed self-abnegation
MNC	multinational corporation
MSC	Military Staff Committee
NAFTA	North American Free Trade Association
NATO	North Atlantic Treaty Organization
NGO	nongovernmental organization
NPT	Non-Proliferation Treaty
OAS	Organization of American States
OAU	Organization of African Unity
OECD	Organization of Economic Cooperation and Development
OECS	Organization of English-Speaking Caribbean States
OPEC	Organization of Petroleum Exporting Countries
OSCE	Organization of Security and Cooperation in Europe (formerly CSCE)
PCA	Permanent Court of Arbitration
PCIJ	Permanent Court of International Justice (predecessor of ICJ)
PD	Prisoner's Dilemma
RUDs	reservations, understandings, and declarations
SALT	Strategic Arms Limitation Treaty
SD	self-determination
START	Strategic Arms Reduction Treaty
Stat.	Statutes at Large
Sup. Ct. of U.S.	Supreme Court of the United States
TIAS	Treaty and Other International Act Series
UNCHE	United Nations Conference on the Human Environment
UNCIO	United Nations Conference on International Organization
UNDP	United Nations Development Programme
UNEP	United Nations Environment Programme
UN Rep. Int'l Arb. Awards	*United Nations Reports of International Arbitral Awards*
UNTAC	United Nations Transitional Authority in Cambodia
UNTS	United Nations Treaty Series
WEU	Western European Union
WTO	World Trade Organization (successor to the GATT)

References

Albrecht-Carrie, Rene. 1958. *A Diplomatic History of Europe Since the Congress of Vienna*. New York: Harper & Row.

Allison, Graham, and Gregory Treverton, eds. 1992. *Rethinking America's Security: Beyond Cold War and to New World Order.* New York: W. W. Norton.

Aron, Raymond. 1955. *The Century of Total War.* Boston: Beacon Press.

Ashley, Richard K. 1986. "Poverty of Neorealism." In Keohane 1986.

Axelrod, Robert. 1970. *Conflict of Interest.* Chicago: Markham.

Baldwin, David A., ed. 1993. *Neorealism and Neoliberalism: The Contemporary Debate.* New York: Columbia University Press.

Barros, James, and Douglas Johnston. 1974. *The International Law of Pollution.* New York: Free Press.

Bartlett, C. J. 1994. *The Global Conflict.* London and New York: Longman.

Barton, John H., and Barry E. Carter. 1992. "The Uneven, but Growing Role of International Law." In Allison and Treverton 1991, 279–294.

Beres, Louis René. 1987. *America Outside the World.* Lexington, MA: D.C. Heath.

Bernstein, Aaron. 1992. "There Is Prison Labor in America, Too!" *Businessweek,* February 21, 1992.

Birnie, Patricia, and Alan E. Boyle. 1992. *International Law and the Environment.* New York and Oxford: Oxford University Press.

Bishop, William W., Jr. 1962. *International Law: Cases and Materials,* 2d ed. Boston: Little, Brown.

Blay, S. K. N. 1992. "New Trends in the Protection of the Antarctic Environment." *AJIL* 86, 2:377–399.

Boutros-Ghali, Boutros. 1992. *Agenda for Peace.* New York: United Nations; reprinted in *ILM* 28:1589.

Bowett, Derek. 1972. "Reprisals Involving Recourse to Armed Force." *AJIL* 66, 3:1–36.

Boyle, Francis Anthony. 1985. *World Politics and International Law.* Durham, NC: Duke University Press.

Brams, Steven J. 1985. *Superpower Games: Applying Game Theory to Superpower Conflict.* New Haven: Yale University Press.

Brierly, James L. 1963. *The Law of Nations: An Introduction to the International Law of Peace,* 6th ed. Edited by Sir Humphrey Waldock. New York and London: Oxford University Press.

Brilmayer, Lea. 1989. *Justifying International Acts.* Ithaca: Cornell University Press.

Brown, Seyom. 1987. *The Causes and Prevention of War.* New York: St. Martin's Press.

Brownlie, Ian. 1973. *Principle of Public International Law,* 2d ed. Oxford and New York: Oxford University Press.

Brownlie, Ian. 1995. *Basic Documents in International Law,* 4th ed. Oxford: Clarendon Press.

Brundtland Commission. 1987. *Our Common Future.* Report of the World

Commission on Environment and Development. Oxford and New York: Oxford University Press.
Bull, Hedley. 1977. *The Anarchical Society: A Study of World Politics.* London: Macmillan.
Burley, Annie-Marie Slaughter. 1993. "International Law and International Relations Theory." *AJIL* 87, 2:205–251.
Buzan, Barry, Charles Jones, and Richard Little. 1993. *The Logic of Anarchy.* New York: Columbia University Press.
Cahier, Philippe. 1969. "Vienna Convention on Diplomatic Relations." In a special issue on Vienna Conventions on Diplomatic and Consular Relations, *International Conciliation,* No. 571 (January). New York: Carnegie Endowment for International Peace.
Caldwell, Lynton Keith. 1980. *International Environmental Policy.* Durham, NC: Duke University Press.
Carr, E. H. 1939. *The Twenty Years' Crisis, 1919–1939.* London: Macmillan. Reissued in 1964 by Harper Torchbooks.
Carr, Edward Hallet. 1945. *Nationalism and After.* London: Macmillan.
Cassirer, Ernest. 1947. *Rousseau, Kant, and Goethe: Two Essays.* Translated by J. Guttmann, et al. Princeton: Princeton University Press.
CBR. 1992. "The Case for China's MFN Status." *China Business Review* 19, 4:14–17.
Charney, Jonathan. 1993. "Universal International Law." *AJIL* 87, 4:529–551.
Charney, Jonathan I. 1994. "U.S. Provisional Application of the 1994 Deep Seabed Agreement." *AJIL* 88, 4:705–714.
Cheng, Bin. 1993. *General Principles of Law as Applied by International Tribunals.* Cambridge and New York: Cambridge University Press.
Chimni, B. S. 1993. *International Law and World Order.* Newbury Park, CA: Sage Publications.
Choucri, Nazli, ed. 1995. *Global Accord: Environmental Challenges and International Responses.* Cambridge: MIT Press.
Christensen, Thomas J., and Jack Snyder. 1990. "Chain Gangs and Passed Bucks: Predicting Alliance Patterns in Multipolarity." *IO* 44, 2:137–168.
Clark, Grenville, and Louis B. Sohn. 1966. *World Peace Through World Law,* 3d ed. Cambridge: Harvard University Press.
Claude, Inis. 1962. *Power in International Relations.* New York: Random House.
Claude, Inis. 1964. *Swords into Plowshares: The Problems and Progress of International Organizations,* 3d ed. New York: Random House.
Claude, Inis L., Jr. 1988. *States and the Global System.* New York: St. Martin's Press.
CLOS III. 1983. The Third UN Convention on the Law of the Sea; opened for signature December 10, 1982. Text in *The Law of the Sea: Official Text of the United Nations Convention of the Law of the Sea, with Annexes and Index.* New York: United Nations.
Cohen, Stephen B. 1982. "Conditioning U.S. Security Assistance on Human Rights Practices." *AJIL* 76, 2.
Coplin, William D. 1966. "International Law and Assumptions About the State." In Falk and Hanrieder, 1968, 15–34.
Crowley, Steven P., and John H. Jackson. 1996. "WTO Dispute Procedures, Standard of Review, and Deference to National Governments." *AJIL* 90, 2:193–213.
D'Amato, Anthony. 1985. "Is International Law Really 'Law'?" *Northwestern University Law Review* 79: 1293–1314.

D'Amato, Anthony. 1990. "The Invasion of Panama Was a Lawful Response to Tyranny." *AJIL* 84, 2:516–524.
D'Amato, Anthony, ed. 1994. *International Law Anthology*. New York: Anderson.
Deudney, Daniel, and G. John Ikenberry. 1991–1992. "The International Sources of Soviet Change." *IS* 16, 3:74–118.
Deutsch, Karl, and Stanley Hoffmann, eds. 1971. *The Relevance of International Law*. Garden City, NY: Doubleday Anchor Books.
Dickinson, E. D. 1929. *Selection of Cases and Other Readings on the Law of Nations*. New York: McGraw Hill.
Dougherty, James E., and Robert L. Pfaltzgraff, Jr. 1990. *Contending Theories of International Relations*, 3d ed. New York: Harper & Row.
Downs, George, and David Rocke. 1990. *Tacit Bargaining, Arms Races, and Arms Control*. Ann Arbor: University of Michigan Press.
Dupuy, T. N. 1980. *The Evolution of Weapons and Warfare*. Bloomington: Indiana University Press.
Eagleton, Clyde. 1928. *The Responsibility of States in International Law*. New York: New York University Press.
Ehrlich, Thomas, and Mary Ellen O'Connell. 1993. *International Law and the Use of Force*. Boston: Little, Brown.
Emerson, Rupert. 1971. "Self-Determination." *AJIL* 65, 2:459.
Erickson, Richard J. 1972. *International Law and the Revolutionary State: A Case Study of the Soviet Union and Customary International Law*. Dobbs Ferry, NY: Oceana Publications.
Falk, Richard A. 1970. *The Status of Law in International Society*. Princeton: Princeton University Press.
Falk, Richard A. 1975. *A Study of Future Worlds*. New York: Free Press.
Falk, Richard A., and Wolfram F. Hanrieder, eds. 1968. *International Law and Organization: An Introductory Reader*. New York and Philadelphia: Lippincott.
Feinerman, James. 1995. "A New World Order: Farewell to the GATT and Welcome to the WTO." *China Business Review* (March- April 1995), 16–18.
Folsom, Ralph H. 1992. *European Community Law in a Nutshell*. St. Paul, MN: West Publishing.
Forsythe, David. 1990. *The Politics of International Law*. Boulder: Lynne Rienner.
Forsythe, David. 1991. *Internationalization of Human Rights*. Boulder: Lynne Rienner.
Franck, Thomas M. 1986. *Judging the World Court*. New York: Priority Press.
Franck, Thomas M. 1990. *The Power of Legitimacy Among Nations*. New York: Oxford University Press.
Franck, Thomas M. 1992a. "The Emerging Right to Democratic Governance." *AJIL* 86, 1:46–91.
Franck, Thomas. 1992b. "Principles of Fairness in International Law." Paper presented at the annual meeting of the American Political Science Association, 1992, in Chicago; cited in Burley 1993, 205.
Frederich, Carl Joachim. 1948. *Inevitable Peace*. Cambridge: Harvard University Press.
Friedmann, Wolfgang. 1964. *The Changing Structure of International Law*. New York: Columbia University Press.
Fry, John. 1993. *The Helsinki Process: Negotiating Security and Arms Control in Europe*. Washington, DC: National Defense University Press.
Funcke, Gail, Billy Wayson, and Neal Miller. 1982. *Assets and Liabilities of Correction Industries*. Lexington, MA: Lexington Books.

Gaddis, John Lewis. 1992–1993. "International Relations Theory and the End of the Cold War." *IS* 17, 1:5–58.
Gardam, Judith. 1993. "Proportionality and Force in International Law." *AJIL* 87, 3:391ff.
Gill, Stephen, and David Law. 1988. *The Global Economy.* Baltimore: Johns Hopkins University Press.
Gilpin, Robert. 1981. *War and Change in World Politics.* Princeton: Princeton University Press.
Glennon, Michael J. 1992. "State-Sponsored Abduction: A Comment on United States v. Alvarez-Machain." *AJIL* 86, 4:746–756.
Gordon, Edward. 1971. "Resolution of the Bahrain Dispute." *AJIL* 65:560–568.
Gottlieb, Gidion. 1993. *Nation Against State.* New York: Council on Foreign Relations.
Grieco, Joseph M. 1990. *Cooperation Among Nations.* Ithaca: Cornell University Press.
Haas, Ernst B. 1968. *The Uniting of Europe.* Stanford: Stanford University Press.
Haas, Ernst B. 1986. *Why We Still Need the United Nations.* Berkeley: Institute of International Studies, University of California.
Haas, Ernst B. 1990. *When Knowledge Is Power.* Berkeley: University of California Press.
Haas, Peter M., with Jan Sundgren. 1995. "Evolving International Environmental Law: Changing Practices of National Sovereignty." In Choucri 1995.
Hackworth, Green H. 1940–1944. *Digest of International Law,* 8 vols. Washington, DC: Government Printing Office.
Hahn, R., and K. Richards. 1989. "The Internationalization of Environmental Regulation." *Harvard International Law Journal* 30:421ff.
Halberstam, Malvina. 1992. "In Defense of the Supreme Court Decision in *Alvarez-Machain.*" *AJIL* 86, 4:736–745.
Halperin, Morton H., and David J. Scheffer. 1992. *Self-Determination in the New World Order.* Washington, DC: Carnegie Endowment for International Peace.
Hanrieder, Wolfram F. 1968. "International Organizations and International Systems." In Falk and Hanrieder 1968.
Hardin, Garret. 1968. "The Tragedy of the Commons." *Science* 162, 124.
Hardin, Russell. 1982. *Collective Action.* Baltimore: Johns Hopkins University Press.
Haus, Leah. 1992. *Globalizing the GATT: Soviet Union's Successor States, Eastern Europe and the International Trading System.* Washington, DC: Brookings Institution.
Hayton, W. 1960. "The Antarctic Settlement of 1959." *AJIL* 54, 2:348ff.
Henkin, Louis. 1968. *How Nations Behave: Law and Foreign Policy.* New York: Praeger.
Henkin, Louis. 1989. "International Law, Politics, Values, and Functions." *Recueil des Cours* 9, 4.
Henkin, Louis. 1995. "U.S. Ratification of Human Rights Conventions: The Ghost of Senator Bricker." *AJIL* 89, 2:341–349.
Henkin, Louis, et al. 1993. *International Law: Cases and Materials,* 3d ed. St. Paul, MN: West Publishing.
Herz, John. 1950. "Idealist Internationalism." *World Politics* 2, 2:157–180.
Herz, John. 1951. *Political Realism and Political Idealism.* Chicago: University of Chicago Press.
Higgins, Rosalyn. 1994. *Problems and Process: International Law and How We Use It.* Oxford: Clarendon Press.

Hinley, John H., Jr., tr. 1951. *The History of the Peloponnesian War* by Thucydides. New York: Modern Library.

Hobbes, Thomas. 1909. *The Leviathan.* Oxford: Clarendon Press.

Hoffmann, Stanley. 1961. "International Systems and International Law." In Klaus Knorr and Sidney Verba, eds., *The International System.* Princeton: Princeton University Press, 205–237. Also reprinted in Falk and Hanrieder 1968, 89–120.

Hsiung, James C. 1972. *Law and Policy in China's Foreign Relations.* New York: Columbia University Press.

Hsiung, James C. 1993a. *Asia Pacific in the New World Politics.* Boulder: Lynne Rienner.

Hsiung, James C. 1993b. "Human Rights and International Relations: Morality, Law, and Politics." In Graziano Batistella, ed., *Human Rights of Migrant Workers.* Quezon City: Scalabrini Center.

Hunter, Robert E. 1992. "The United States in a New Era." In Brad Roberts 1992, 3–18.

Huntley, Wade L. 1996. "Kant's Third Image: Systemic Sources of the Liberal Peace," *ISQ* 40, 1:45–76.

ICJ. 1992. *Summaries of Judgments, Advisory Opinions, and Orders of the International Court of Justice: 1948–1991.* New York: United Nations.

Independent Commission of Inquiry on the U.S. Invasion of Panama. 1991. *The U.S. Invasion of Panama: The Truth Behind Operation Just Cause.* Boston: South End Press.

Issues 40. 1985. *Issues Before the 40th General Assembly of the United Nations.* New York: UNA-USA.

Issues 46. 1991. *Issues Before the 46th General Assembly of the United Nations.* New York: UNA-USA.

Jacob, Philip E., Alexine L. Atherton, and Arthur M. Wallenstein. 1972. *The Dynamics of International Organization,* rev. ed. Homewood, IL: Dorsey Press.

Jacobson, Harold K., William M. Reisinger, and Todd Mathers. 1986. "National Entanglements in International Governmental Organizations." *American Political Science Review* 80, 1:141–159.

James, Alan. 1986. "Comment on J. D. B. Miller." *Review of International Studies* 12:91–93.

Janis, Mark W. 1988. *An Introduction to International Law,* 1st ed. Boston: Little, Brown.

Janis, Mark W. 1993. *An Introduction to International Law,* 2d ed. Boston: Little, Brown.

Jensen, Lloyd. 1988. *Negotiating Nuclear Arms Control.* Columbia: University of South Carolina Press.

Jervis, Robert. 1978. "Cooperation Under the Security Dilemma." *World Politics* 30, 2:167–214.

Johnson, Harold S. 1967. *Self-Determination Within the Community of Nations.* Leiden: Sijthoff.

Joyner, Christopher C. 1984. "The United States Action in Grenada: Reflections on the Lawlessness of Invasion." *AJIL* 78, 1:131–134.

Joyner, Christopher C. 1992. "The Reality and Relevance of International Law." In Kegley and Wittkopf, 1992.

Kant, Immanuel. 1957. *The Perpetual Peace.* Edited and translated by Lewis White Beck. Indianapolis: Bobbs-Merrill.

Kaplan, Morton A., and Nicholas deB. Katzenbach. 1961. *The Political Foundations of International Law.* New York: John Wiley.

Katzarov, Koustantin. 1964. *The Theory of Nationalization.* The Hague: Martinus Nijhoff.

Kay, David A. 1972. "The United Nations and Decolonization." In James Barros, ed., *The United Nations.* New York: Free Press.

Kegley, Charles W., Jr., ed. 1995. *Controversies in International Relations Theory: Realism and the Neoliberal Challenge.* New York: St. Martin's Press.

Kegley, Charles W., Jr., and Gregory Raymond. 1994. *A Multipolar Peace? Great Power Politics in the Twenty-First Century.* New York: St. Martin's Press.

Kegley, Charles W., and Eugene R. Wittkopf, eds. 1992. *The Global Agenda: Issues and Perspectives.* New York: McGraw-Hill.

Kelsen, Hans. 1945. *General Theory of International Law and State.* Berkeley: University of California Press.

Kennen, George. 1954. *The Realities of American Foreign Policy.* Princeton: Princeton University Press.

Keohane, Robert. 1984. *After Hegemony.* Princeton: Princeton University Press.

Keohane, Robert, ed. 1986. *Neorealism and Its Critics.* New York: Columbia University Press. See especially his own chapter: "Realism, Neorealism, and the Study of World Politics," 1–26.

Keohane, Robert O., and Lisa L. Martin. 1995. "The Promise of Institutionalist Theory," *IS* 20, 1:39–51.

Keohane, Robert O., and Joseph S. Nye. 1977. *Power and Interdependence.* Boston: Little, Brown.

Kertesz, Stephen D. 1967. *The Quest for Peace Through Diplomacy.* Englewood Cliffs, NJ: Prentice-Hall.

Kindleberger, Charles P. 1986. *The World in Depression: 1929–1939.* Berkeley: University of California Press.

Kiss, Alexander. 1992. "The Implications of Global Change for the International Legal System." In Weiss 1992, 315–339.

Knorr, Klaus. 1975. *The Power of Nations: The Political Economy of International Relations.* New York: Basic Books.

Kocks, Stephen A. 1994. "Explaining the Strategic Behavior of States: International Law as System Structure." *ISQ* 38, 4:535–556.

Kohona, Palitha Tikiri Bandara. 1985. *The Regulation of International Economic Relations Through Law.* Dordrecht and Boston: Martinus Nijhoff.

Koslowski, Rey, and Friedrich Kratochwil. 1994. "Understanding Change in International Politics: The Soviet Empire's Demise and the International System." *IO* 48, 2:215–248.

Krasner, Stephen D. 1985. *Structural Conflict: The Third World Against Global Liberalism.* Berkeley: University of California Press.

Krasner, Stephen D., ed. 1982. *International Regimes,* a special issue of *International Organization* (spring); also published as a monograph by Cornell University Press, 1983.

Kratochwil, Friedrich V. 1989. *Rules, Norms, and Decisions.* Cambridge: Cambridge University Press.

Kratochwil, Frederich, and John Ruggie. 1986. "International Organization: A State of the Art on the Art of the State." *IO* 40, 4:754–775.

Krickus, Richard J. 1987. *The Superpowers in Crisis.* Washington, DC: Pergamon-Brassey.

Lapid, Yosef. 1991. "Theorizing the 'National' in International Relations Theory: Reflection on Nationalism and Neorealism." Paper presented at the International Studies Association (ISA) annual meeting, Vancouver, March 20–23, 1991.

Lasswell, Harold D., and Myres McDougal. 1943. "Legal Education and Public Policy: Professional Training in the Public Interest." *Yale Law Journal* 52:203.

Lauterpacht, Hersch. *Oppenheim*. 1955. L.F.L. Oppenheim, *International Law: A Treatise*. Vol. 1, Peace (8th ed., by Hersch Lauterpacht). London and New York: Longmans, Green.

Lauterpacht, Hersch. 1970. *Private Law Sources and Analogies of International Law*. Hamden, CT: Archo Books. Reprint of 1927 edition, published by Longmans, Green, London.

Levi, Werner. 1991. *Contemporary International Law*. Boulder: Westview Press.

Lieber, Robert J. 1988. *No Common Power: Understanding International Relations*. Boston: Scott, Foresman.

Lissitzyn, Oliver J. 1965. *International Law Today and Tomorrow*. Dobbs Ferry, NY: Oceana Publications.

Lowenfeld, Andreas. 1989. "U.S. Law Enforcement Abroad: The Constitution and International Law." *AJIL* 83, 4:880–893.

Lowenfeld, Andreas. 1990. "U.S. Law Enforcement Abroad: The Constitution and International Law, Continued." *AJIL* 84, 2:444–493.

Luce, R. D., and Howard Raiffa. 1957. *Games and Decisions*. New York: John Wiley.

Luttwak, Edward N. 1987. *The Paradoxical Logic of Strategy*. Berkeley: Institute of International Studies, University of California.

McClanahan, Grant V. 1989. *Diplomatic Immunity: Principles, Practices, Problems*. New York: St. Martin's Press.

McCormack, Thomas. 1989. *America's Half-Century: United States Foreign Policy in the Cold War*. Baltimore: Johns Hopkins University Press.

McDougal, Myres S. 1953. "International Law, Power, and Policy: A Contemporary Conception." *Recueil des Cours* 82:137.

McDougal, Myres S., et al. 1960. *Studies in World Public Order*. New Haven: Yale University Press.

Mandelbaum, Michael. 1988. *The Fate of Nations*. New York: Cambridge University Press.

Mandelbaum, Michael. 1996. "Foreign Policy as Social Work." *Foreign Affairs* 75, 1:16–32.

Mansbach, Richard, Yale H. Ferguson, and Donald Lampert. 1976. *The Web of World Politics: Nonstate Actors in the Global System*. Englewood Cliffs, NJ: Prentice-Hall.

Masters, Ruth. 1964. "World Politics as a Primitive System." *World Politics* 16, 3:595–619.

Mearsheimer, John J. 1994. "The False Promise of International Institutions." *IS* 19, 3:5–49.

Mercer, Jonathan. 1995. "Anarchy and Identity." *IO* 49, 2:229–252.

Milner, H. 1991. "The Assumption of Anarchy in International Relations Theory: A Critique." *Review of International Studies* 17, 1:67–85.

Mingst, Karen A., and Margaret P. Karns. 1995. *The United Nations in the Post–Cold War Era*. Boulder: Westview Press.

Mitrany, David. 1946. *A Working Peace System*. London and New York: Royal Institute of International Affairs.

Mittelman, James H., ed. 1996. *Globalization: Critical Reflections*. Boulder: Lynne Rienner.

Modelski, George. 1978. "The Long Cycle of Global Politics and the Nation-State." *Comparative Studies of Society and History* 20: 214–235.

Moore, John B. 1906. *Digest of International Law,* 8 vols. Washington, DC: U.S. Government Printing Office.
Morgenstern, Felice. 1986. *Legal Problems of International Organizations.* Cambridge: Grotius Publications.
Morgenthau, Hans. 1981. *In Defense of National Interest.* Lanham, MD: University Press of America; reissue of 1951 edition published by Alfred Knopf.
Morgenthau, Hans (updated by Kenneth Thompson). 1985. *Politics Among Nations: The Struggle for Power and Peace,* 6th ed. New York: Alfred Knopf.
Mower, A. Glenn, Jr. 1985. *International Cooperation for Social Justice: Global and Regional Protection of Economic and Social Rights.* Westport, CT: Greenwood Press.
Mower, A. Glenn, Jr. 1987. *Human Rights and American Foreign Policy: The Carter and Reagan Experiences.* Westport, CT: Greenwood Press.
Mueller, John. 1989. *Retreat from Doomsday: The Obsolescence of Major War.* New York: Basic Books.
Muller, Sam, and Wim Mijs, eds. 1994. *The Flame Rekindled: New Hopes for International Arbitration.* Dordrecht: Martinus Nijhoff.
Müllerson, Rein. 1994. *International Law, Rights, and Politics: Developments in Eastern Europe and the CIS.* London and New York: Routledge.
Nanda, Ved P. 1972. "Self-Determination in International Law: The Tragic Tale of Two Cities—Islamabad (West Pakistan) and Dacca (East Pakistan)." *AJIL* 66:321–336.
Nardin, Terry. 1992. "International Ethics and International Law." *Review of International Studies* 18, 1:19–30.
Nayar, Baldev Raj. 1995. "Regimes, Power, and International Aviation." *IO* 49, 1:139–170.
NZMERAT. 1991. *United Nations Handbook.* Published by the New Zealand Ministry of External Relations and Trade. Auckland: New House Publishers.
O'Brien, James C. 1993. "The International Tribunal for Violations of International Humanitarian Law in the Former Yugoslavia." *AJIL* 87, 4:639–659.
Oliver, Covey T. 1991. "The Jurisdiction (Competence) of States." In M. Bedjaoui, ed., *International Law: Achievements and Prospects.* Dordrecht: Martinus Nijhoff.
Olson, Mancur, Jr. 1971. *The Logic of Collective Action,* rev. ed. New York: Shocken Books.
Oneal, John R. 1990. "The Theory of Collective Action and Burden Sharing in NATO." *IO* 44, 3:379–402.
Onuf, Nicholas, and Franklin F. Klink. 1989. "Anarchy, Authority, and Rule." *ISQ* 33, 2:149–173.
Oppenheim, Lassa. 1992. *International Law,* vol. 1 (9th ed. Jennings and Watts). London: Longmans Green.
Oxman, Bernard H. 1994. "The 1994 Agreement and the [1982 LOS] Convention," part of the "Law of the Sea Forum: The 1994 Agreement on Implementation of the Seabed Provisions of the Convention on the Law of the Sea." *AJIL* 88, 2:687–715.
Oye, Kenneth A. 1985. "Explaining Cooperation Under Anarchy," *World Politics* 38, 1:1–24.
Palmer, Geoffrey. 1992. "New Ways to Make International Environmental Law." *AJIL* 86, 2:259–283.
Parry, Clive. 1965. *The Sources and Evidence of International Law.* Manchester: Manchester University Press; Dobbs Ferry, NY: Oceana Publications.

Perkins, John. 1981. *The Prudent Peace: Law as Foreign Policy.* Chicago: University of Chicago Press.

Pfaff, William. 1995. "A New Colonialism? Europe Must Go Back into Africa." *Foreign Affairs* 74, 2:2–6.

Porter, Gareth, and Janet Welsh Brown. 1996. *Global Environmental Politics,* 2d ed. Boulder: Westview Press.

Posen, Barry. 1984. *The Sources of Military Doctrine.* Ithaca: Cornell University Press.

Poulsen, Thomas, and Dimitri Sharkov. 1995. *Nations and States.* Englewood Cliffs, NJ: Prentice-Hall.

Ralston, J. 1929. *International Arbitration from Athens to Locarno.* Stanford: Stanford University Press.

Ramundo, Bernard A. 1967. *Peaceful Coexistence: International Law in the Building of Communism.* Baltimore: Johns Hopkins University Press.

Rapoport, Anatol, and Albert Chammah. 1965. *Prisoner's Dilemma.* Ann Arbor: University of Michigan Press.

Rasler, Karen A., and William R. Thompson. 1989. "Global Wars, Public Debts, and the Long Cycle." In Russet, Starr, and Stoll 1989, 42–61.

Ray, James Lee. 1987. *Global Politics,* 3d ed. Boston: Houghton Mifflin.

Re, Edward. 1966. *Report of the Foreign Claims Settlement Commission.* In *Hearing Before the Subcommittee on the Far East and the Pacific of the Committee of Foreign Affairs,* House of Representatives, 89th Cong. 2nd Sess., on S. 3675. Washington, DC: Government Printing Office.

Reisman, W. Michael. 1990. "Editorial Comments: International Law After the Cold War." *AJIL* 84, 4:859–866.

Ringmar, Erik. 1995. "The Relevance of International Law: A Hegelian Interpretation of a Peculiar Seventeenth-Century Preoccupation." *Review of International Studies* 21, 1:87–103.

Rittberger, Voker, ed. 1990. *International Regimes in East-West Politics.* London: Pinter.

Rivera, Joseph. 1968. *The Psychological Dimensions of Foreign Policy.* Columbus, OH: Charles Merrill.

Roberts, Brad, ed. 1992. *U.S. Foreign Policy After the Cold War.* Cambridge: MIT Press.

Rochester, J. Martin. 1995. "The United Nations in a New World Order: Reviving the Theory and Practice of International Organization." In Kegley 1995, 199–222.

Rosenau, James. 1986. "Before Cooperation: Hegemons, Regimes, and Habit-Driven Actors in World Politics." *IO* 40, 4:849–894.

Rosenne, Shabti. 1985. *The Law and Practice of the International Court.* Dordrecht: Martinus Nijhoff.

Ruggie, John Gerard. 1993. "Territoriality and Beyond: Problematizing Modernity in International Relations." *IO* 47, 1:139–174.

Ruggie, John Gerard. 1995. "The False Promise of Realism." *IS* 20, 1:62–70.

Russett, Bruce, and Harvey Starr. 1992. *World Politics,* 4th ed. New York: W. H. Freeman.

Russett, Bruce, Harvey Starr, and Richard Stoll, eds. 1989. *Choices in World Politics: Sovereignty and Interdependence.* New York: W. H. Freeman.

Safran, Nadav. 1969. *From War to War: The Arab-Israeli Confrontation, 1948–1967.* New York: Pegasus.

Sands, Philippe. 1995. *Principles of International Environmental Law,* vol. 1. Manchester and New York: Manchester University Press.

Sbragia, Alberta M., ed. 1992. *Euro-Politics: Institutions and Policymaking in the "New" European Community*. Washington, DC: Brookings Institution.

Schachter, Oscar. 1991a. "The Jurisdiction of States." In Schachter, *International Law in Theory and Practice*. Dordrecht: Martinus Nijhoff, chap. 12.

Schachter, Oscar. 1991b. "United Nations Law in the Gulf Conflict." *AJIL* 85, 3:452–473.

Schattuck, Petra, and Jill Norgren. 1991. *Partial Justice*. Oxford: Berg Publishers.

Schelling, Thomas C. 1966. *Arms and Influence*. New Haven: Yale University Press.

Schwarzenberger, Georg. 1965. *The Inductive Approach to International Law*. Dobbs Ferry, NY: Oceana Publications.

Schwarzenberger, Georg. 1967. *A Manual of International Law*, 5th ed. New York: Praeger.

Schwebel, Stephen. 1987. "Ad Hoc Chambers of the International Court of Justice." *AJIL* 81:831ff.

Shafritz, Jay M. 1993. *The Dictionary of 20th Century World Politics*. New York: Henry Holt.

Shaw, W. F., and L. Albert. 1980. *Partition: The Price of Quebec's Independence*. Montreal: Thorhill Publishing.

Shirer, William L. 1960. *The Collapse of the Third Reich*. New York: Simon and Schuster.

Slomanson, William R. 1995. *Fundamental Perspectives on International Law*. Minneapolis: West Publishing.

Smith, Wayne. 1996. "Shackled to the Past: The United States and Cuba." *Current History* (February):49–54.

Spegele, Roger D. 1987. "Three Forms of Political Realism." *Political Studies* 35: 189–210.

Starr, Harvey. 1995. "International Law and International Order." In Kegley 1995, 269–316.

Stein, Arthur. 1990. *Why Nations Cooperate*. Ithaca: Cornell University Press.

Stein, Janice Gross. 1994. "Political Learning by Doing: Gorbachev as Uncommitted Thinker and Motivated Learner." *IO* 48, 2:155–184.

Stent, Angela. 1987. "Economic Containment." In Terry L. Deibel and John Lewis Gaddis, eds., *Containing the Soviet Union*. New York: Pergamon-Brassy, 59–77.

Stuyt, A. 1990. *Survey of International Arbitrations: 1794–1889*. Dordrecht: Martinus Nijhoff.

Szasz, C. Paul. 1992. "International Norm-Making." In Weiss 1992, 41–80.

Szyliowicz, Joseph, and Bard E. O'Neill, eds. 1975. *The Energy Crisis and U.S. Foreign Policy*. New York: Praeger.

Thompson, Janice E. 1995. "State Sovereignty in International Relations: The Gap Between Theory and Empirical Research." *ISQ* 39, 2:213–233.

Tolley, Howard, Jr. 1986. *The U.N. Commission on Human Rights*. Boulder: Westview Press.

Tucker, Robert W. 1972. "Reprisals and Self-Defense: The Customary Law." *AJIL* 66, 3:586–596.

Vagts, Detlev F. 1984. "International Law Under Time Pressure: Grading the Grenada Take-Home Examination." *AJIL* 78, 1:169–172.

van Dyke, Vernon. 1970. *Human Rights, the United States, and the World Community*. New York: Oxford University Press.

von Glahn, Gerhard. 1992. *Law Among Nations*, 6th ed. New York: Macmillan. Also the 5th ed. (1986).

Walker, R. B. J. 1987. "History and Structure in the Theory of International Relations." *Millennium* 18, 2:163–183.
Walt, Stephen. 1987. *The Origins of Alliances.* Ithaca: Cornell University Press.
Walters, Robert S., and David H. Blake. 1992. *The Politics of Global Economic Relations.* Englewood Cliffs, NJ: Prentice-Hall.
Waltz, Kenneth N. 1959. *Man, State, and War.* New York: Columbia University Press.
Waltz, Kenneth N. 1979. *Theory of International Politics.* Reading, MA: Addison-Wesley.
Waltz, Kenneth N. 1988. "The Origins of War in Neorealist Theory." *Journal of Interdisciplinary History* 18, 4:39–52.
Waltz, Kenneth N. 1993. "The Emerging Structure of International Politics." *IS* 18, 1:44–79.
Weiss, Edith Brown, ed. 1992. *Environmental Change and International Law: New Challenges and Dimensions.* Tokyo: United Nations University Press.
Weiss, Edith Brown. 1994. "Notes from the President." *ASIL Newsletter* (November-December).
Weiss, Thomas, ed. 1993. *Collective Security in a Changing World.* Boulder: Westview Press.
Weiss, Thomas G., David Forsythe, and Roger A. Coate. 1994. *The United Nations and Changing World Politics.* Boulder: Westview Press.
Wendt, Alexander E. 1987. "The Agent-Structure Problem in International Relations Theory." *IO* 41, 3:335–370.
Wendt, Alexander. 1995. "Constructing International Politics." *IS* 20, 1:71–81.
Whiteman, Marjorie M. 1970. *Digest of International Law, 1963–1970,* 15 vols. Washington, DC: Government Printing Office.
Winham, Gilbert R. 1992. *The Evolution of International Trade Agreements.* Toronto: University of Toronto Press.
World Bank. 1993. *The East Asian Miracle: Economic Growth and Public Policy.* World Bank Policy Research Report. New York: Oxford University Press.
Wright, Quincy. 1949. "Modern Technology and the World Order." In W. F. Ogburn, ed., *Technology and International Relations.* Chicago: University of Chicago Press.
Wright, Quincy. 1955. *The Study of International Relations.* New York: Appleton-Century-Crofts.
Young, Oran R. 1989. "The Politics of International Regime Formation: Managing Natural Resources and Environment." *IO* 43:349–375.
Young, Oran R., and Gail Osherenko, eds. 1993. *Creating International Environmental Regimes.* Ithaca: Cornell University Press.
Yu, Yiping. 1996. "England, the Self-Appointed Defender of Human Rights, Is Lobbying for an EU Crackdown on the European Court of Human Rights." A special report printed in *Qiao Bao* (China Press, New York), April 4, 1996, 3.
Zimmerman, James Michael. 1992. "U.S. Law and Convict-Produced Imports." *China Business Review* 19, 2:41–43.

Index

About the Book

This is a study of the political parameters of international law and, conversely, the law's relevance and reach in international politics. At the theoretical level, it bridges the competing dominant paradigms—neorealism and neoliberalism—in the contemporary IR literature.

The neorealist and neoliberal paradigms converge on the interstice where, because of their urge for order, sovereign states act collaboratively to mitigate the effects of anarchy. This collaboration results in the creation of norms, regimes, and institutions for regulating and facilitating international relations. The very fact that the system's anarchic condition is conducive to, rather than obstructive of, cooperation is a giant paradox. Hsiung ably unravels this contradiction and explores—through empirical analyses of the interplay of international law and international politics—the challenge it poses for the neorealist central belief regarding systemic anarchy.

JAMES C. HSIUNG is professor of politics at New York University, where he teaches international politics theory, international law, and international organization. He is author or editor of fifteen books including *Asia Pacific in the New World Politics* and *Beyond China's Independent Foreign Policy.* Dr. Hsiung has held visiting professorships in Taiwan, mainland China, and most recently, at Lingnan University in Hong Kong, and he is a consulting member of the Shanghai Academy of Social Sciences.